THE WARNING

Created by MIKE MIGNOLA

ABE SAPIEN

An amphibious man discovered in a primitive stasis chamber in a long-forgotten subbasement beneath a Washington, D.C., hospital. Recent events have confirmed a previous life, dating back to the Civil War, as scientist and occult investigator Langdon Everett Caul.

LIZ SHERMAN

A fire-starter since the age of eleven, when she accidentally burned her entire family to death. She has been a ward of the B.P.R.D. since then, learning to control her pyrokinetic abilities and cope with the trauma those abilities have wrought. Recently, she has been troubled by visions of a mysterious gentleman and the end of the world.

DR. KATE CORRIGAN

A former professor at New York University and an authority on folklore and occult history. Dr. Corrigan has been a B.P.R.D. consultant for over ten years and now serves as Special Liaison to the enhanced-talents task force.

PANYA

An ancient Egyptian mummy who returned to life during an unrolling ceremony in the nineteenth century. After her resurrection, Panya was a prisoner first of the Heliopic Brotherhood of Ra, and later of the Oannes Society, until she made contact with and subsequently was freed by the B.P.R.D. She has demonstrated psychic abilities, although their precise nature and range remain unknown.

JOHANN KRAUS

A medium whose physical form was destroyed while his ectoplasmic projection was out-of-body. A psychic empath, Johann can create temporary forms for the dead to speak to the living.

MIKE MIGNOLA'S

B.P.R.D.

THE WARNING

Story by
MIKE MIGNOLA and JOHN ARCUDI

Art by
GUY DAVIS

Colors by
DAVE STEWART

Letters by
CLEM ROBINS

Cover by
MIKE MIGNOLA

Series Covers by
MIKE MIGNOLA and KEVIN NOWLAN

Editor
SCOTT ALLIE

Assistant Editor
RACHEL EDIDIN

Collection Designer
AMY ARENDTS

Publisher
MIKE RICHARDSON

DARK HORSE BOOKS®

Neil Hankerson ♦ *executive vice president*
Tom Weddle ♦ *chief financial officer*
Randy Stradley ♦ *vice president of publishing*
Michael Martens ♦ *vice president of business development*
Anita Nelson ♦ *vice president of marketing, sales, & licensing*
David Scroggy ♦ *vice president of product development*
Dale LaFountain ♦ *vice president of information technology*
Darlene Vogel ♦ *director of purchasing*
Ken Lizzi ♦ *general counsel*
Davey Estrada ♦ *editorial director*
Scott Allie ♦ *senior managing editor*
Chris Warner ♦ *senior books editor, Dark Horse Books*
Rob Simpson ♦ *senior books editor, M Press/DH Press*
Diana Schutz ♦ *executive editor*
Cary Grazzini ♦ *director of design & production*
Lia Ribacchi ♦ *art director*
Cara Niece ♦ *director of scheduling*

Special thanks to Jason Hvam

www.hellboy.com

Published by Dark Horse Books
A division of Dark Horse Comics, Inc.
10956 SE Main Street
Milwaukie, OR 97222

First Edition: May 2009
ISBN 978-1-59582-304-5

3 5 7 9 10 8 6 4 2

Printed at Midas Printing International, Ltd., Huizhou, China

B.P.R.D.: The Warning

This book collects the *B.P.R.D.: The Warning* comic-book series, issues #1–#5, and the short story "Out of Reach," from *Free Comic Book Day 2008*, published by Dark Horse Comics.

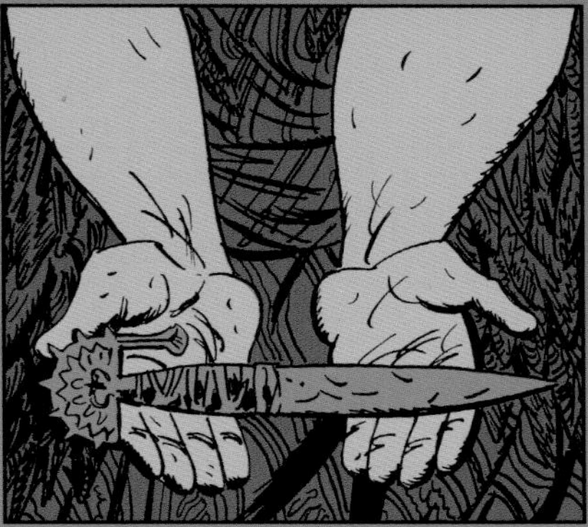

PROLOGUE

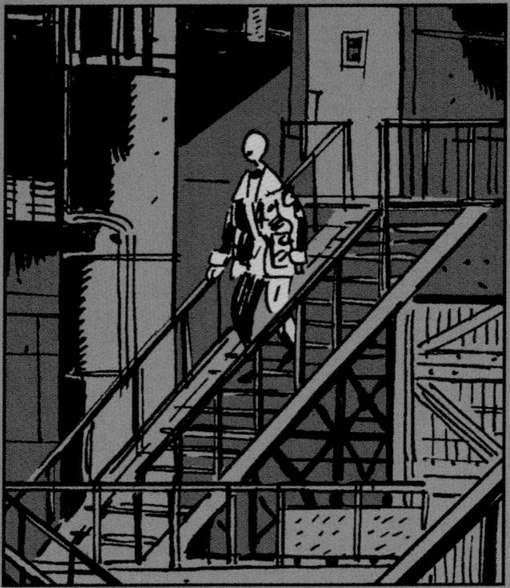

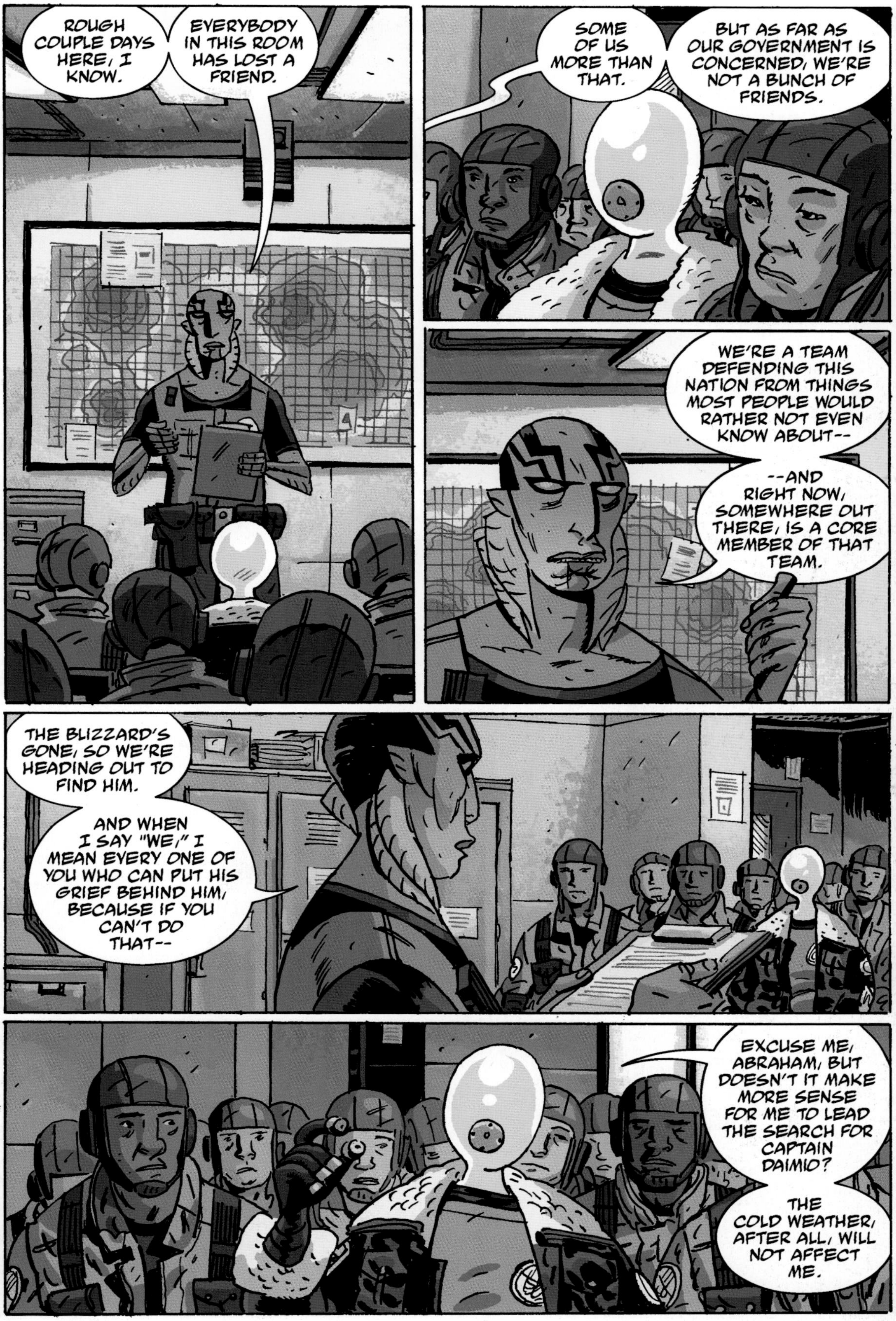
ROUGH COUPLE DAYS HERE, I KNOW.
EVERYBODY IN THIS ROOM HAS LOST A FRIEND.
SOME OF US MORE THAN THAT.
BUT AS FAR AS OUR GOVERNMENT IS CONCERNED, WE'RE NOT A BUNCH OF FRIENDS.
WE'RE A TEAM DEFENDING THIS NATION FROM THINGS MOST PEOPLE WOULD RATHER NOT EVEN KNOW ABOUT--
--AND RIGHT NOW, SOMEWHERE OUT THERE, IS A CORE MEMBER OF THAT TEAM.
THE BLIZZARD'S GONE, SO WE'RE HEADING OUT TO FIND HIM.
AND WHEN I SAY "WE," I MEAN EVERY ONE OF YOU WHO CAN PUT HIS GRIEF BEHIND HIM, BECAUSE IF YOU CAN'T DO THAT--
EXCUSE ME, ABRAHAM, BUT DOESN'T IT MAKE MORE SENSE FOR ME TO LEAD THE SEARCH FOR CAPTAIN DAIMIO?
THE COLD WEATHER, AFTER ALL, WILL NOT AFFECT ME.

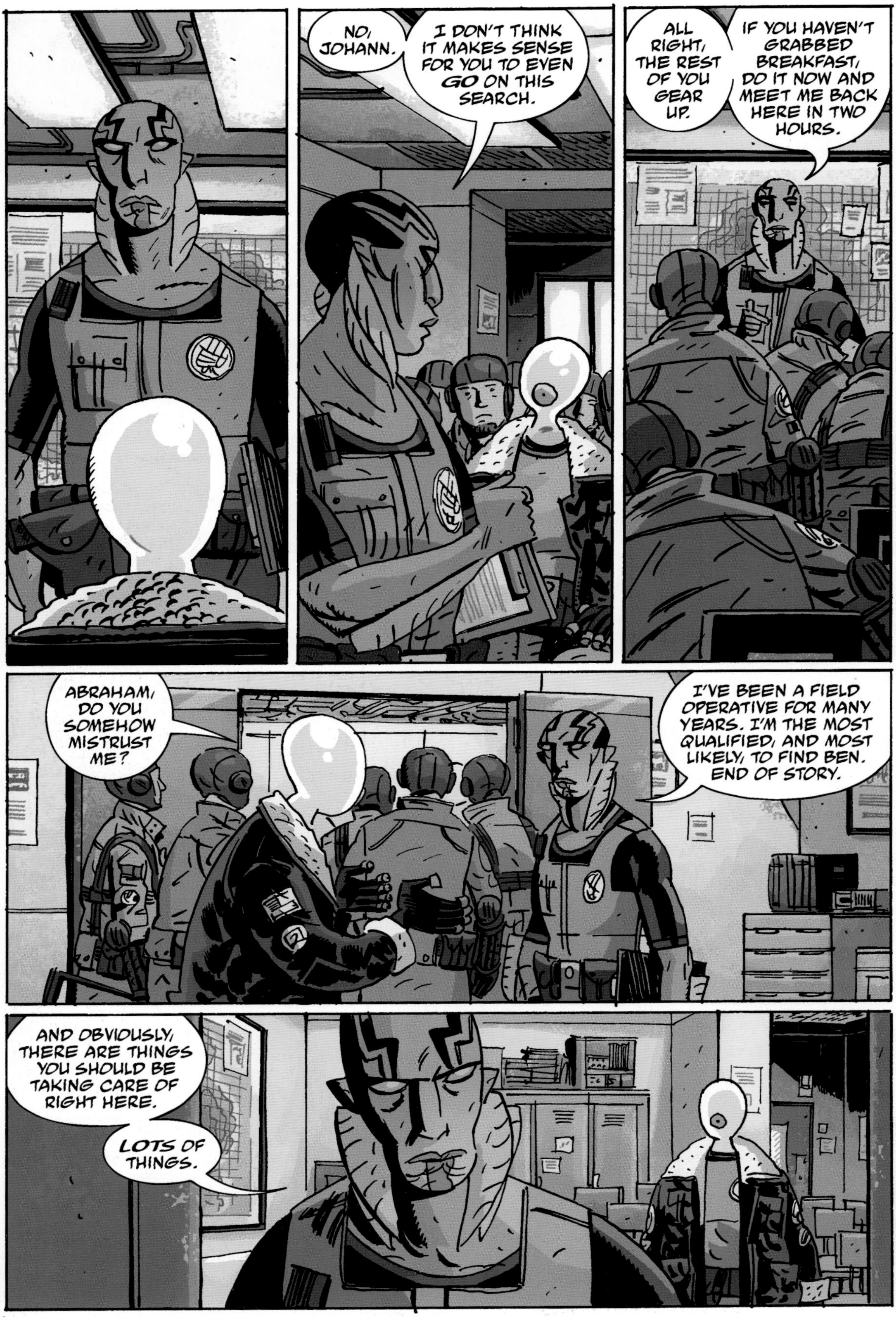
NO, JOHANN.
I DON'T THINK IT MAKES SENSE FOR YOU TO EVEN GO ON THIS SEARCH.
ALL RIGHT, THE REST OF YOU GEAR UP.
IF YOU HAVEN'T GRABBED BREAKFAST, DO IT NOW AND MEET ME BACK HERE IN TWO HOURS.
ABRAHAM, DO YOU SOMEHOW MISTRUST ME?
I'VE BEEN A FIELD OPERATIVE FOR MANY YEARS. I'M THE MOST QUALIFIED, AND MOST LIKELY, TO FIND BEN. END OF STORY.
AND OBVIOUSLY, THERE ARE THINGS YOU SHOULD BE TAKING CARE OF RIGHT HERE.
LOTS OF THINGS.

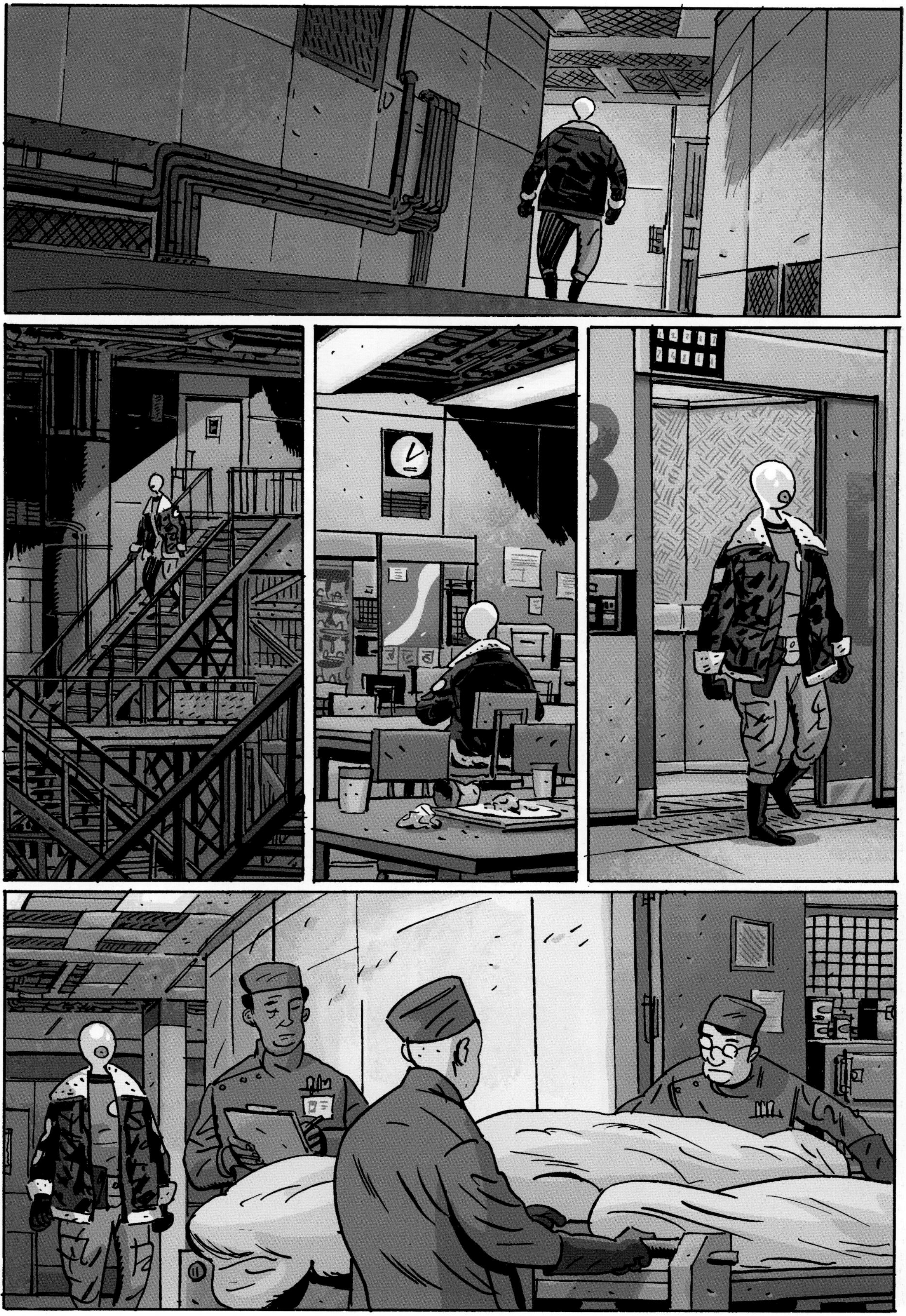

OH. MORNING, AGENT KRAUS.

GUTEN TAG.

SO, YOU ARE REMOVING THE BODIES.

TO WHERE?

CHAVES IS HEADED TO WASHINGTON. THEY'LL TRY TO LOCATE ANY NEXT OF KIN. AS FOR THE--

--OTHER... TWO...

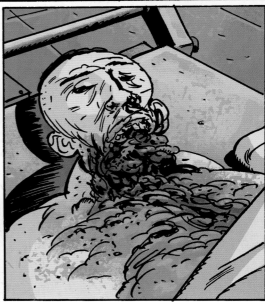

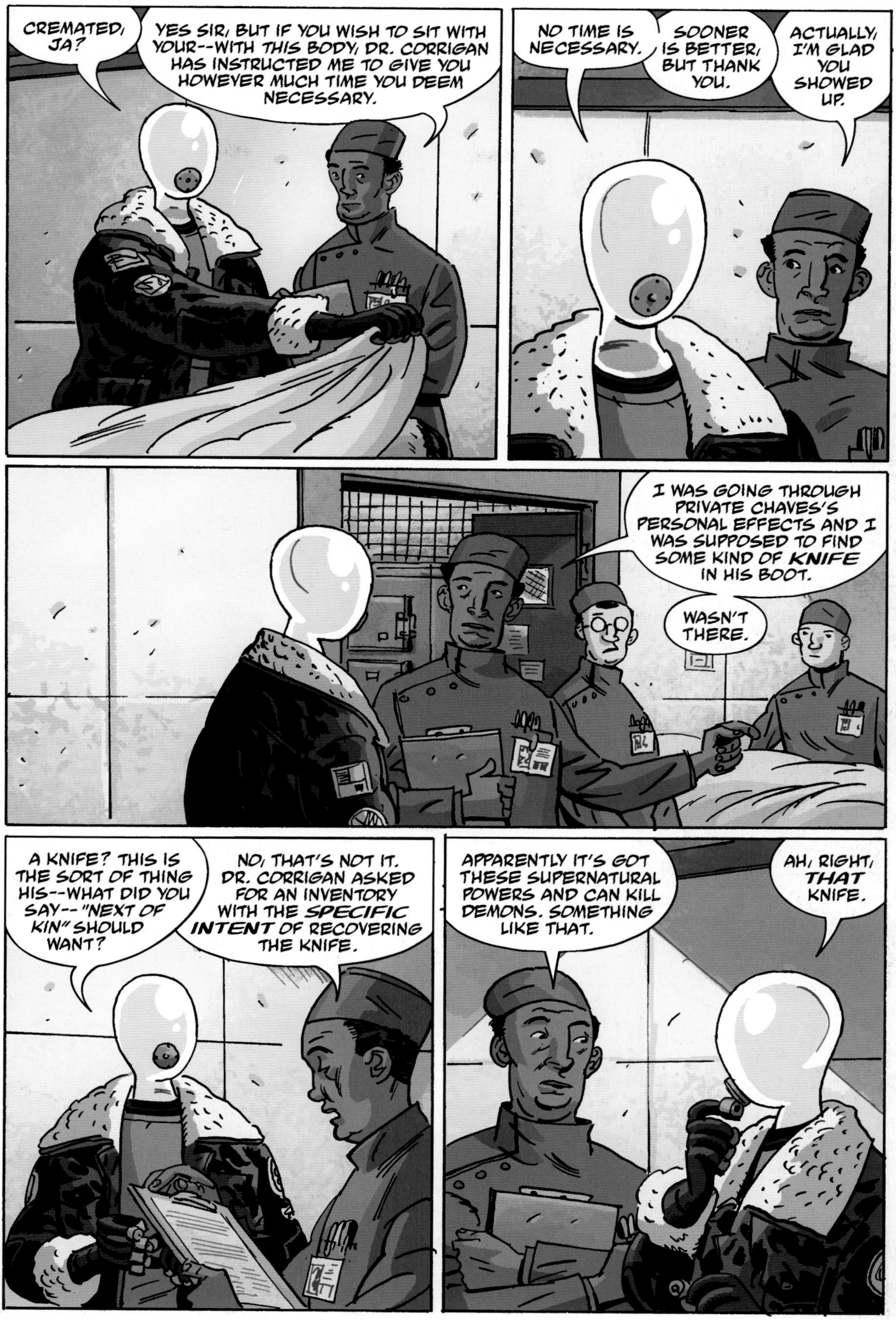
CREMATED, JA?
YES SIR, BUT IF YOU WISH TO SIT WITH YOUR--WITH THIS BODY, DR. CORRIGAN HAS INSTRUCTED ME TO GIVE YOU HOWEVER MUCH TIME YOU DEEM NECESSARY.
NO TIME IS NECESSARY.
SOONER IS BETTER, BUT THANK YOU.
ACTUALLY, I'M GLAD YOU SHOWED UP.
I WAS GOING THROUGH PRIVATE CHAVES'S PERSONAL EFFECTS AND I WAS SUPPOSED TO FIND SOME KIND OF KNIFE IN HIS BOOT.
WASN'T THERE.
A KNIFE? THIS IS THE SORT OF THING HIS--WHAT DID YOU SAY-- "NEXT OF KIN" SHOULD WANT?
NO, THAT'S NOT IT. DR. CORRIGAN ASKED FOR AN INVENTORY WITH THE SPECIFIC INTENT OF RECOVERING THE KNIFE.
APPARENTLY IT'S GOT THESE SUPERNATURAL POWERS AND CAN KILL DEMONS. SOMETHING LIKE THAT.
AH, RIGHT, THAT KNIFE.

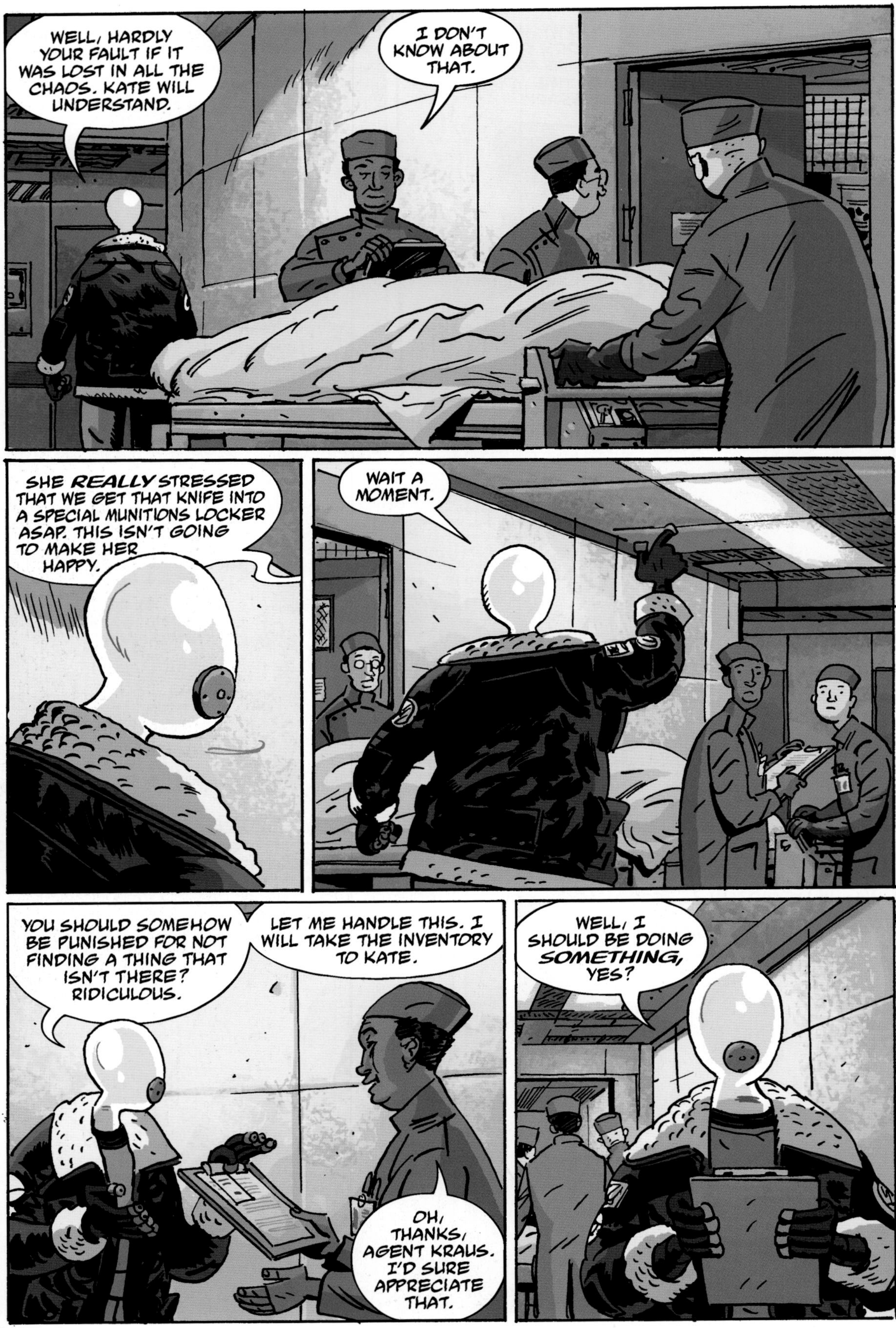
WELL, HARDLY YOUR FAULT IF IT WAS LOST IN ALL THE CHAOS. KATE WILL UNDERSTAND.
I DON'T KNOW ABOUT THAT.
SHE REALLY STRESSED THAT WE GET THAT KNIFE INTO A SPECIAL MUNITIONS LOCKER ASAP. THIS ISN'T GOING TO MAKE HER HAPPY.
WAIT A MOMENT.
YOU SHOULD SOMEHOW BE PUNISHED FOR NOT FINDING A THING THAT ISN'T THERE? RIDICULOUS.
LET ME HANDLE THIS. I WILL TAKE THE INVENTORY TO KATE.
OH, THANKS, AGENT KRAUS. I'D SURE APPRECIATE THAT.
WELL, I SHOULD BE DOING SOMETHING, YES?

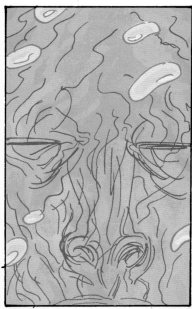

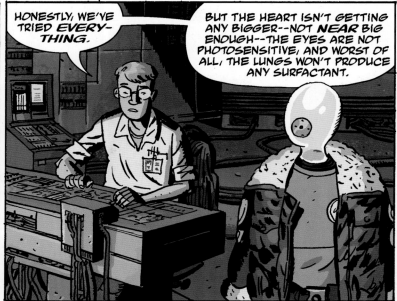

HONESTLY, WE'VE TRIED *EVERY-THING.*

BUT THE HEART ISN'T GETTING ANY BIGGER--NOT *NEAR* BIG ENOUGH--THE EYES ARE NOT PHOTOSENSITIVE, AND WORST OF ALL, THE LUNGS WON'T PRODUCE ANY SURFACTANT.

WHATEVER THOSE CRAZY ROBOTS WERE DOING OUT THERE, WE JUST CAN'T REPRODUCE IT HERE.

THIS GUY WON'T SURVIVE EMERSION.

SORRY.

HEY, I'M GOING UP TO GO GRAB SOME BREAKFAST. YOU STAYING, OR DO I HAVE TO LOCK UP?

I THINK I WOULD LIKE TO STAY.

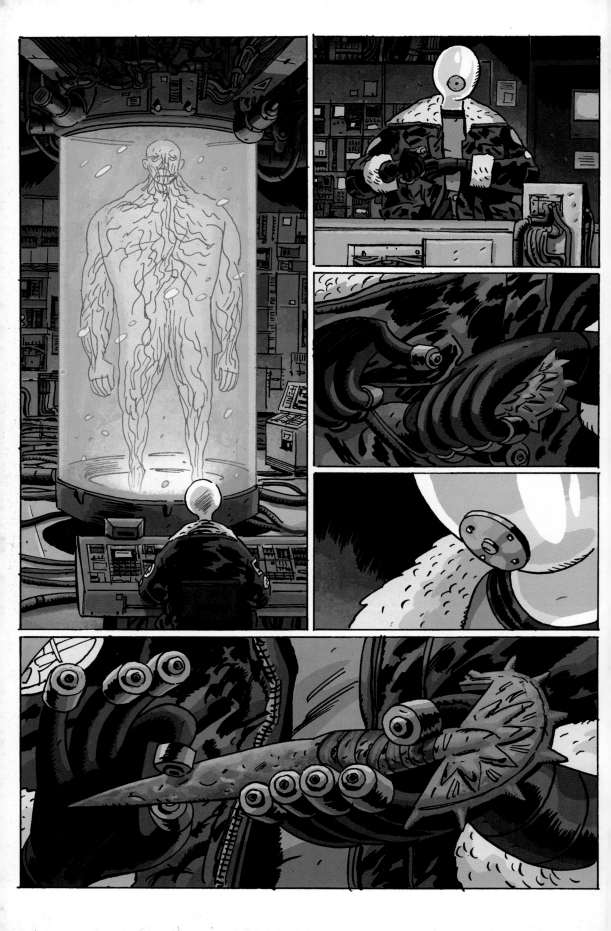

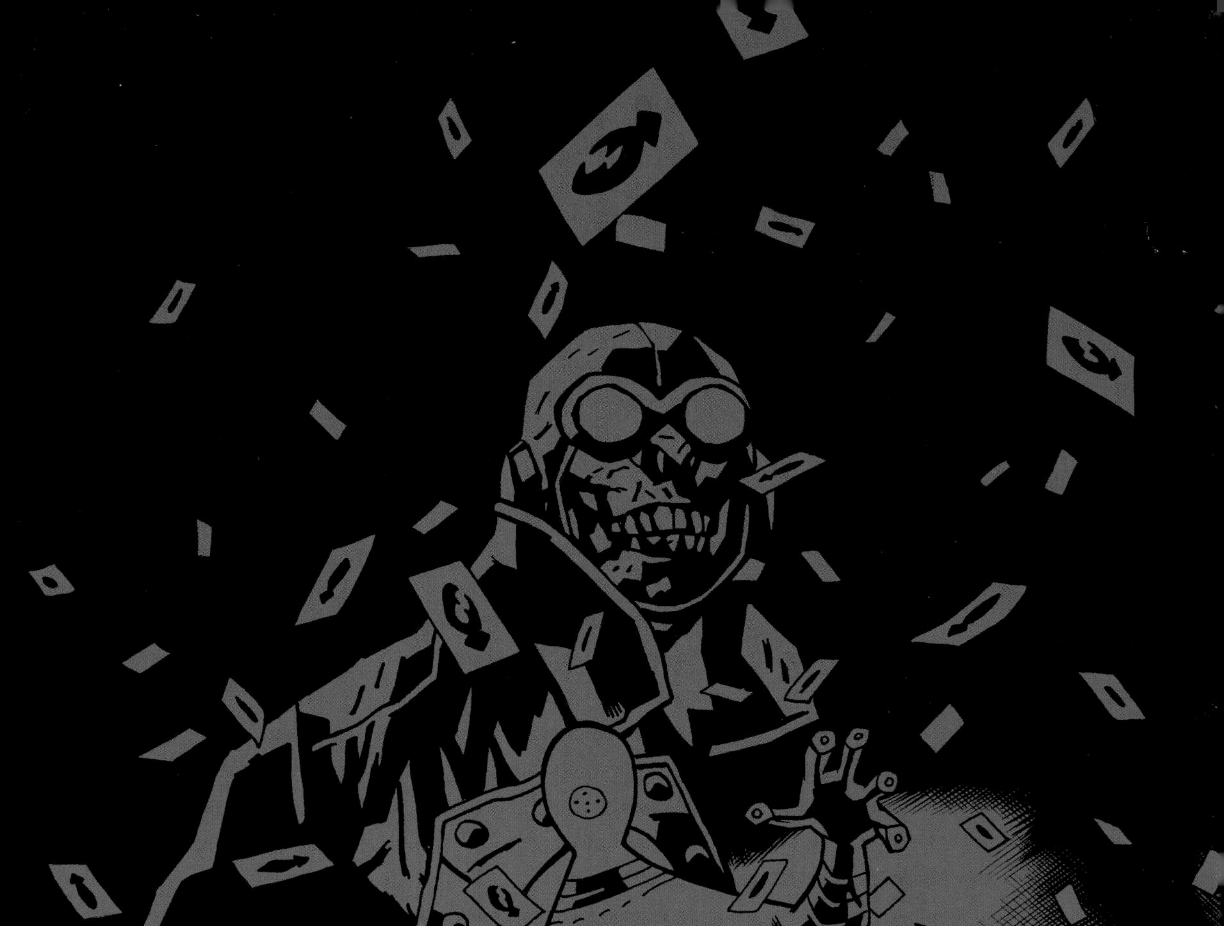
M
NOWLAN

CHAPTER ONE

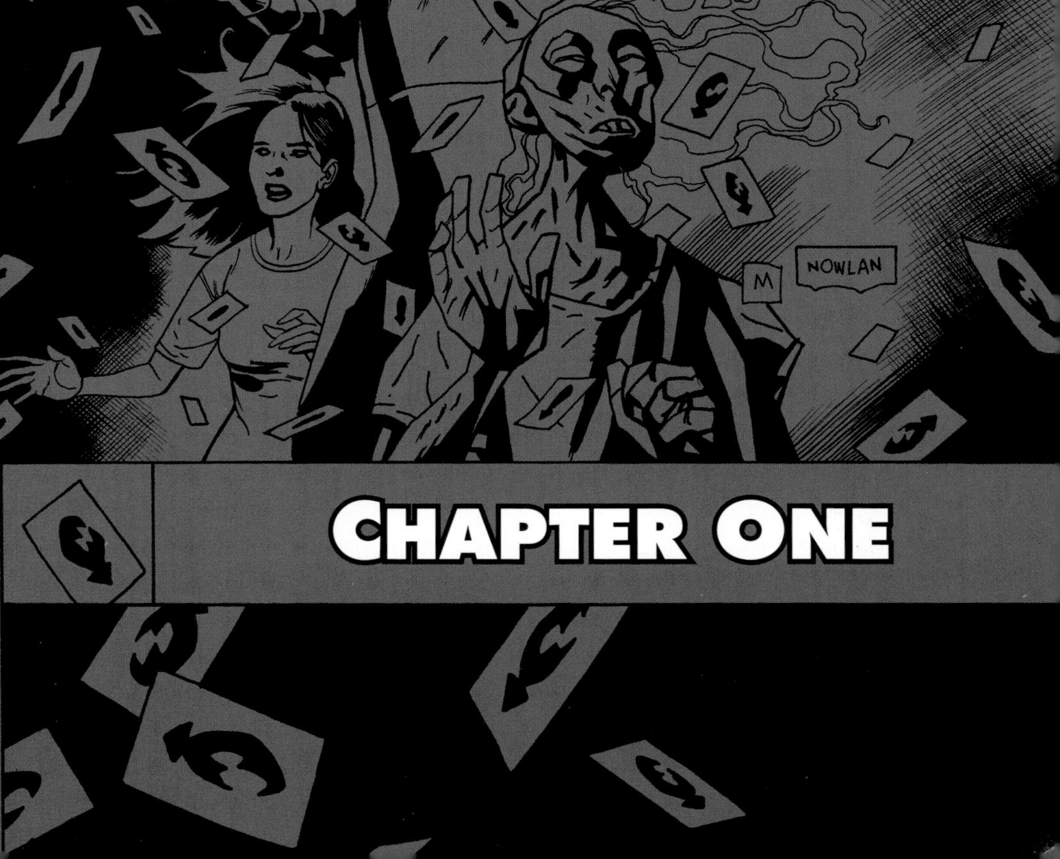

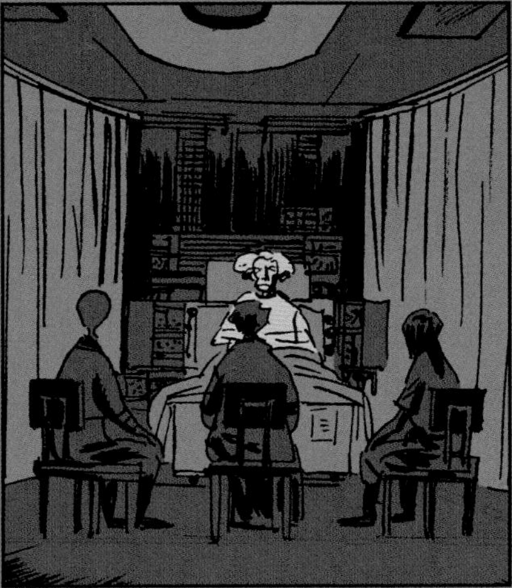

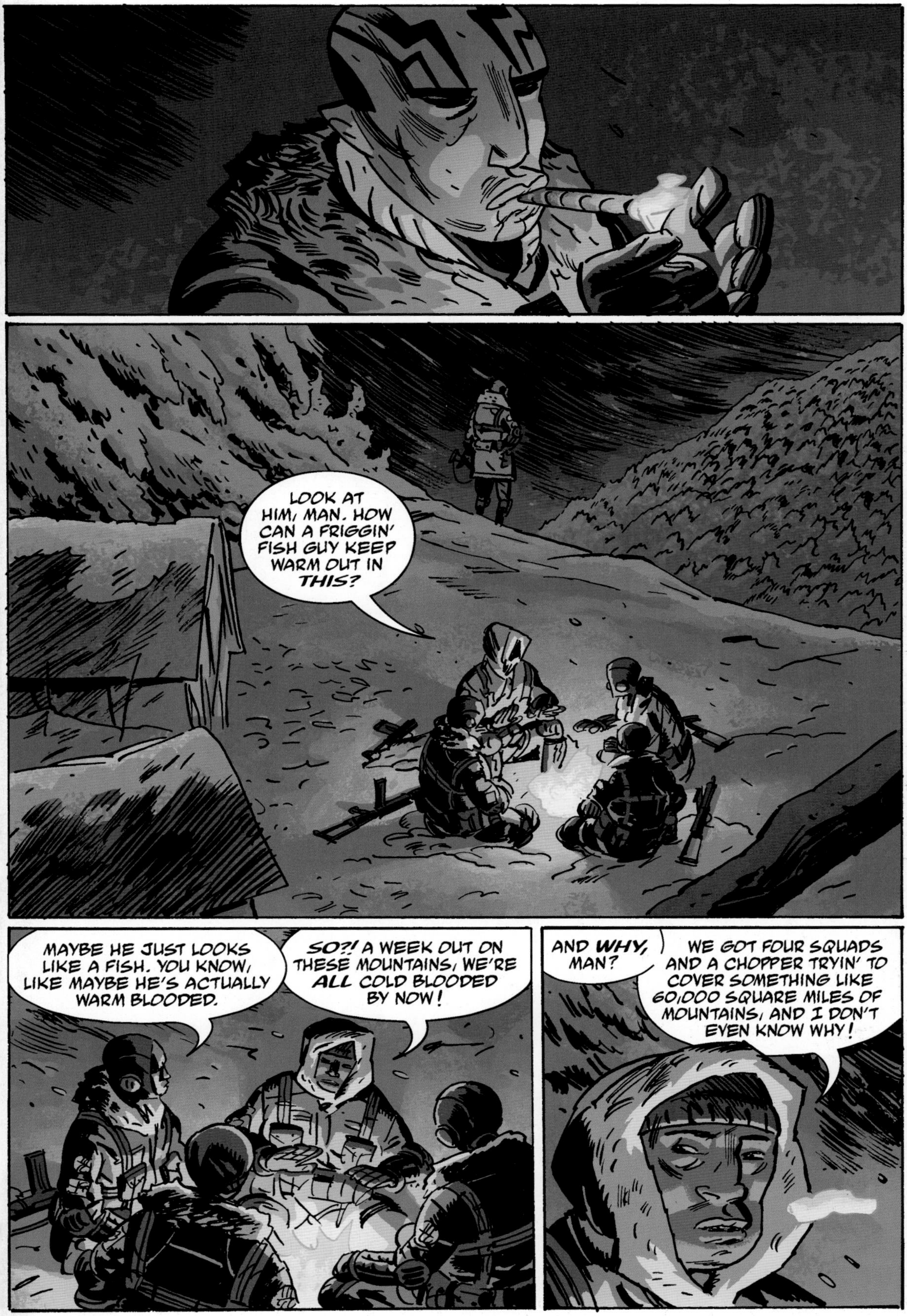

LOOK AT HIM, MAN. HOW CAN A FRIGGIN' FISH GUY KEEP WARM OUT IN THIS?
MAYBE HE JUST LOOKS LIKE A FISH. YOU KNOW, LIKE MAYBE HE'S ACTUALLY WARM BLOODED.
SO?! A WEEK OUT ON THESE MOUNTAINS, WE'RE ALL COLD BLOODED BY NOW!
AND WHY, MAN?
WE GOT FOUR SQUADS AND A CHOPPER TRYIN' TO COVER SOMETHING LIKE 60,000 SQUARE MILES OF MOUNTAINS, AND I DON'T EVEN KNOW WHY!

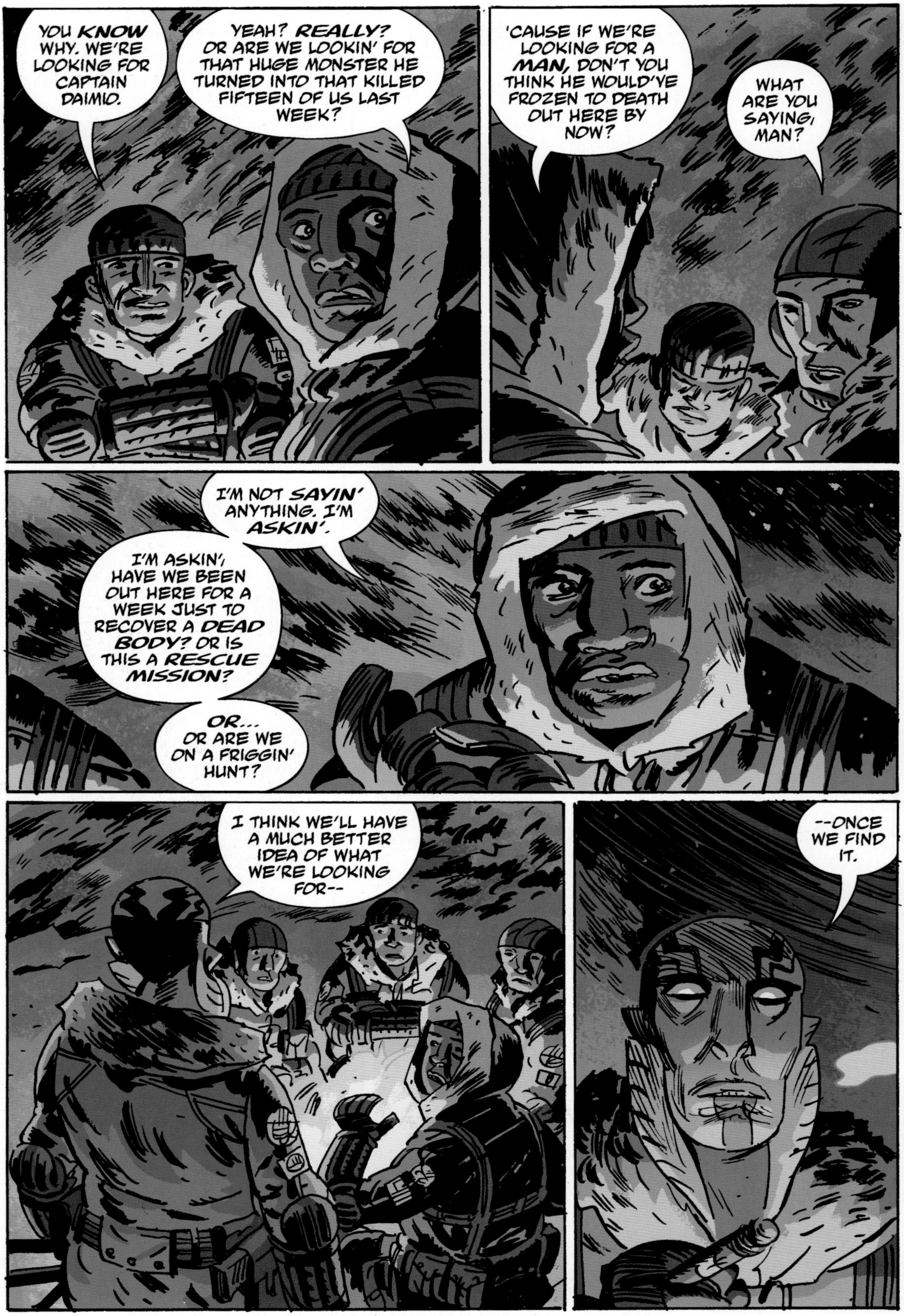

YOU KNOW WHY. WE'RE LOOKING FOR CAPTAIN DAIMIO.
YEAH? REALLY? OR ARE WE LOOKIN' FOR THAT HUGE MONSTER HE TURNED INTO THAT KILLED FIFTEEN OF US LAST WEEK?
'CAUSE IF WE'RE LOOKING FOR A MAN, DON'T YOU THINK HE WOULD'VE FROZEN TO DEATH OUT HERE BY NOW?
WHAT ARE YOU SAYING, MAN?
I'M NOT SAYIN' ANYTHING. I'M ASKIN'.
I'M ASKIN', HAVE WE BEEN OUT HERE FOR A WEEK JUST TO RECOVER A DEAD BODY? OR IS THIS A RESCUE MISSION?
OR... OR ARE WE ON A FRIGGIN' HUNT?
I THINK WE'LL HAVE A MUCH BETTER IDEA OF WHAT WE'RE LOOKING FOR--
--ONCE WE FIND IT.

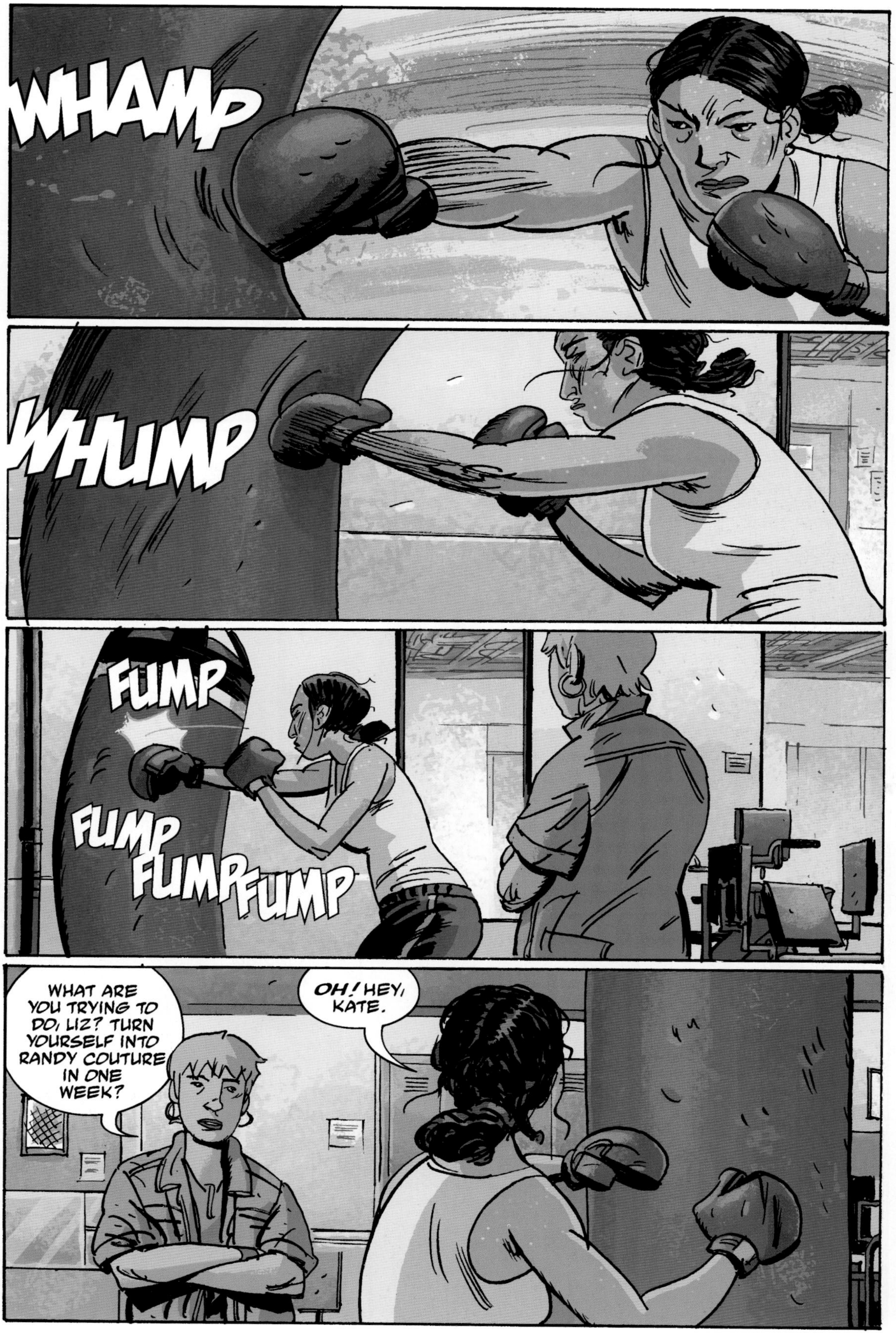
WHAMP
WHUMP
FUMP
FUMP
FUMP FUMP
WHAT ARE YOU TRYING TO DO, LIZ? TURN YOURSELF INTO RANDY COUTURE IN ONE WEEK?
OH! HEY, KATE.

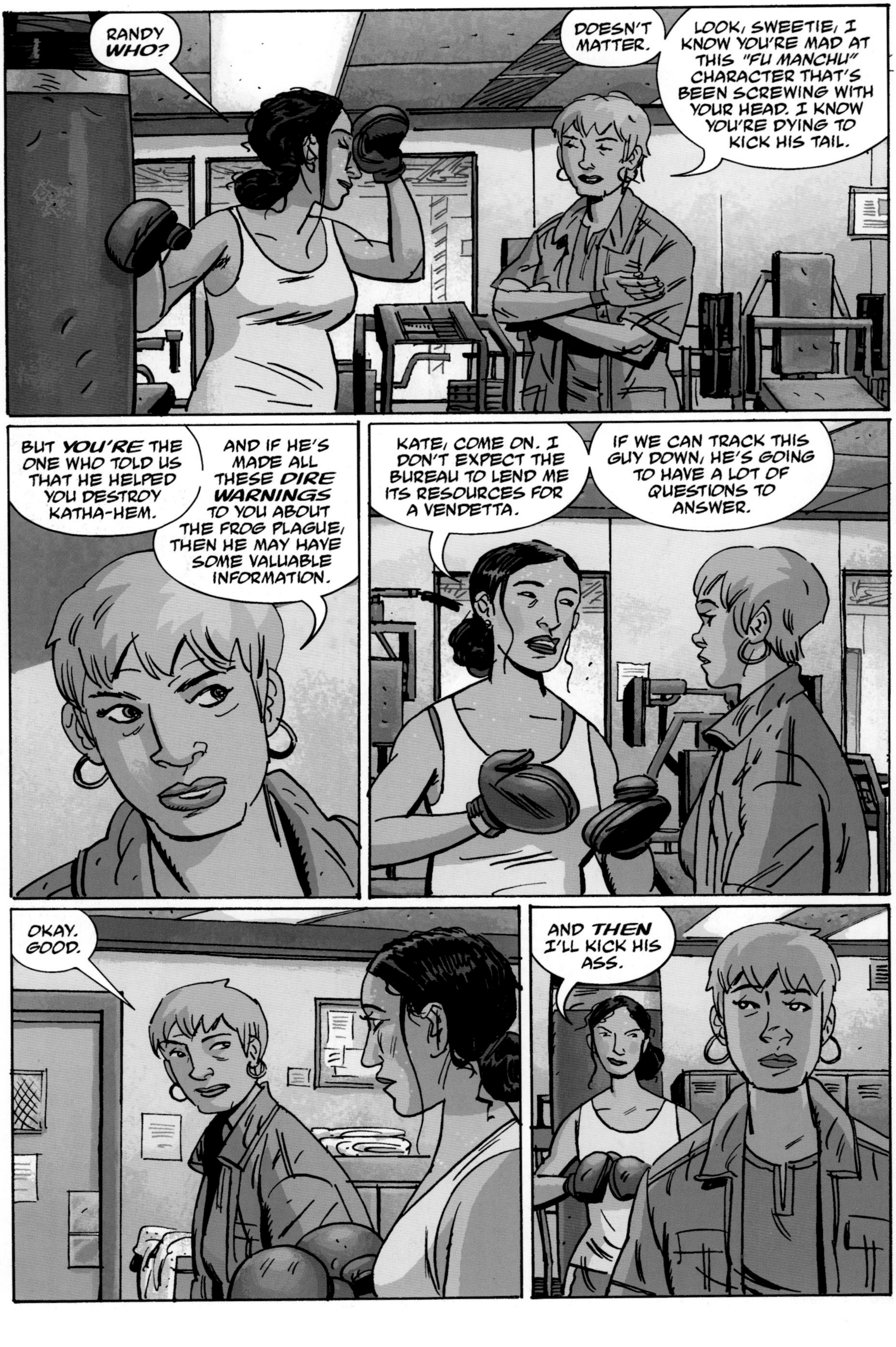
RANDY *WHO?*
DOESN'T MATTER.
LOOK, SWEETIE, I KNOW YOU'RE MAD AT THIS "FU MANCHU" CHARACTER THAT'S BEEN SCREWING WITH YOUR HEAD. I KNOW YOU'RE DYING TO KICK HIS TAIL.
BUT *YOU'RE* THE ONE WHO TOLD US THAT HE HELPED YOU DESTROY KATHA-HEM.
AND IF HE'S MADE ALL THESE *DIRE WARNINGS* TO YOU ABOUT THE FROG PLAGUE, THEN HE MAY HAVE SOME VALUABLE INFORMATION.
KATE, COME ON. I DON'T EXPECT THE BUREAU TO LEND ME ITS RESOURCES FOR A VENDETTA.
IF WE CAN TRACK THIS GUY DOWN, HE'S GOING TO HAVE A LOT OF QUESTIONS TO ANSWER.
OKAY. GOOD.
AND *THEN* I'LL KICK HIS ASS.

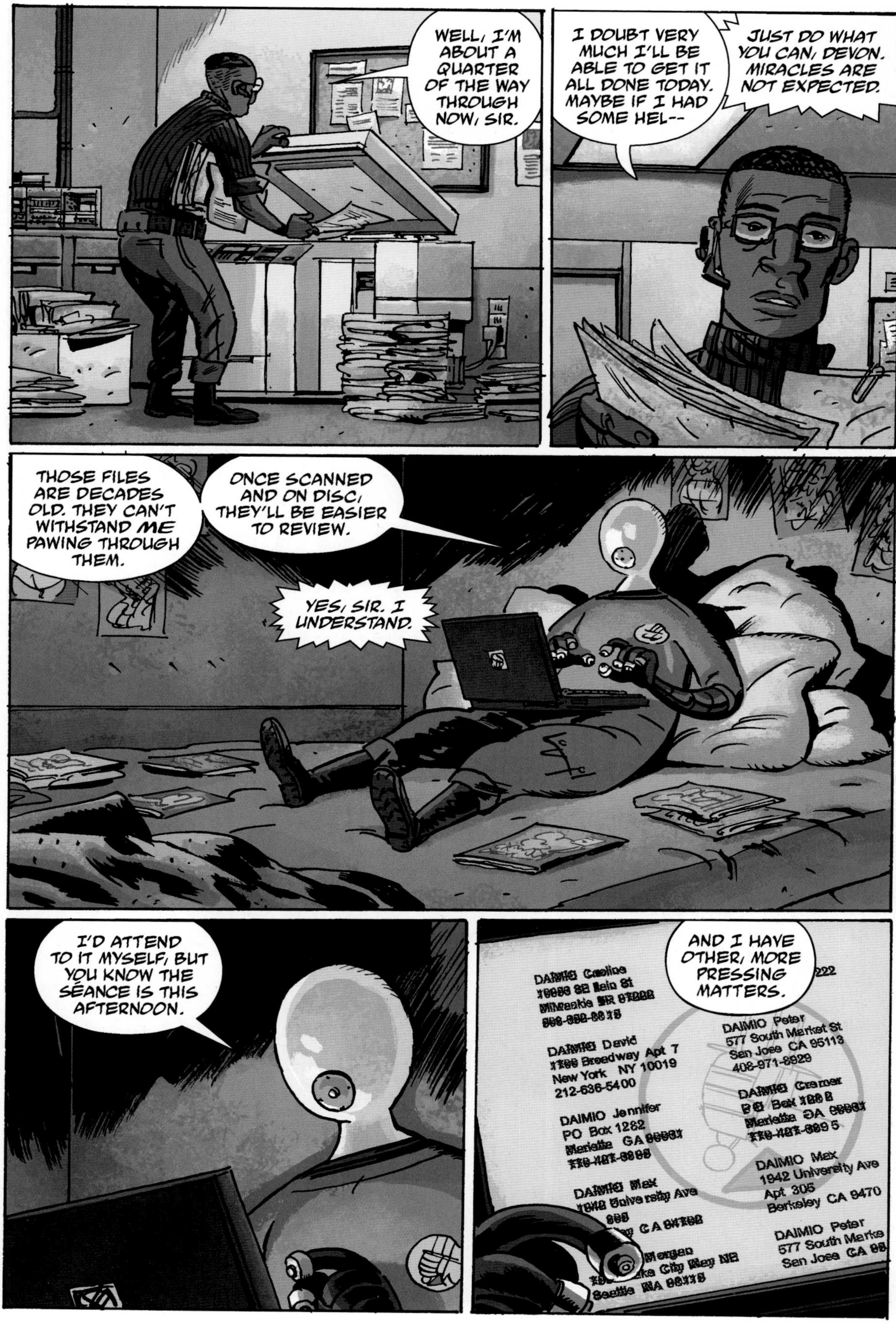
WELL, I'M ABOUT A QUARTER OF THE WAY THROUGH NOW, SIR.
I DOUBT VERY MUCH I'LL BE ABLE TO GET IT ALL DONE TODAY. MAYBE IF I HAD SOME HEL--
JUST DO WHAT YOU CAN, DEVON. MIRACLES ARE NOT EXPECTED.
THOSE FILES ARE DECADES OLD. THEY CAN'T WITHSTAND *ME* PAWING THROUGH THEM.
ONCE SCANNED AND ON DISC, THEY'LL BE EASIER TO REVIEW.
YES, SIR. I UNDERSTAND.
I'D ATTEND TO IT MYSELF, BUT YOU KNOW THE SÉANCE IS THIS AFTERNOON.
AND I HAVE OTHER, MORE PRESSING MATTERS.
New York NY 10019
212-636-5400
DAIMIO Peter
577 South Market St
San Jose CA 95113
408-971-6929
DAIMIO Jennifer
PO Box 1282
DAIMIO Max
1942 University Ave
Apt 305
Berkeley CA 9470

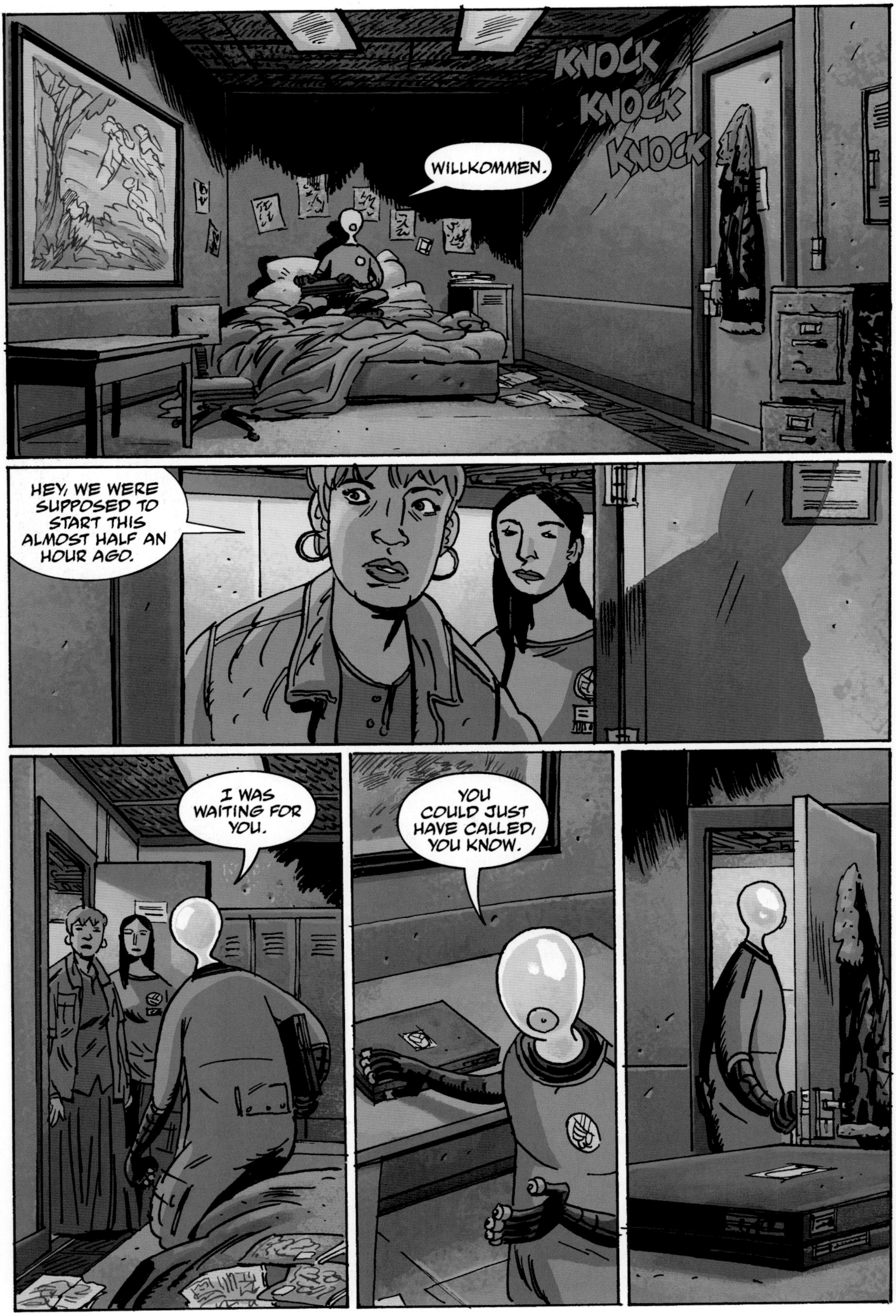
KNOCK
KNOCK
KNOCK
WILLKOMMEN.
HEY, WE WERE SUPPOSED TO START THIS ALMOST HALF AN HOUR AGO.
I WAS WAITING FOR YOU.
YOU COULD JUST HAVE CALLED, YOU KNOW.

WAIT. THE INFIRMARY? WHY HAVE WE COME HERE?

YOU SAID YOU WANTED AT LEAST FOUR OF US TO PARTICIPATE, AND WE CAN'T VERY WELL MOVE PANYA OUT OF HERE YET.

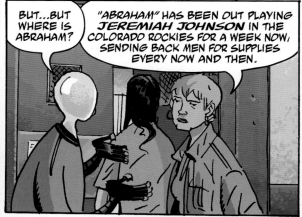

BUT...BUT WHERE IS ABRAHAM?

"ABRAHAM" HAS BEEN OUT PLAYING *JEREMIAH JOHNSON* IN THE COLORADO ROCKIES FOR A WEEK NOW, SENDING BACK MEN FOR SUPPLIES EVERY NOW AND THEN.

AND OUT THERE, HIS CELL PHONE DOESN'T WORK-- OR MAYBE HE JUST TURNED IT OFF.

EITHER WAY, WE'VE GOT PANYA.

DO YOU OBJECT, HERR KRAUS?

NO, NO. ONLY SURPRISED.

YOU KNOW, YOU PLAN FOR ONE THING, AND IT GOES ANOTHER WAY. IT THROWS YOU OFF.

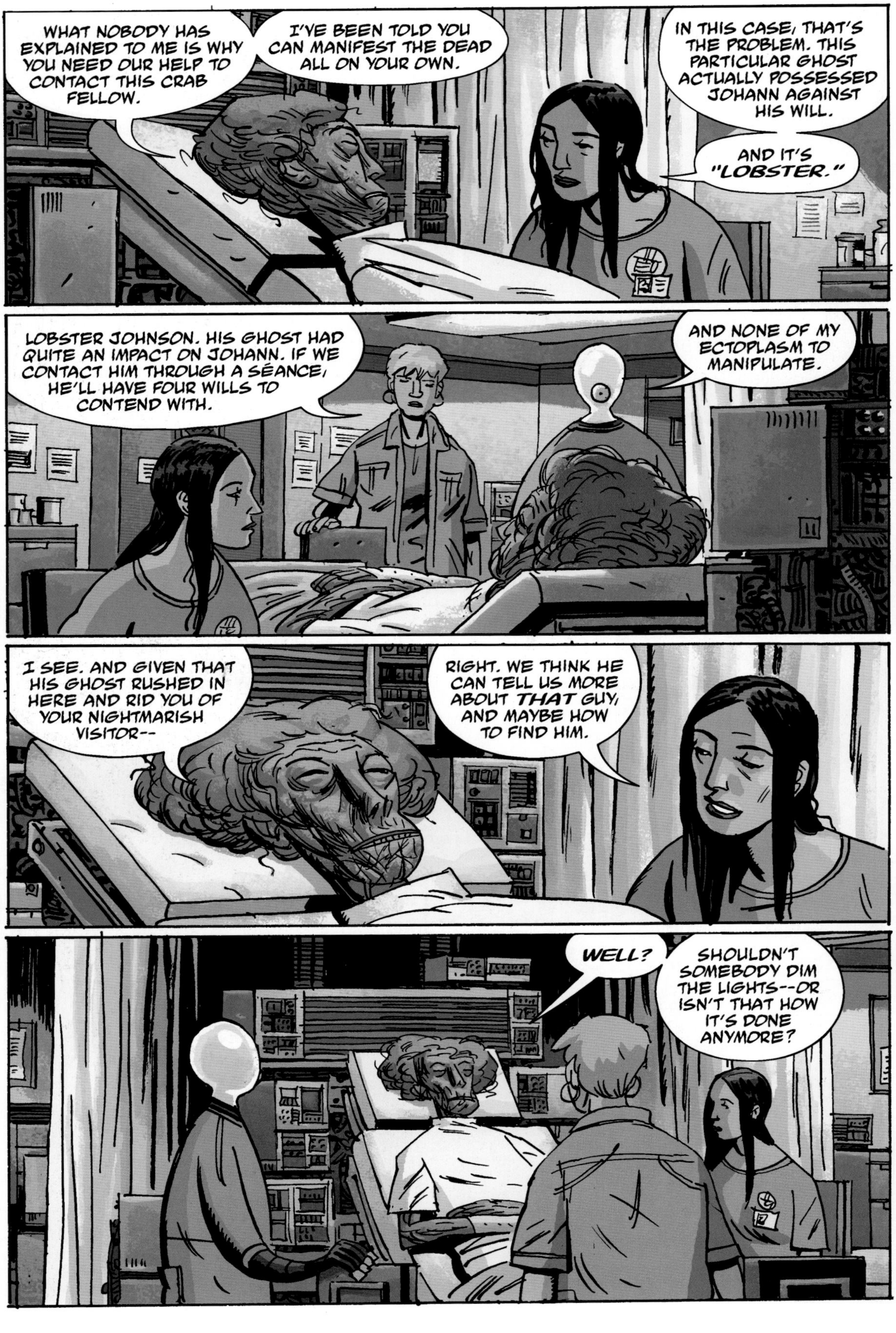
WHAT NOBODY HAS EXPLAINED TO ME IS WHY YOU NEED OUR HELP TO CONTACT THIS CRAB FELLOW.
I'VE BEEN TOLD YOU CAN MANIFEST THE DEAD ALL ON YOUR OWN.
IN THIS CASE, THAT'S THE PROBLEM. THIS PARTICULAR GHOST ACTUALLY POSSESSED JOHANN AGAINST HIS WILL.
AND IT'S "LOBSTER."
LOBSTER JOHNSON. HIS GHOST HAD QUITE AN IMPACT ON JOHANN. IF WE CONTACT HIM THROUGH A SÉANCE, HE'LL HAVE FOUR WILLS TO CONTEND WITH.
AND NONE OF MY ECTOPLASM TO MANIPULATE.
I SEE. AND GIVEN THAT HIS GHOST RUSHED IN HERE AND RID YOU OF YOUR NIGHTMARISH VISITOR--
RIGHT. WE THINK HE CAN TELL US MORE ABOUT THAT GUY, AND MAYBE HOW TO FIND HIM.
WELL?
SHOULDN'T SOMEBODY DIM THE LIGHTS--OR ISN'T THAT HOW IT'S DONE ANYMORE?

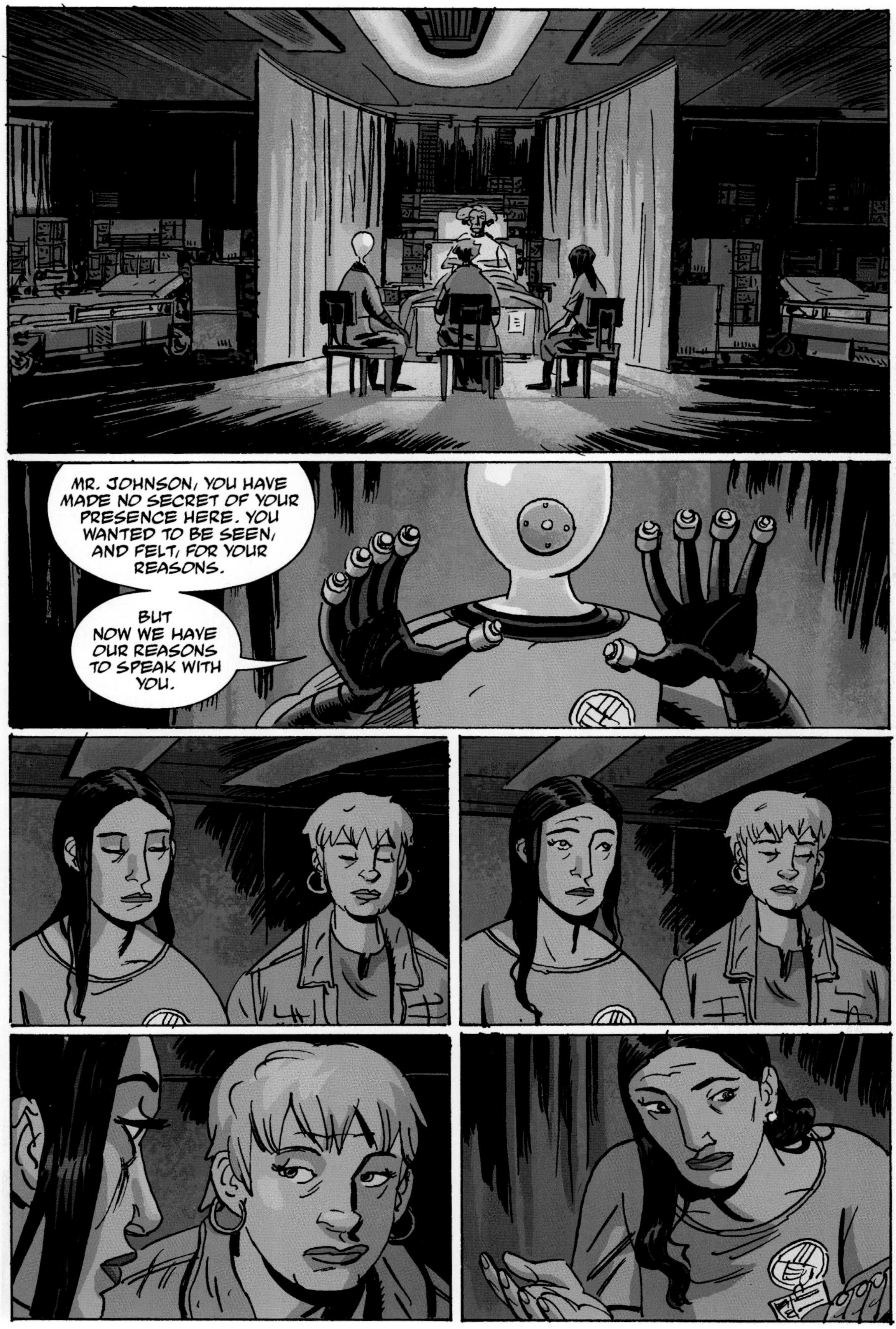
MR. JOHNSON, YOU HAVE MADE NO SECRET OF YOUR PRESENCE HERE. YOU WANTED TO BE SEEN, AND FELT, FOR YOUR REASONS.
BUT NOW WE HAVE OUR REASONS TO SPEAK WITH YOU.

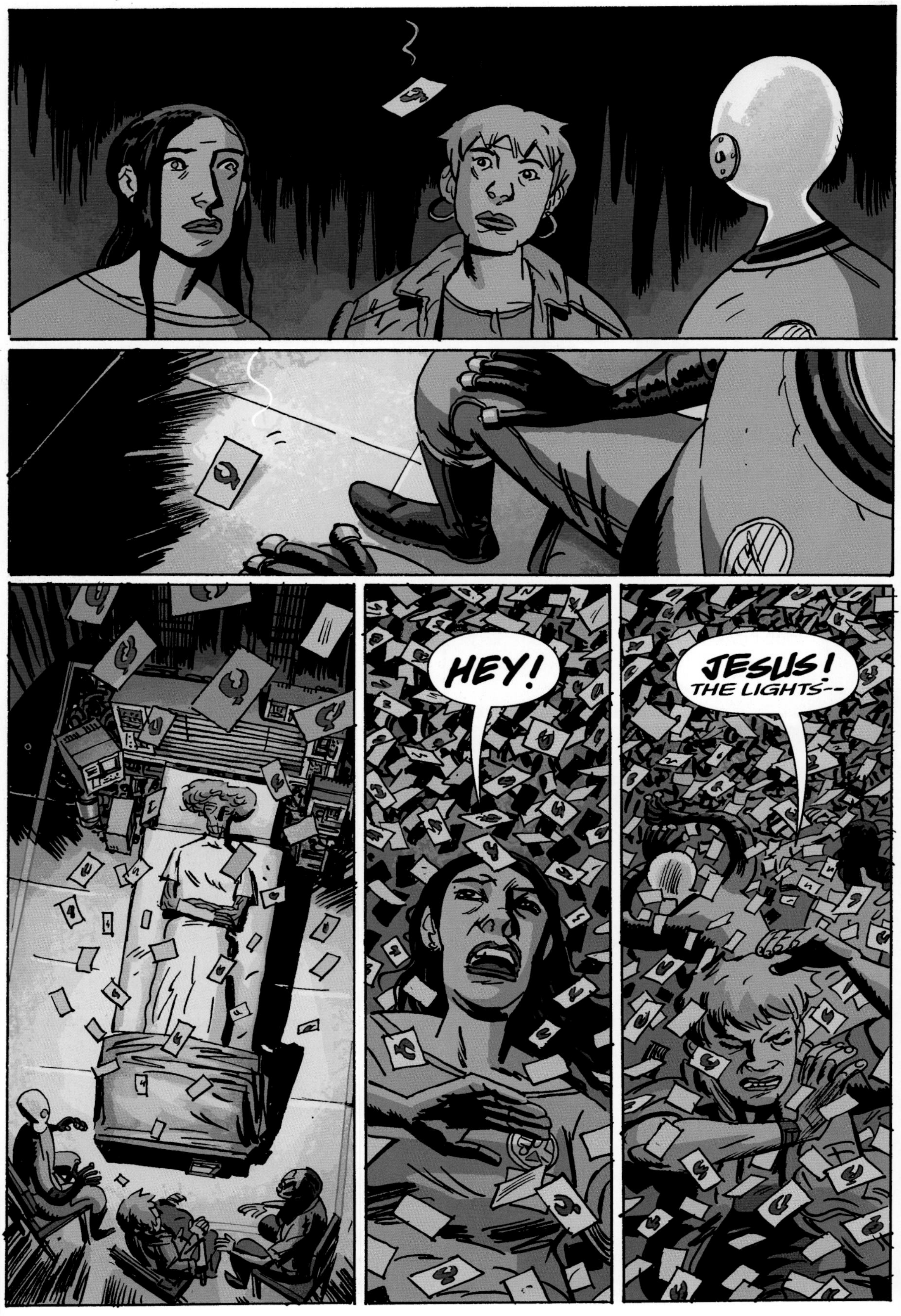
HEY!
JESUS! THE LIGHTS--

--SOMEBODY GET--

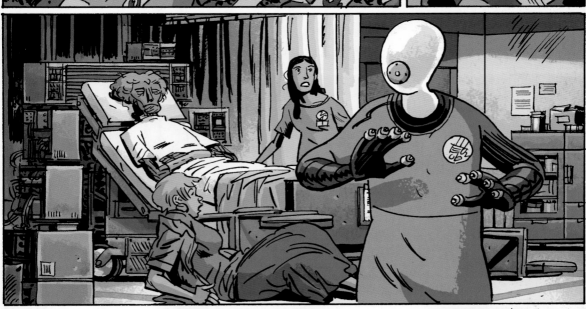

WHAT THE F--

LOOK!

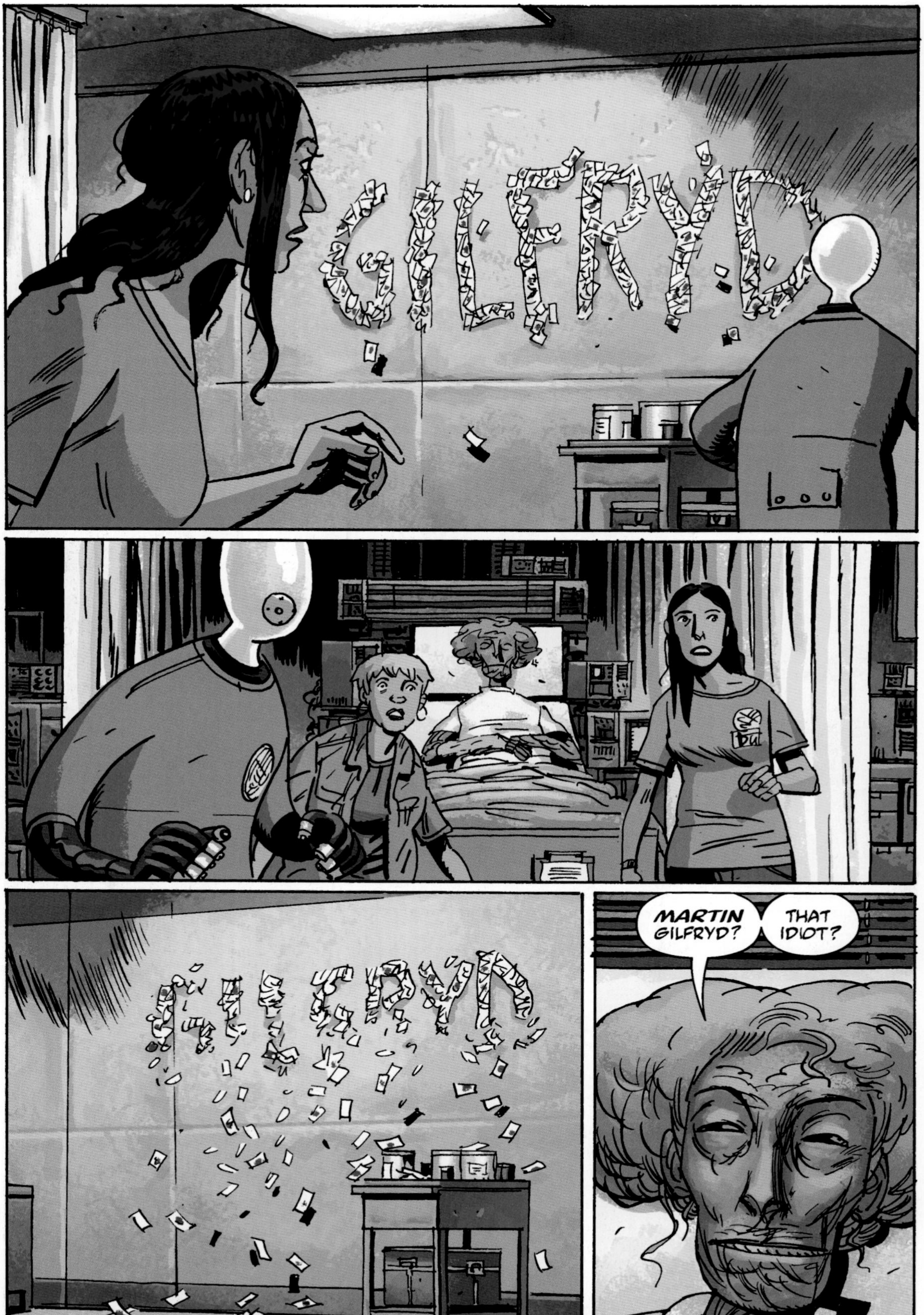
GILFRYD
MARTIN GILFRYD?
THAT IDIOT?

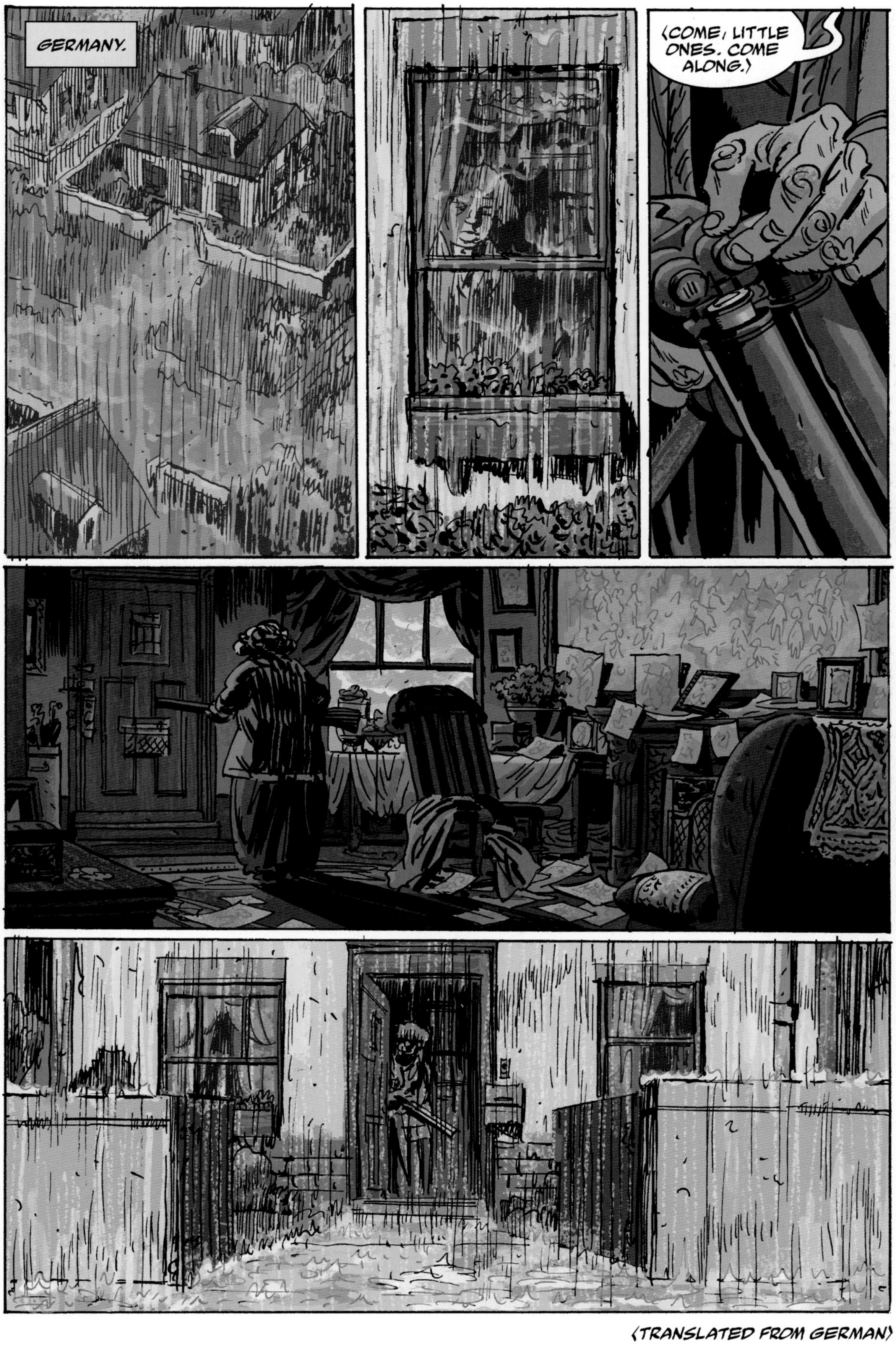
GERMANY.
⟨COME, LITTLE ONES. COME ALONG.⟩

⟨TRANSLATED FROM GERMAN⟩

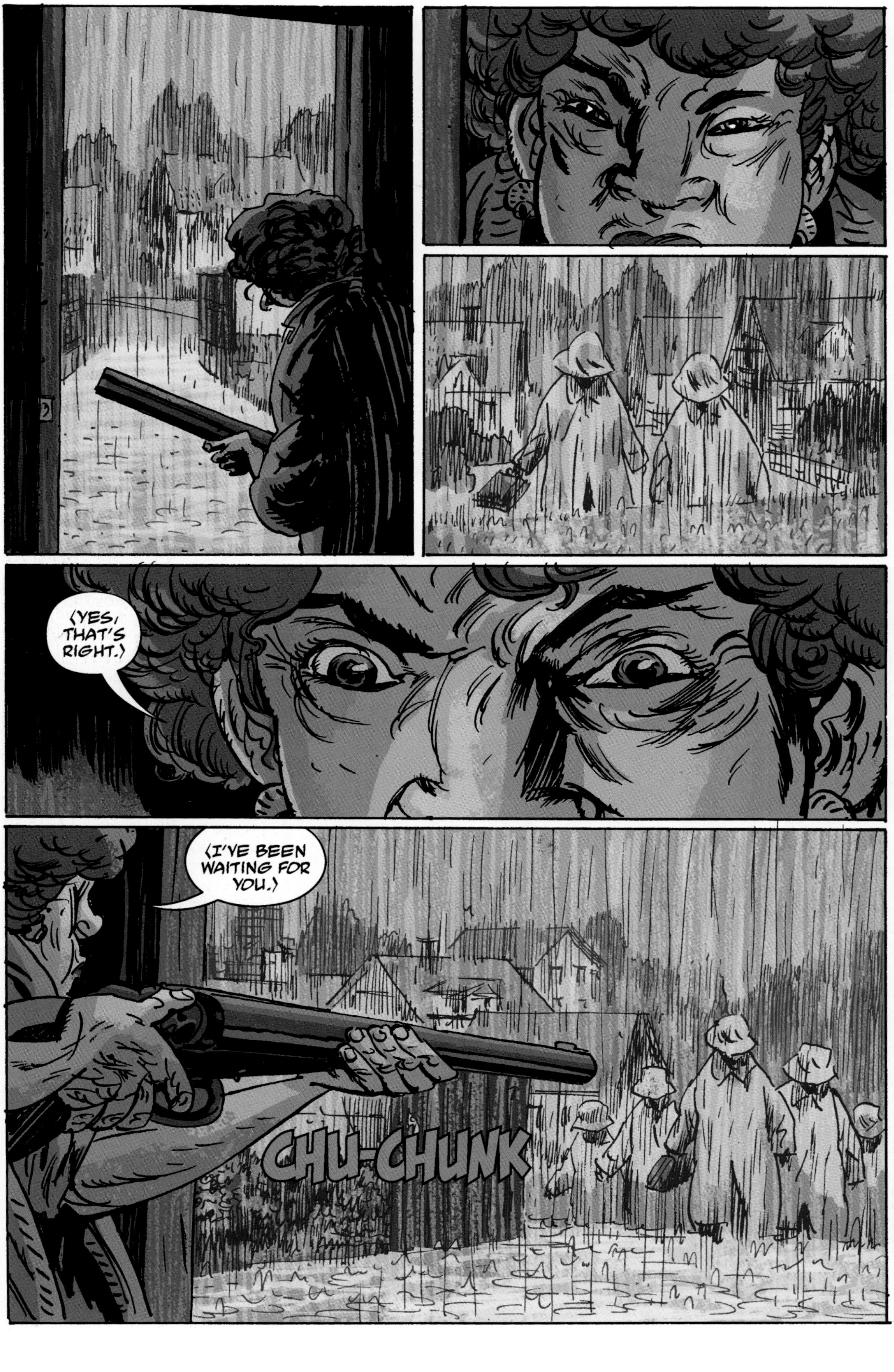

⟨YES, THAT'S RIGHT.⟩
⟨I'VE BEEN WAITING FOR YOU.⟩
CHU-CHUNK

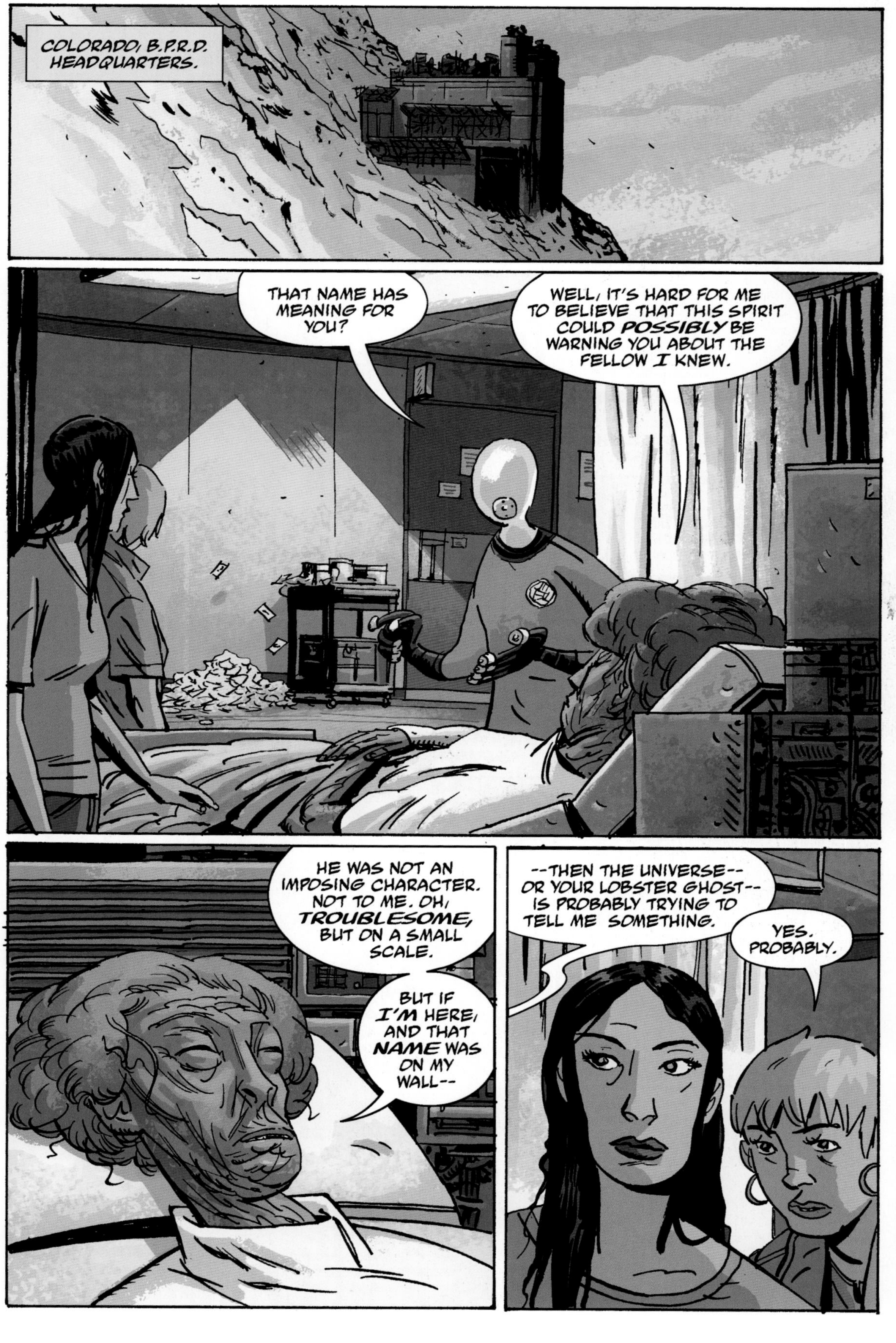
COLORADO, B.P.R.D. HEADQUARTERS.
THAT NAME HAS MEANING FOR YOU?
WELL, IT'S HARD FOR ME TO BELIEVE THAT THIS SPIRIT COULD POSSIBLY BE WARNING YOU ABOUT THE FELLOW I KNEW.
HE WAS NOT AN IMPOSING CHARACTER. NOT TO ME. OH, TROUBLESOME, BUT ON A SMALL SCALE.
BUT IF I'M HERE, AND THAT NAME WAS ON MY WALL--
--THEN THE UNIVERSE-- OR YOUR LOBSTER GHOST-- IS PROBABLY TRYING TO TELL ME SOMETHING.
YES. PROBABLY.

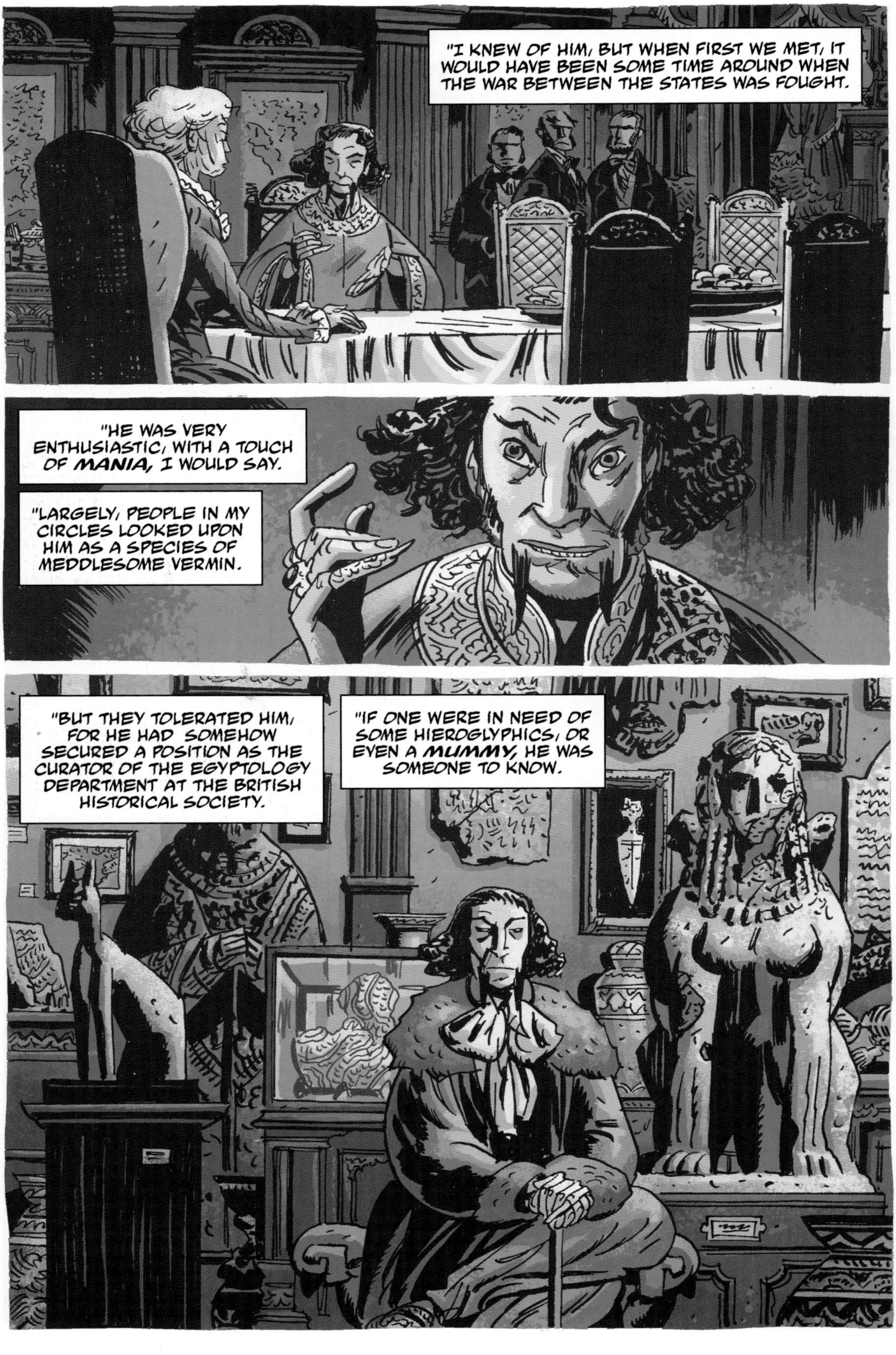
"I KNEW OF HIM, BUT WHEN FIRST WE MET, IT WOULD HAVE BEEN SOME TIME AROUND WHEN THE WAR BETWEEN THE STATES WAS FOUGHT.
"HE WAS VERY ENTHUSIASTIC, WITH A TOUCH OF MANIA, I WOULD SAY.
"LARGELY, PEOPLE IN MY CIRCLES LOOKED UPON HIM AS A SPECIES OF MEDDLESOME VERMIN.
"BUT THEY TOLERATED HIM, FOR HE HAD SOMEHOW SECURED A POSITION AS THE CURATOR OF THE EGYPTOLOGY DEPARTMENT AT THE BRITISH HISTORICAL SOCIETY.
"IF ONE WERE IN NEED OF SOME HIEROGLYPHICS, OR EVEN A MUMMY, HE WAS SOMEONE TO KNOW.

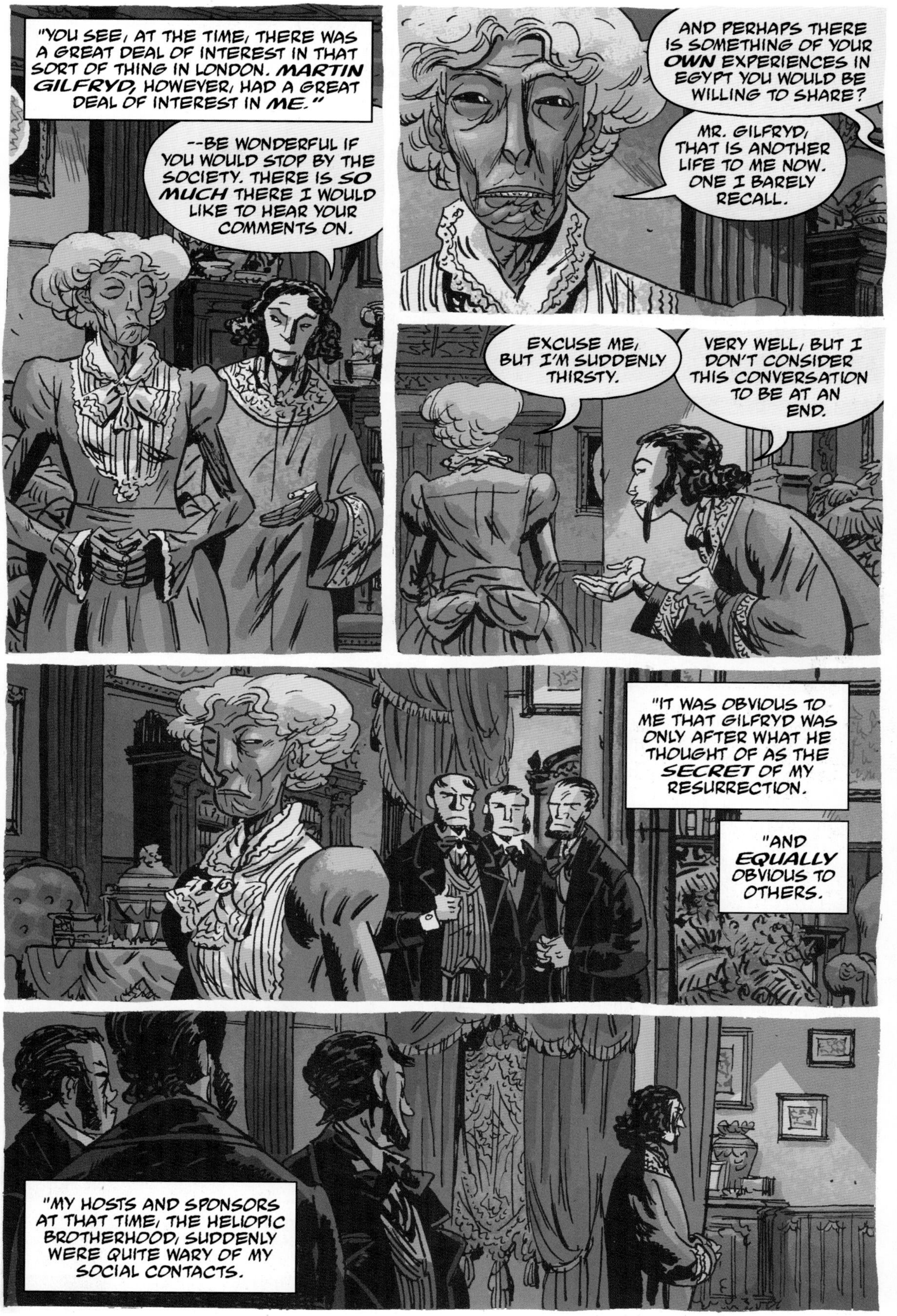
"YOU SEE, AT THE TIME, THERE WAS A GREAT DEAL OF INTEREST IN THAT SORT OF THING IN LONDON. MARTIN GILFRYD, HOWEVER, HAD A GREAT DEAL OF INTEREST IN ME."
--BE WONDERFUL IF YOU WOULD STOP BY THE SOCIETY. THERE IS SO MUCH THERE I WOULD LIKE TO HEAR YOUR COMMENTS ON.
AND PERHAPS THERE IS SOMETHING OF YOUR OWN EXPERIENCES IN EGYPT YOU WOULD BE WILLING TO SHARE?
MR. GILFRYD, THAT IS ANOTHER LIFE TO ME NOW. ONE I BARELY RECALL.
EXCUSE ME, BUT I'M SUDDENLY THIRSTY.
VERY WELL, BUT I DON'T CONSIDER THIS CONVERSATION TO BE AT AN END.
"IT WAS OBVIOUS TO ME THAT GILFRYD WAS ONLY AFTER WHAT HE THOUGHT OF AS THE SECRET OF MY RESURRECTION.
"AND EQUALLY OBVIOUS TO OTHERS.
"MY HOSTS AND SPONSORS AT THAT TIME, THE HELIOPIC BROTHERHOOD, SUDDENLY WERE QUITE WARY OF MY SOCIAL CONTACTS.

"SOON THEREAFTER, AS YOU MAY HAVE HEARD, I WAS CONFINED BY THE BROTHERS TO THEIR LONDON MANOR.

"I SAW NO MORE OF GILFRYD, OR *ANYONE ELSE*, FOR THAT MATTER...

"...ALTHOUGH I HEARD OF HIM NOW AND AGAIN.

"HE APPARENTLY FELL ON HARD TIMES IN ENSUING YEARS, AND TOOK UP WITH A PARTICULARLY VILE *OCCULTIST*.

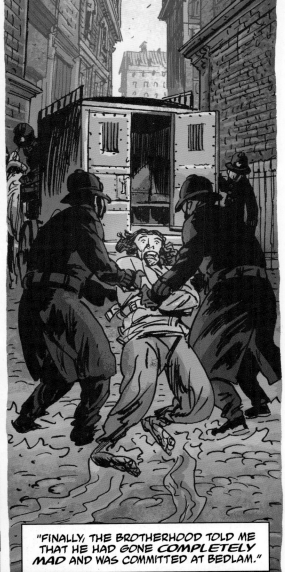

"FINALLY, THE BROTHERHOOD TOLD ME THAT HE HAD GONE *COMPLETELY MAD* AND WAS COMMITTED AT BEDLAM."

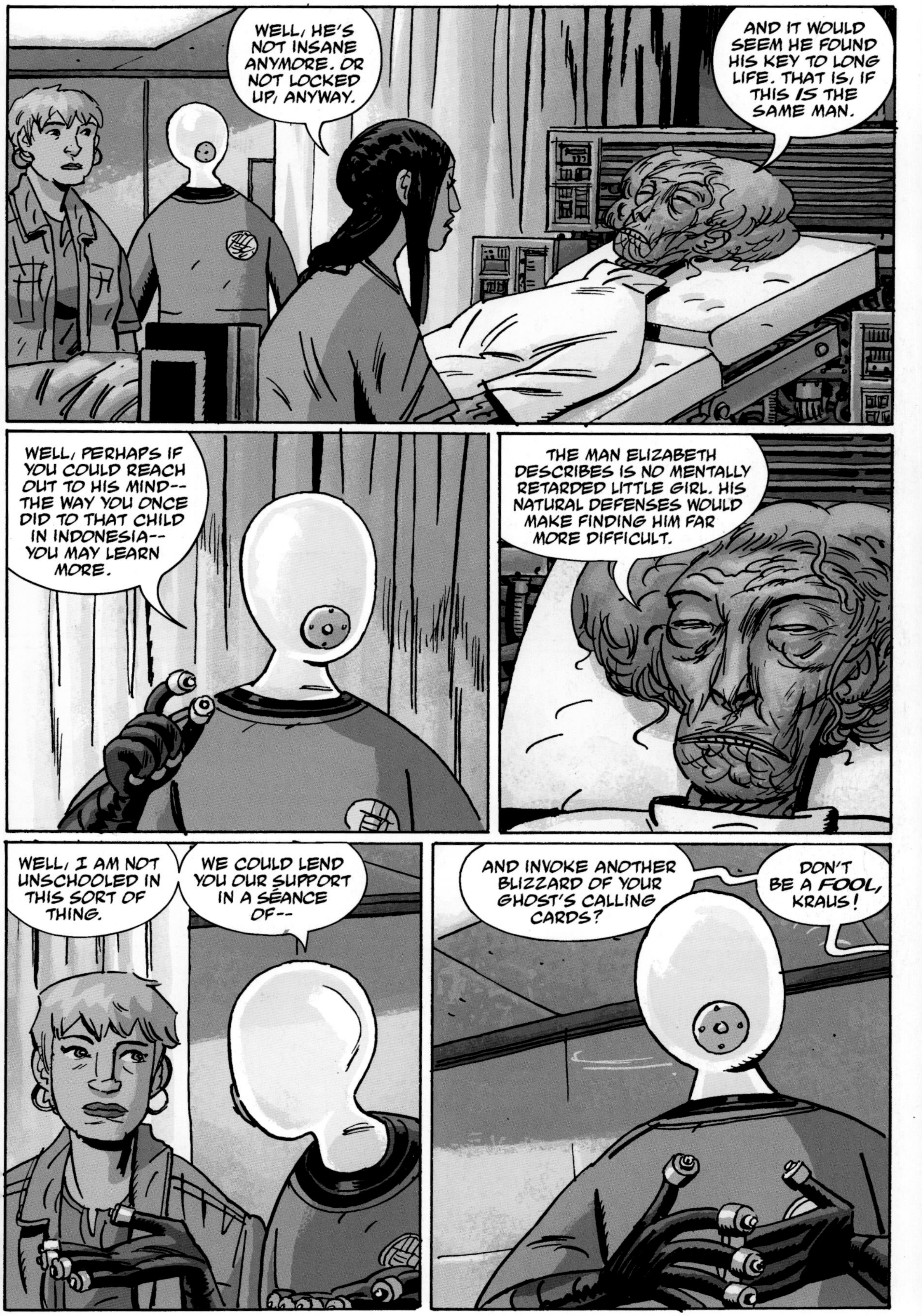
WELL, HE'S NOT INSANE ANYMORE. OR NOT LOCKED UP, ANYWAY.
AND IT WOULD SEEM HE FOUND HIS KEY TO LONG LIFE. THAT IS, IF THIS IS THE SAME MAN.
WELL, PERHAPS IF YOU COULD REACH OUT TO HIS MIND-- THE WAY YOU ONCE DID TO THAT CHILD IN INDONESIA-- YOU MAY LEARN MORE.
THE MAN ELIZABETH DESCRIBES IS NO MENTALLY RETARDED LITTLE GIRL. HIS NATURAL DEFENSES WOULD MAKE FINDING HIM FAR MORE DIFFICULT.
WELL, I AM NOT UNSCHOOLED IN THIS SORT OF THING.
WE COULD LEND YOU OUR SUPPORT IN A SÉANCE OF--
AND INVOKE ANOTHER BLIZZARD OF YOUR GHOST'S CALLING CARDS?
DON'T BE A FOOL, KRAUS!

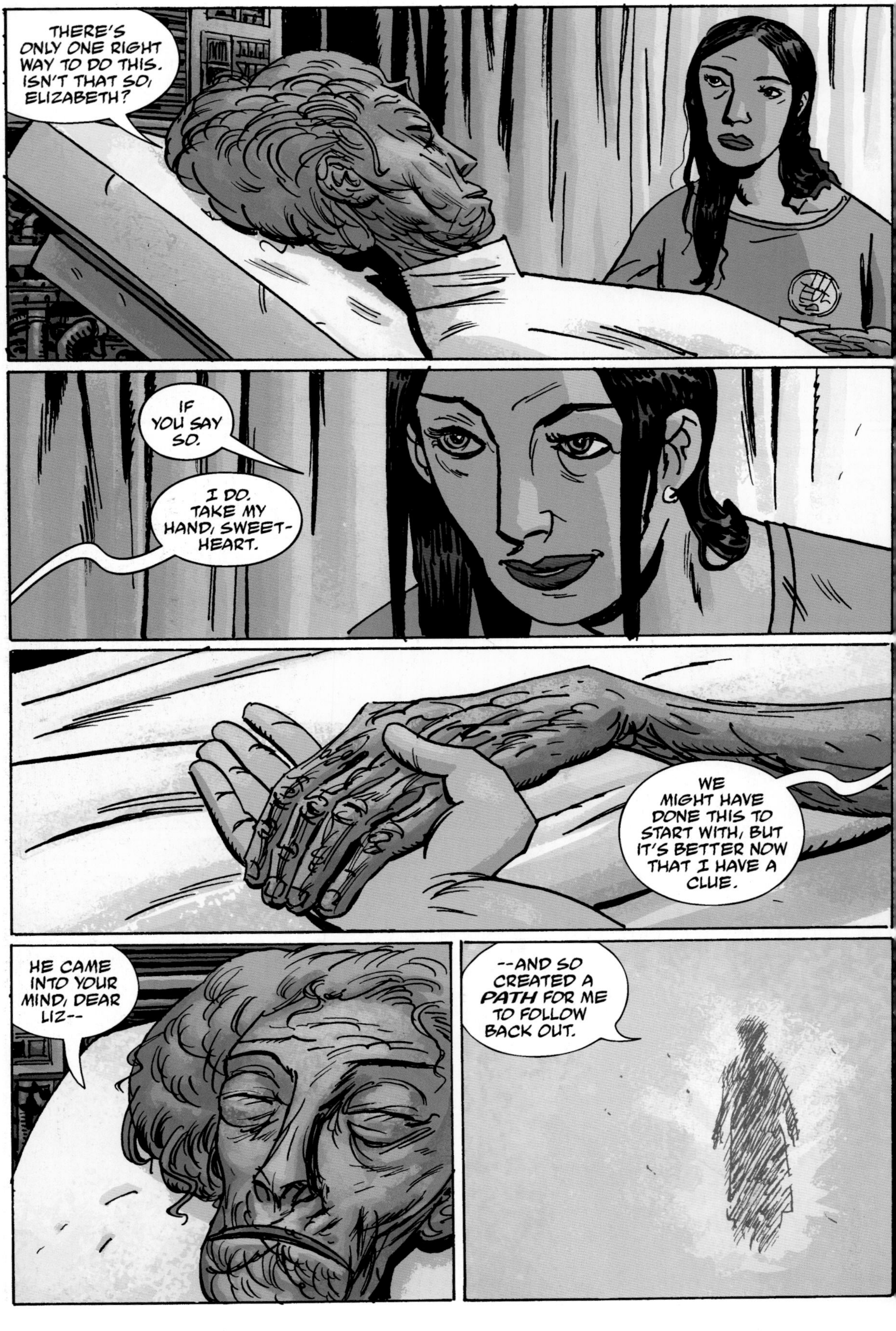
THERE'S ONLY ONE RIGHT WAY TO DO THIS. ISN'T THAT SO, ELIZABETH?
IF YOU SAY SO.
I DO. TAKE MY HAND, SWEET-HEART.
WE MIGHT HAVE DONE THIS TO START WITH, BUT IT'S BETTER NOW THAT I HAVE A CLUE.
HE CAME INTO YOUR MIND, DEAR LIZ--
--AND SO CREATED A PATH FOR ME TO FOLLOW BACK OUT.

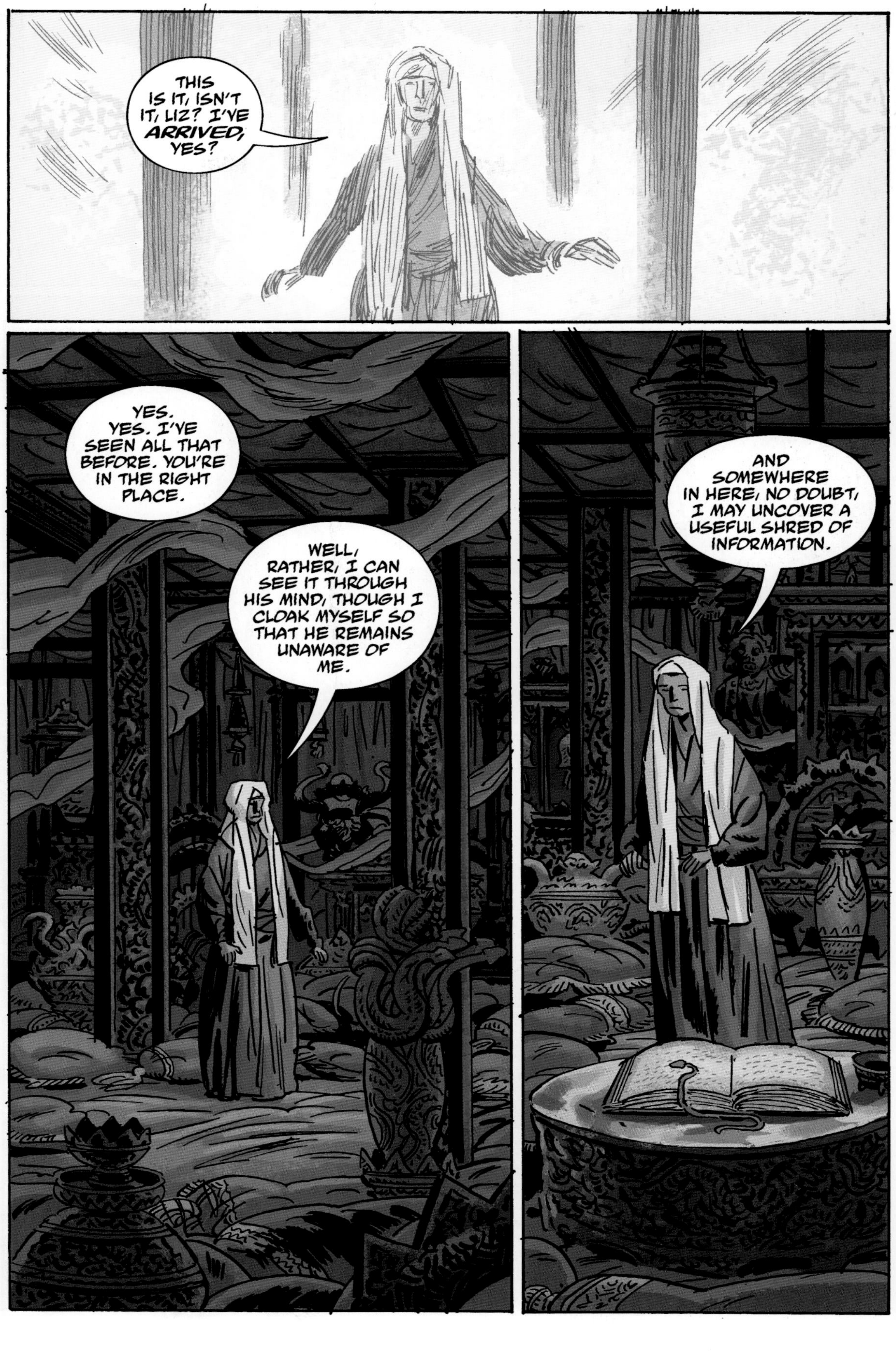
THIS IS IT, ISN'T IT, LIZ? I'VE *ARRIVED,* YES?
YES. YES. I'VE SEEN ALL THAT BEFORE. YOU'RE IN THE RIGHT PLACE.
WELL, RATHER, I CAN SEE IT THROUGH HIS MIND, THOUGH I CLOAK MYSELF SO THAT HE REMAINS UNAWARE OF ME.
AND SOMEWHERE IN HERE, NO DOUBT, I MAY UNCOVER A USEFUL SHRED OF INFORMATION.

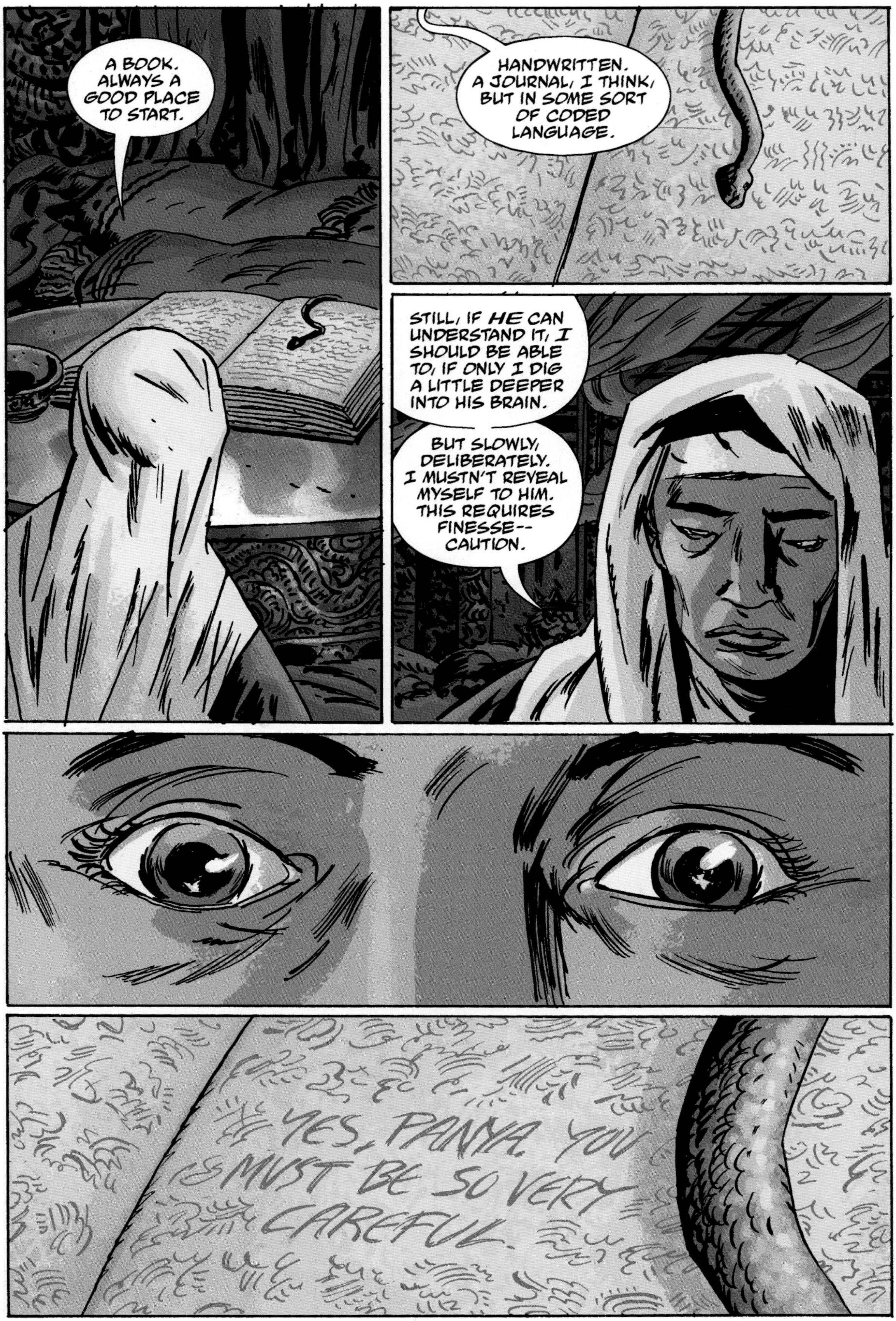
A BOOK. ALWAYS A GOOD PLACE TO START.
HANDWRITTEN. A JOURNAL, I THINK, BUT IN SOME SORT OF CODED LANGUAGE.
STILL, IF HE CAN UNDERSTAND IT, I SHOULD BE ABLE TO, IF ONLY I DIG A LITTLE DEEPER INTO HIS BRAIN.
BUT SLOWLY, DELIBERATELY. I MUSTN'T REVEAL MYSELF TO HIM. THIS REQUIRES FINESSE-- CAUTION.
YES, PANYA. YOU MUST BE SO VERY CAREFUL.

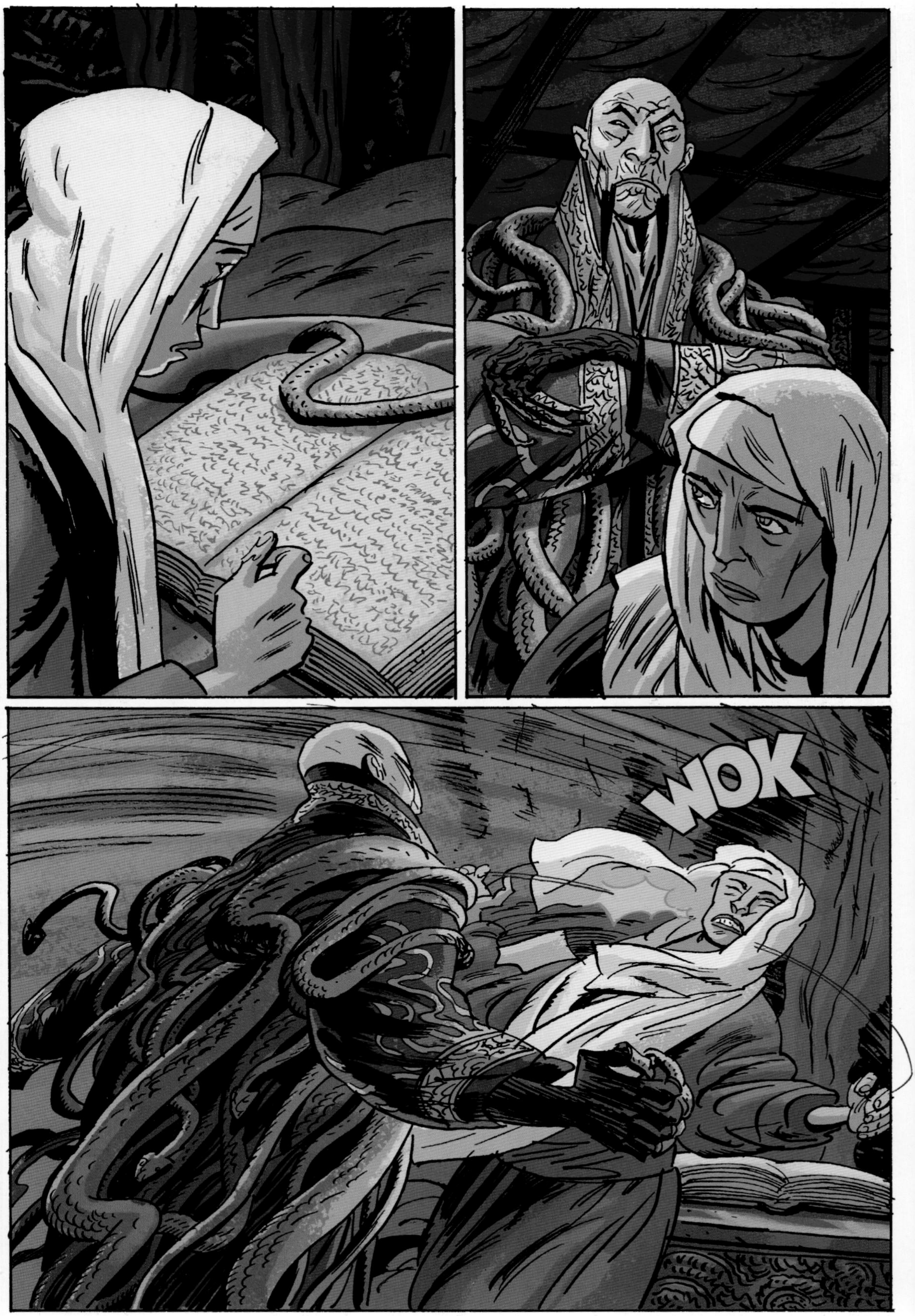
WOK

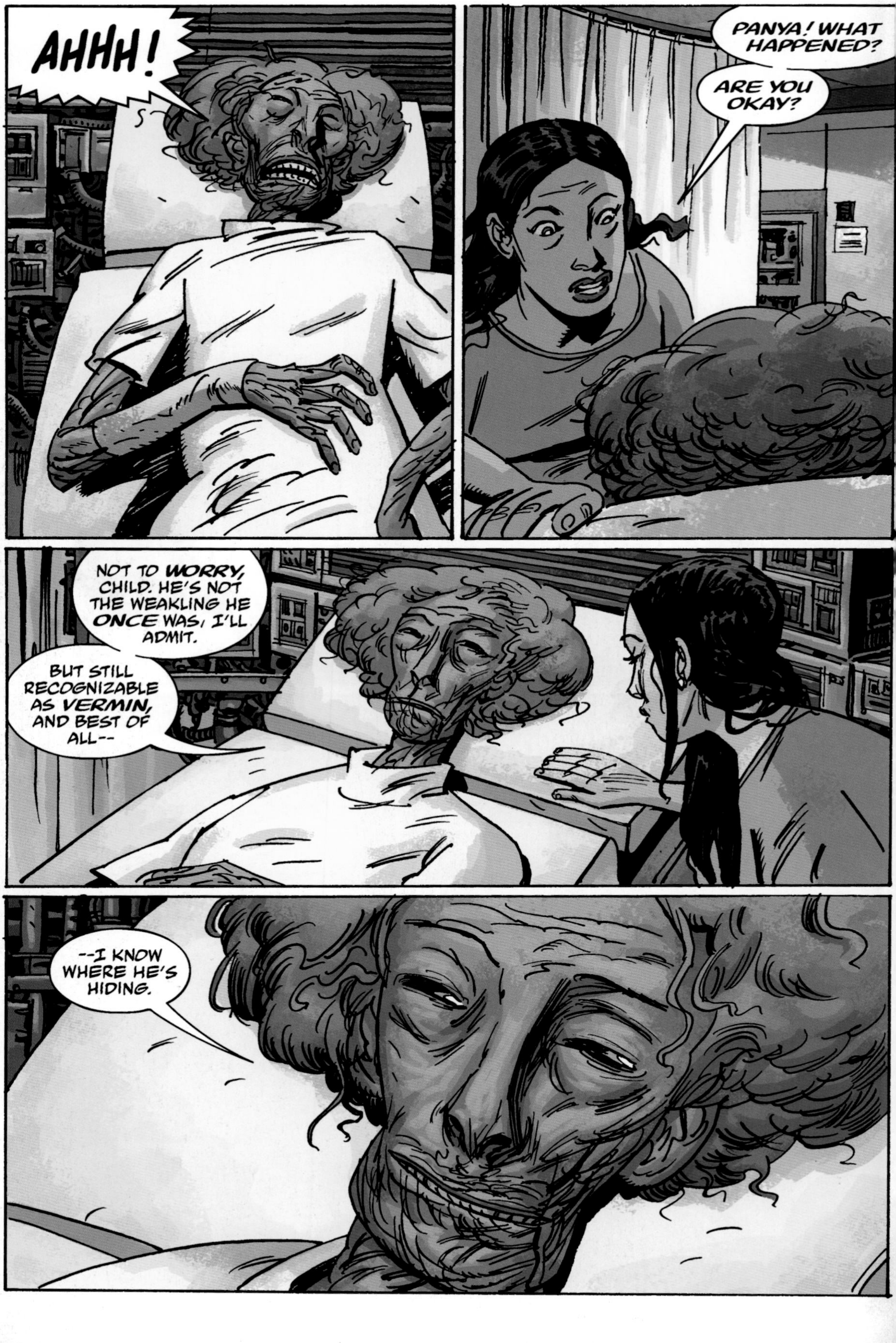
AHHH!
PANYA! WHAT HAPPENED?
ARE YOU OKAY?
NOT TO WORRY, CHILD. HE'S NOT THE WEAKLING HE ONCE WAS, I'LL ADMIT.
BUT STILL RECOGNIZABLE AS VERMIN, AND BEST OF ALL--
--I KNOW WHERE HE'S HIDING.

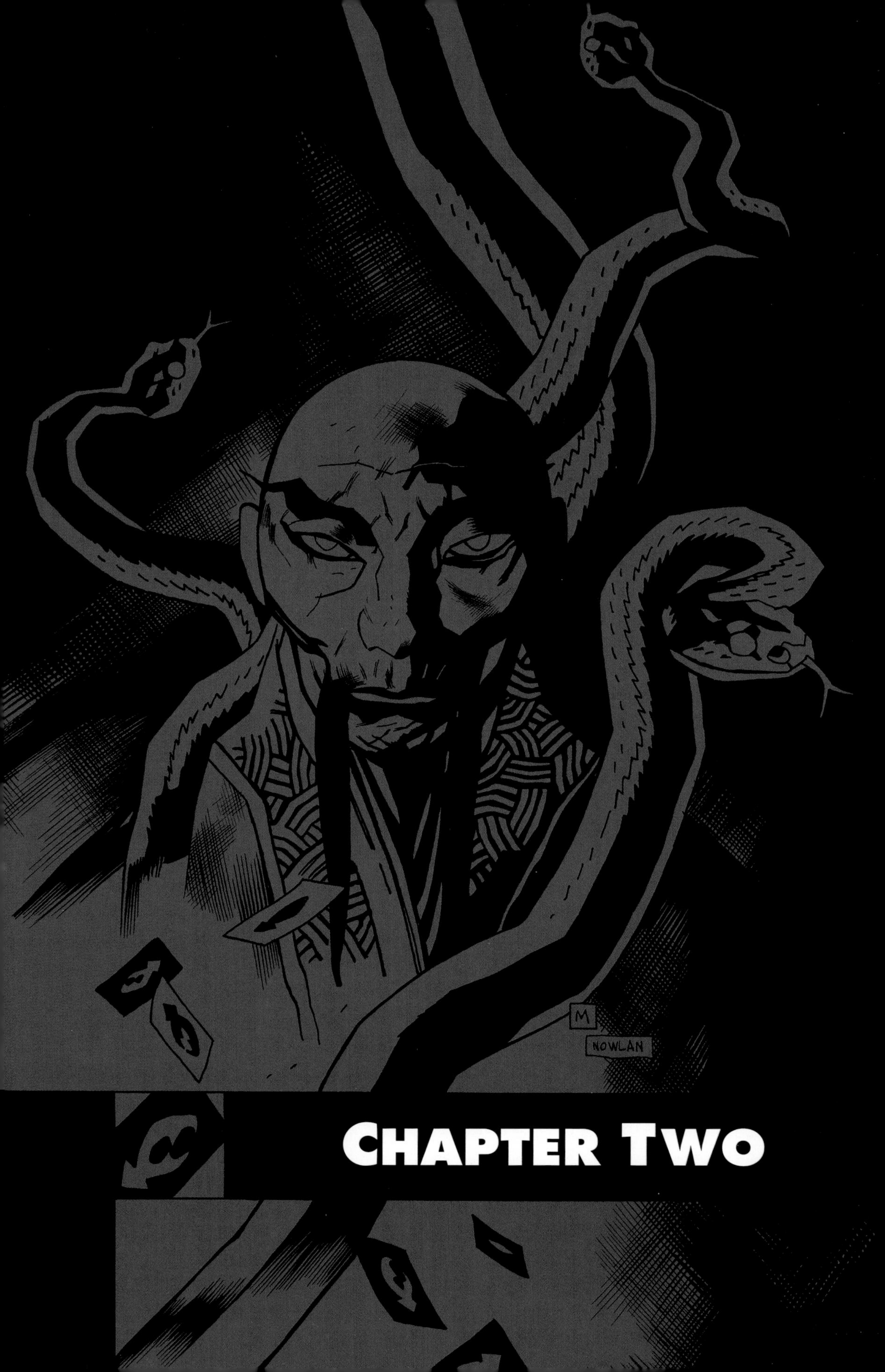
M
NOWLAN

CHAPTER TWO

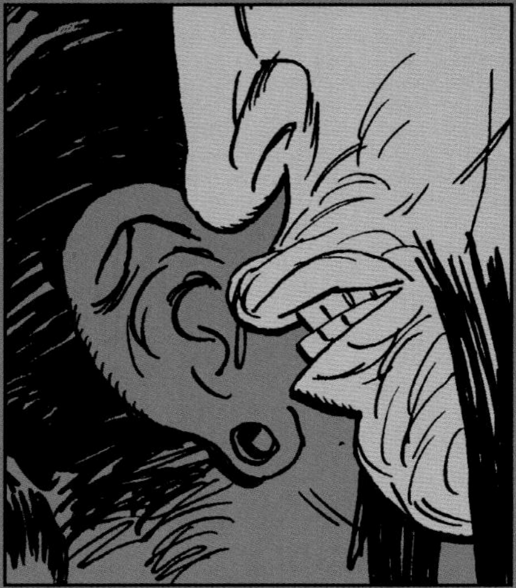

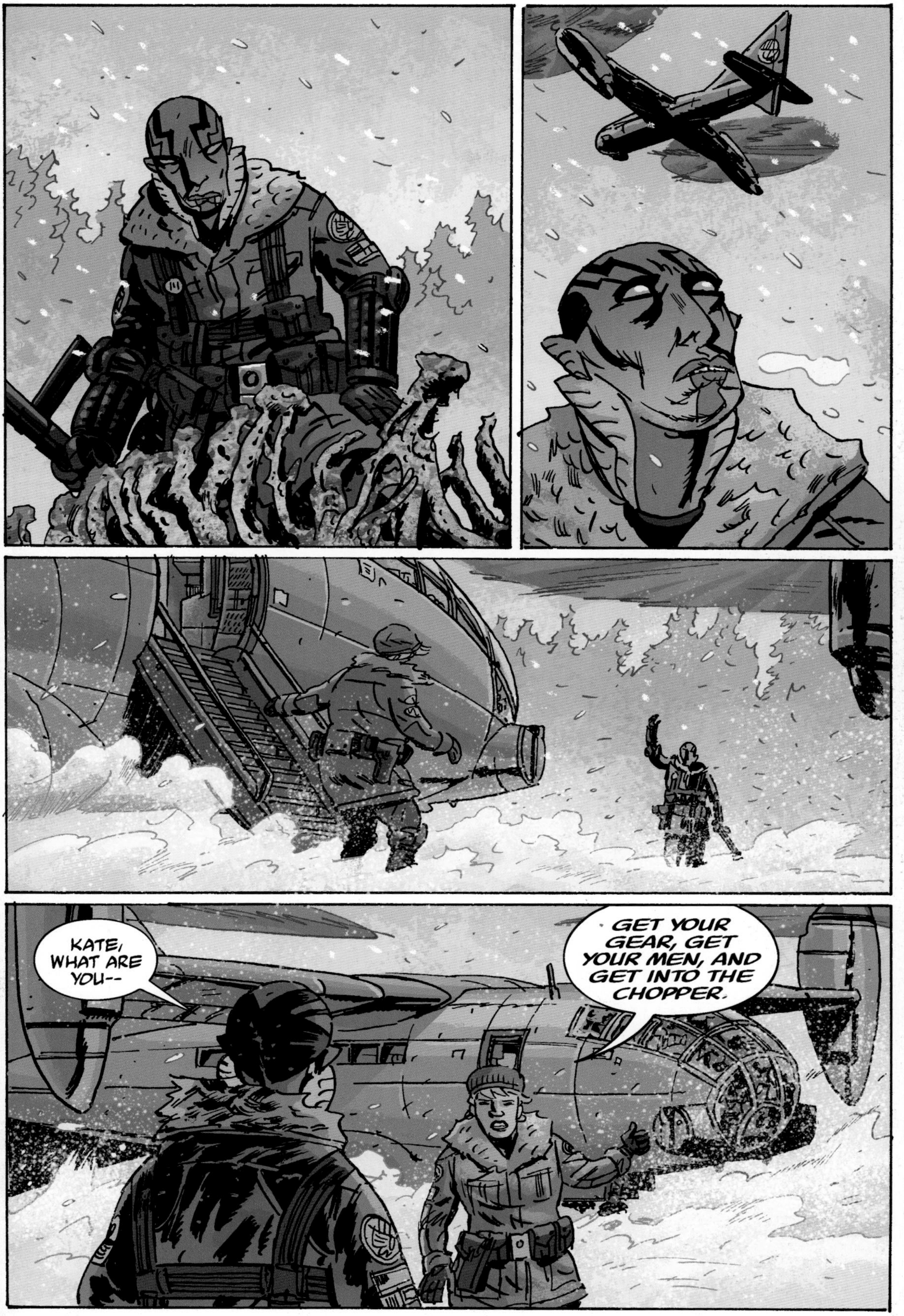
KATE, WHAT ARE YOU--
GET YOUR GEAR, GET YOUR MEN, AND GET INTO THE CHOPPER.

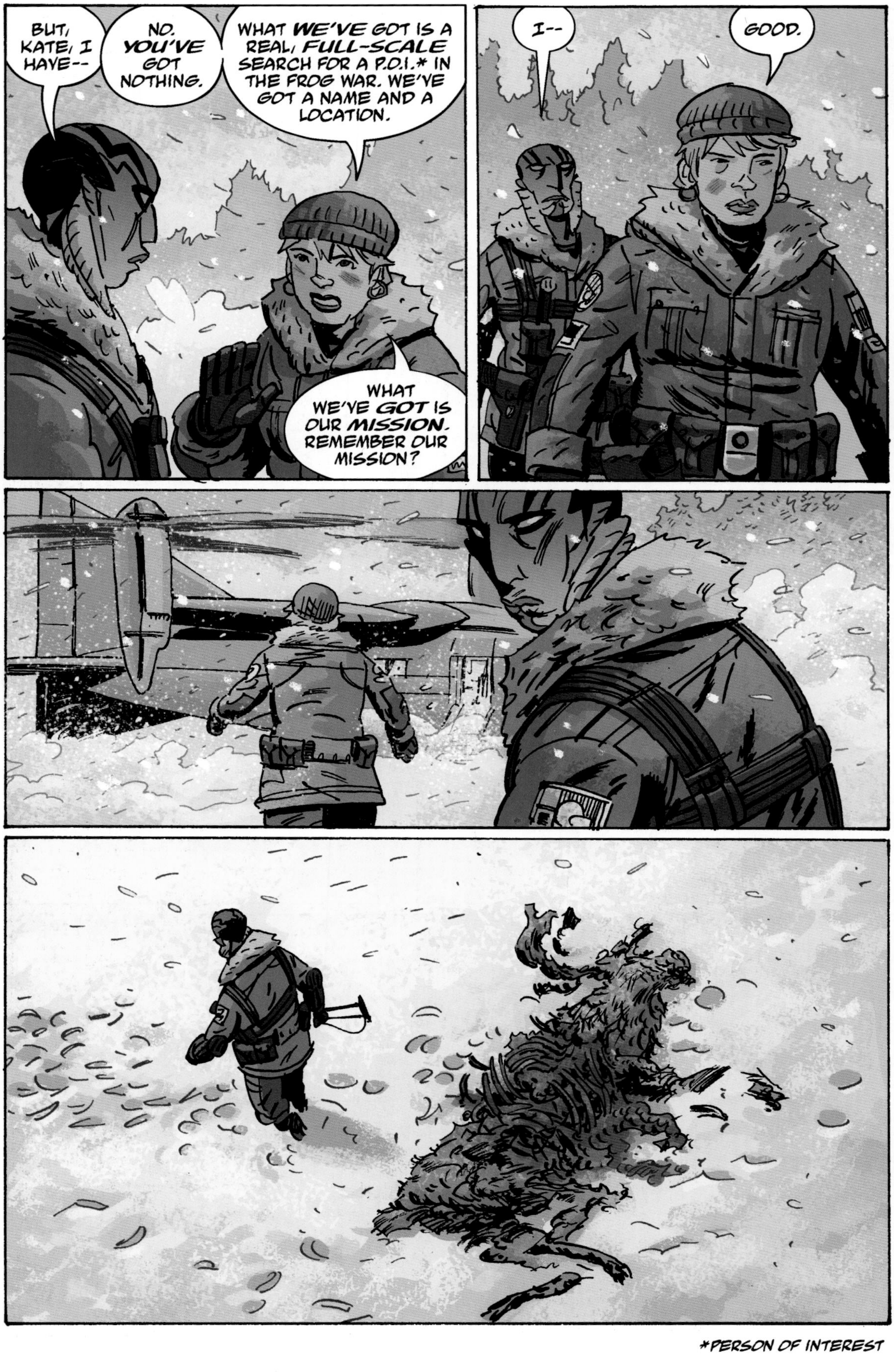
BUT, KATE, I HAVE--
NO. YOU'VE GOT NOTHING.
WHAT WE'VE GOT IS A REAL, FULL-SCALE SEARCH FOR A P.O.I.* IN THE FROG WAR. WE'VE GOT A NAME AND A LOCATION.
WHAT WE'VE GOT IS OUR MISSION. REMEMBER OUR MISSION?
I--
GOOD.

*PERSON OF INTEREST

PLEASE TO EXCUSE ME.

YOU HAVE A BIG TRIP TO MAKE. SHOULDN'T YOU BE PREPARING?

WELL, I JUST WANTED TO THANK YOU FOR LOCATING THAT GILFRYD GENTLEMAN. HE'S BEEN A TROUBLE TO ELIZABETH FOR SO LONG NOW.

THAT'S EXACTLY WHY I HAD TO HELP. SHE'S SUCH A DEAR.

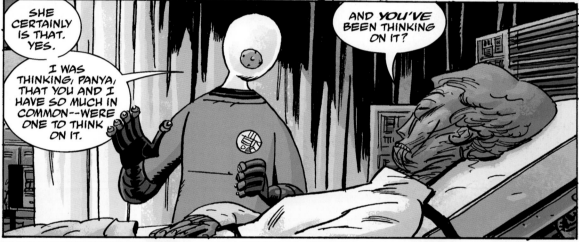

SHE CERTAINLY IS THAT. YES.

I WAS THINKING, PANYA, THAT YOU AND I HAVE SO MUCH IN COMMON--WERE ONE TO THINK ON IT.

AND *YOU'VE* BEEN THINKING ON IT?

WHAT I MEAN IS, EACH OF US IS A MEDIUM. EACH OF US IS ABLE TO CONNECT PEOPLE--FIND THE MISSING, BRING THEM TO THOSE WHO SEEK.

I CAN LOCATE A SOUL AMONG THE DEAD, WHILE YOU CAN TRACK DOWN A MIND AMONG THE LIVING.

THAT'S NOT EXACTLY WHAT I DO.

I WAS ABLE TO REACH GILFRYD THROUGH HIS INVASION OF LIZ'S PSYCHE, BUT THINKING THAT I CAN "FIND" A SPECIFIC PERSON WOULD BE A MISTAKE.

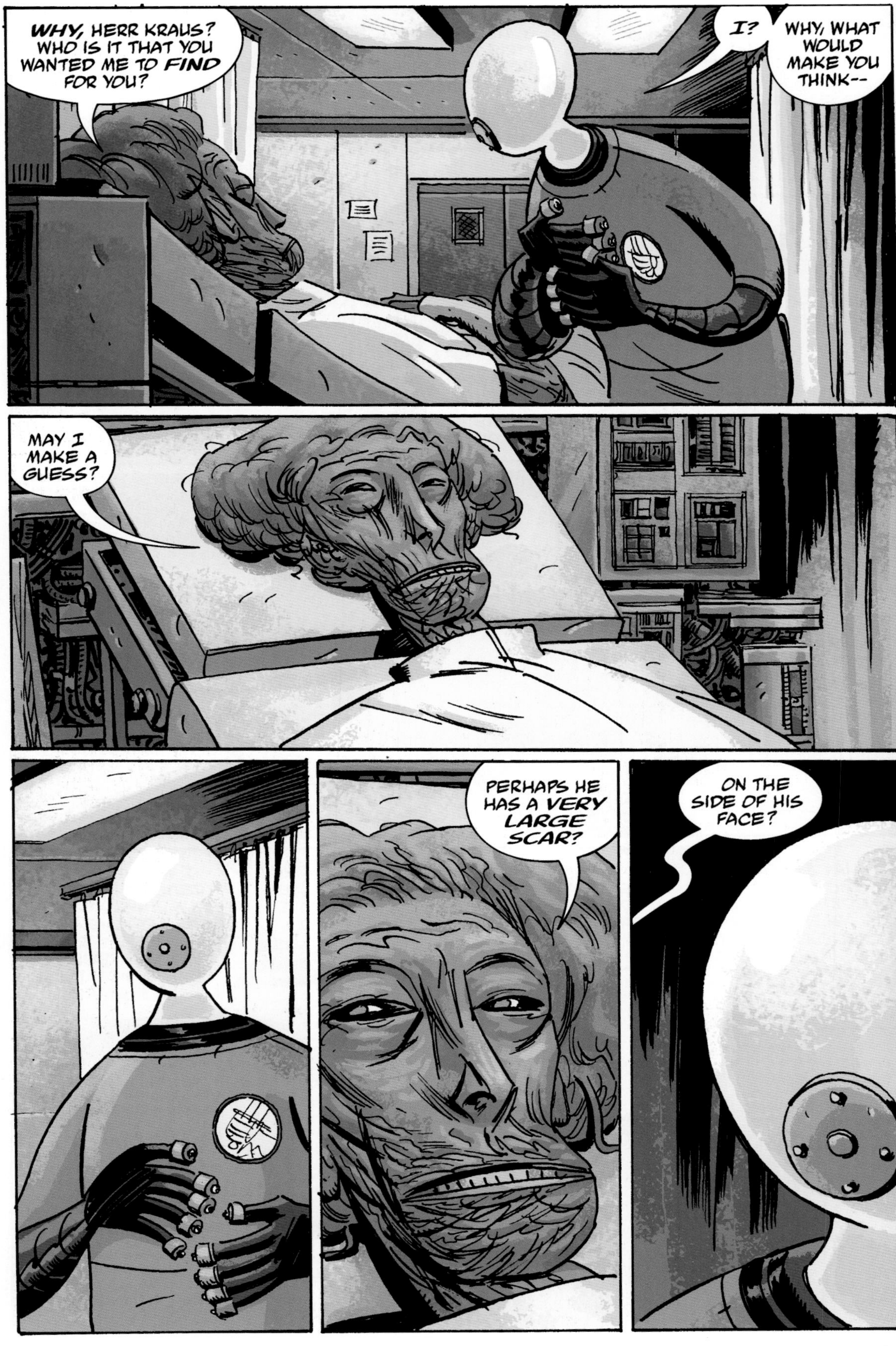
WHY, HERR KRAUS? WHO IS IT THAT YOU WANTED ME TO FIND FOR YOU?
I?
WHY, WHAT WOULD MAKE YOU THINK--
MAY I MAKE A GUESS?
PERHAPS HE HAS A VERY LARGE SCAR?
ON THE SIDE OF HIS FACE?

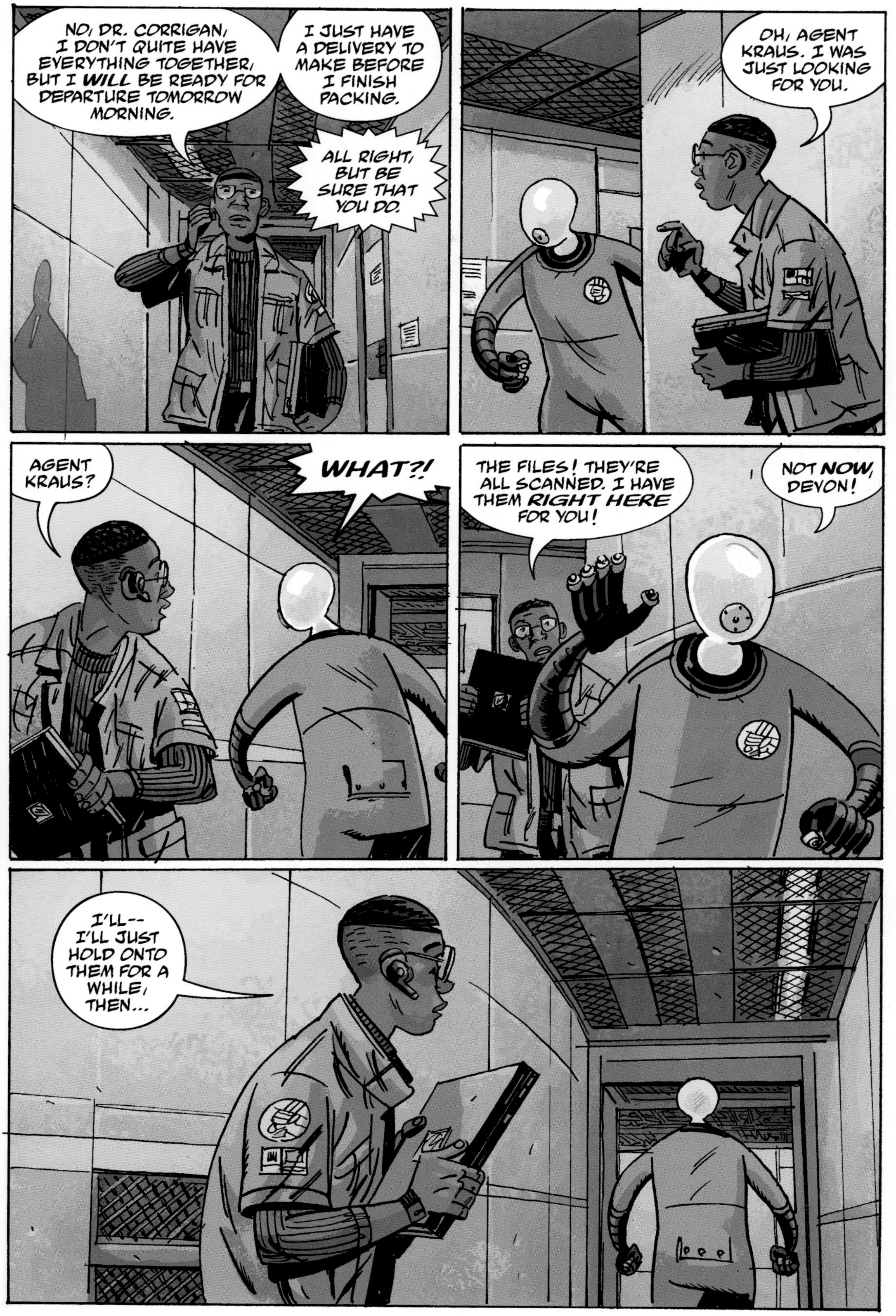
NO, DR. CORRIGAN, I DON'T QUITE HAVE EVERYTHING TOGETHER, BUT I **WILL** BE READY FOR DEPARTURE TOMORROW MORNING.
I JUST HAVE A DELIVERY TO MAKE BEFORE I FINISH PACKING.
ALL RIGHT, BUT BE SURE THAT YOU DO.
OH, AGENT KRAUS. I WAS JUST LOOKING FOR YOU.
AGENT KRAUS?
WHAT?!
THE FILES! THEY'RE ALL SCANNED. I HAVE THEM **RIGHT HERE** FOR YOU!
NOT **NOW**, DEVON!
I'LL-- I'LL JUST HOLD ONTO THEM FOR A WHILE, THEN...

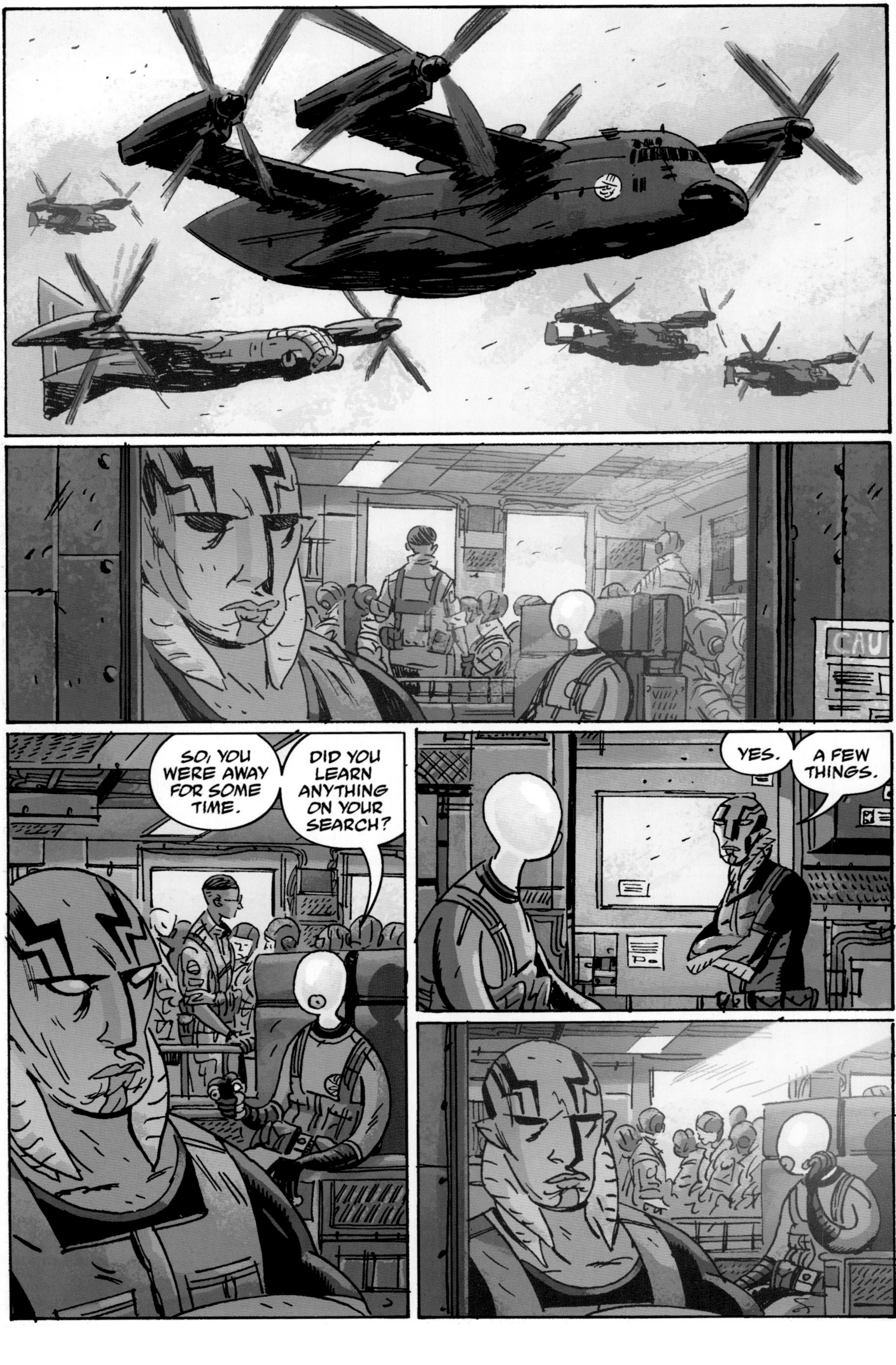
SO, YOU WERE AWAY FOR SOME TIME.
DID YOU LEARN ANYTHING ON YOUR SEARCH?
YES.
A FEW THINGS.

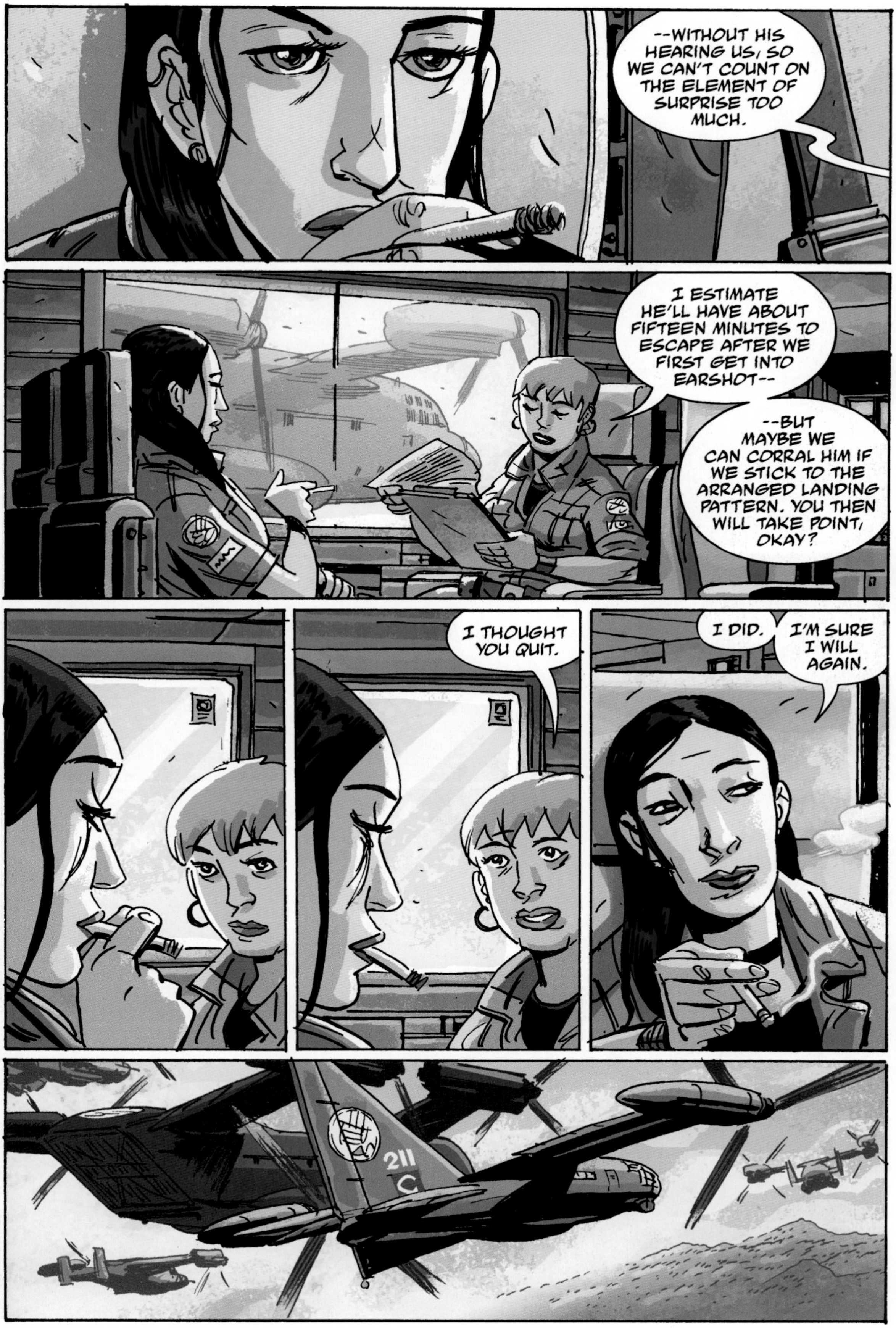
--WITHOUT HIS HEARING US, SO WE CAN'T COUNT ON THE ELEMENT OF SURPRISE TOO MUCH.
I ESTIMATE HE'LL HAVE ABOUT FIFTEEN MINUTES TO ESCAPE AFTER WE FIRST GET INTO EARSHOT--
--BUT MAYBE WE CAN CORRAL HIM IF WE STICK TO THE ARRANGED LANDING PATTERN. YOU THEN WILL TAKE POINT, OKAY?
I THOUGHT YOU QUIT.
I DID.
I'M SURE I WILL AGAIN.
211
C

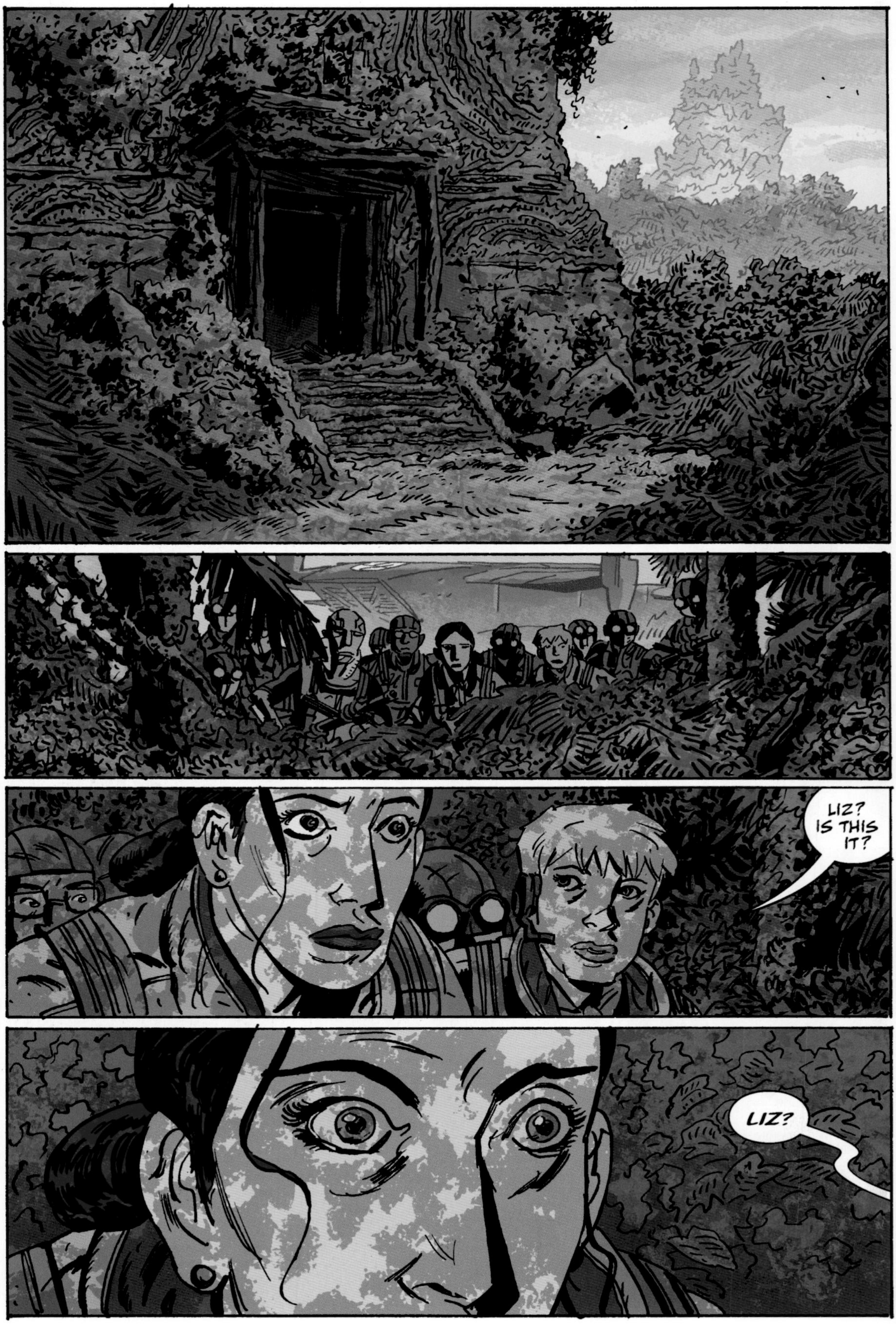
LIZ? IS THIS IT?
LIZ?

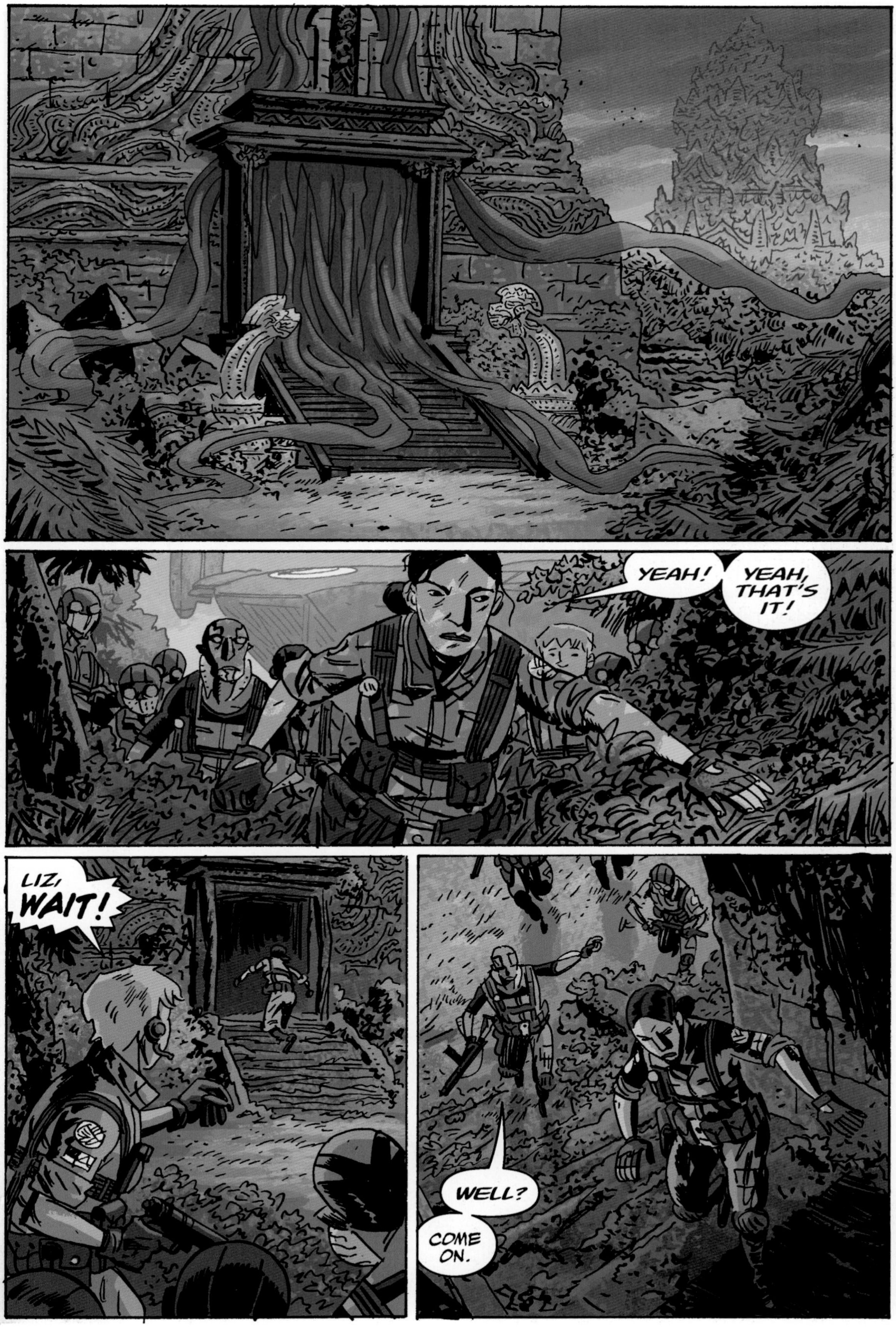
YEAH!
YEAH, THAT'S IT!
LIZ, WAIT!
WELL?
COME ON.

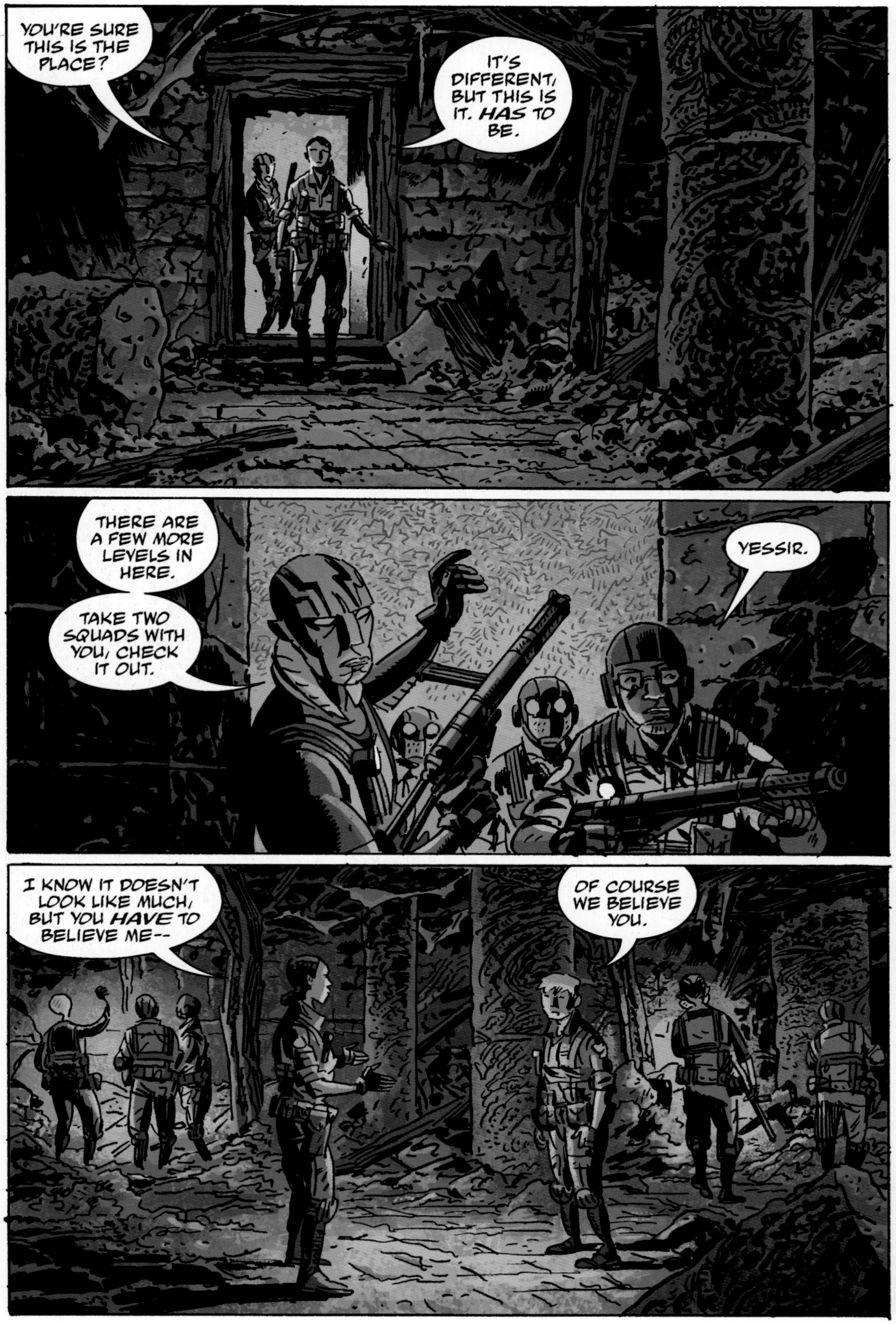
YOU'RE SURE THIS IS THE PLACE?
IT'S DIFFERENT, BUT THIS IS IT. HAS TO BE.
THERE ARE A FEW MORE LEVELS IN HERE.
TAKE TWO SQUADS WITH YOU, CHECK IT OUT.
YESSIR.
I KNOW IT DOESN'T LOOK LIKE MUCH, BUT YOU HAVE TO BELIEVE ME--
OF COURSE WE BELIEVE YOU.

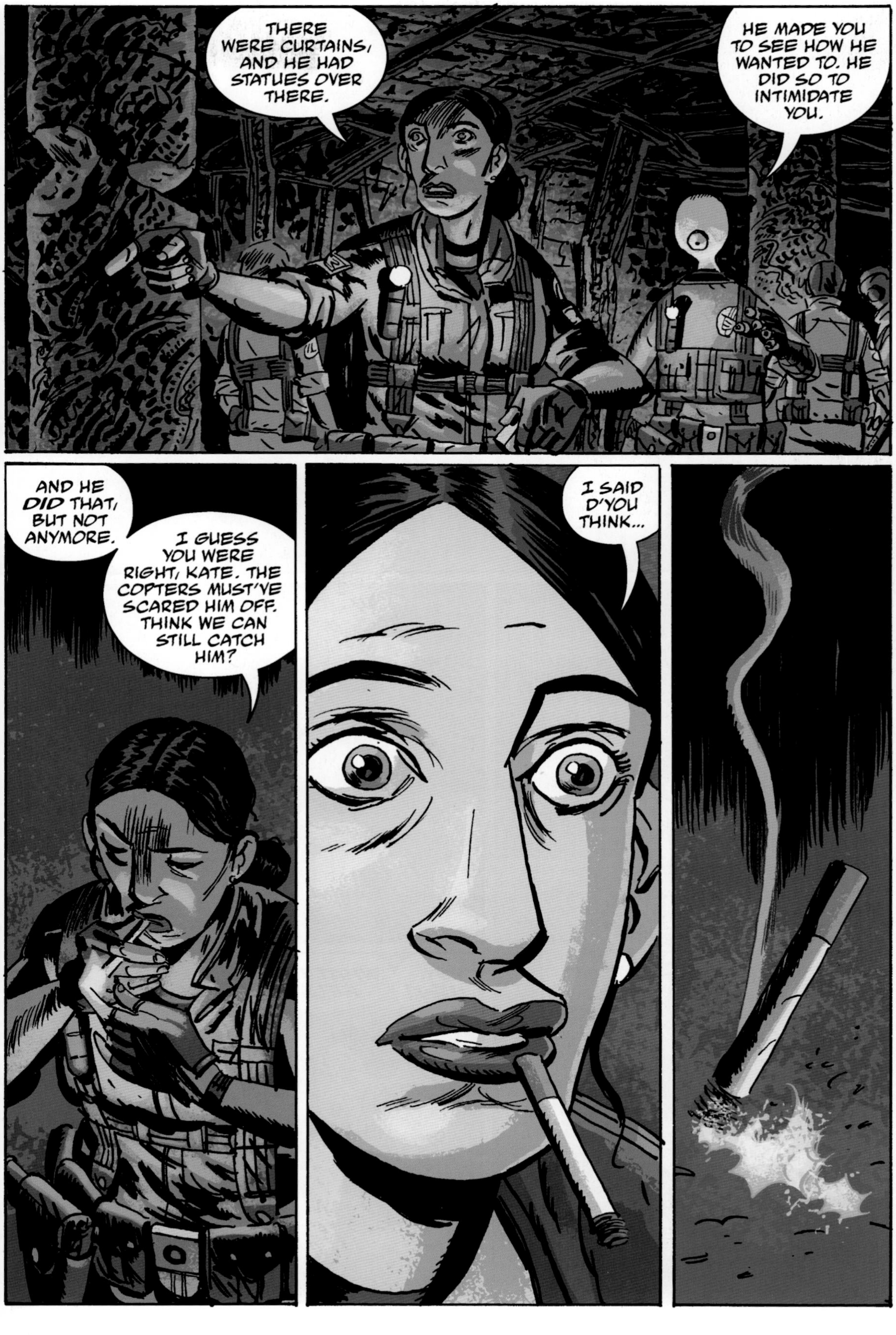
THERE WERE CURTAINS, AND HE HAD STATUES OVER THERE.
HE MADE YOU TO SEE HOW HE WANTED TO. HE DID SO TO INTIMIDATE YOU.
AND HE DID THAT, BUT NOT ANYMORE.
I GUESS YOU WERE RIGHT, KATE. THE COPTERS MUST'VE SCARED HIM OFF. THINK WE CAN STILL CATCH HIM?
I SAID D'YOU THINK...

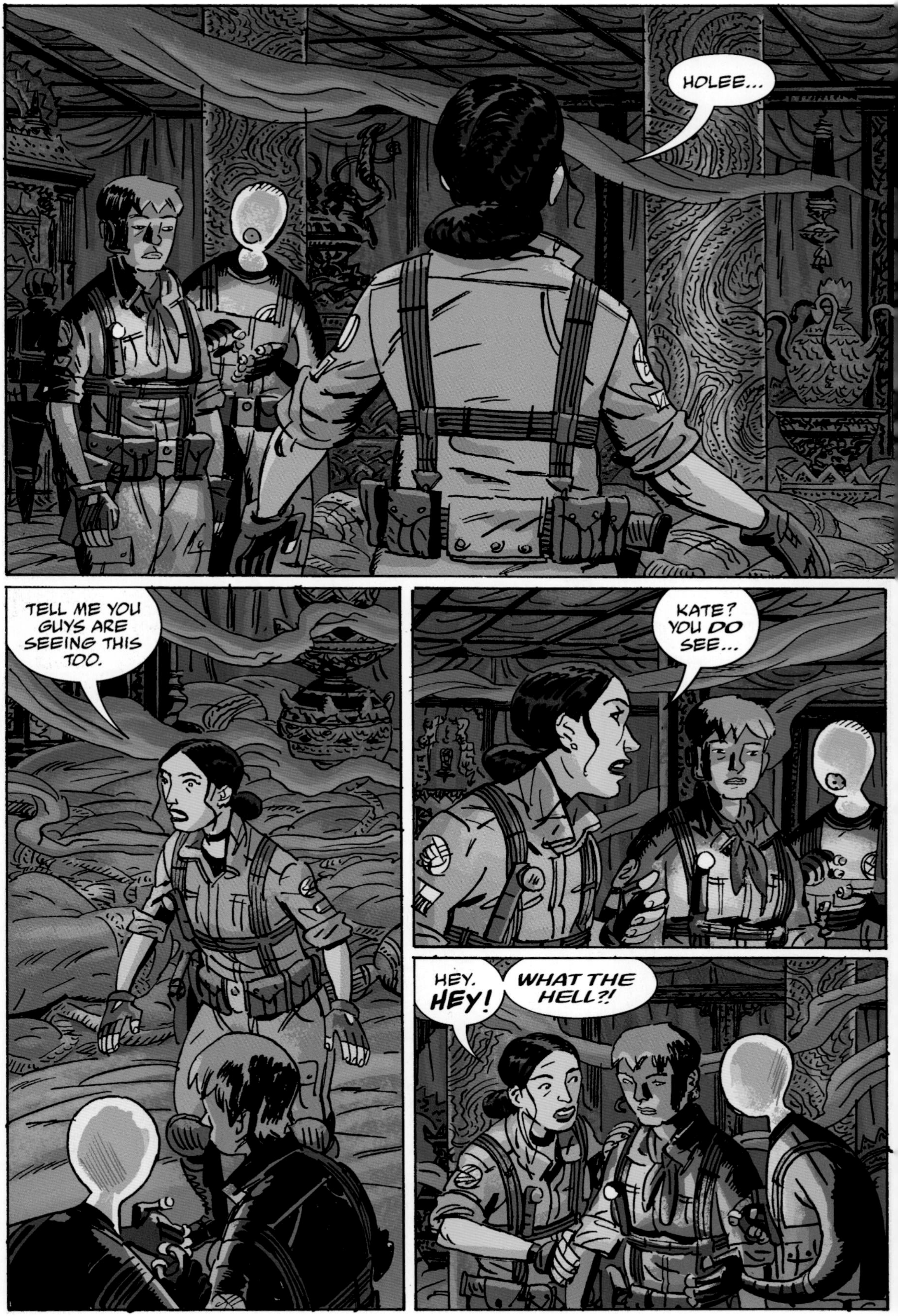
HOLEE...
TELL ME YOU GUYS ARE SEEING THIS TOO.
KATE? YOU DO SEE...
HEY. HEY!
WHAT THE HELL?!

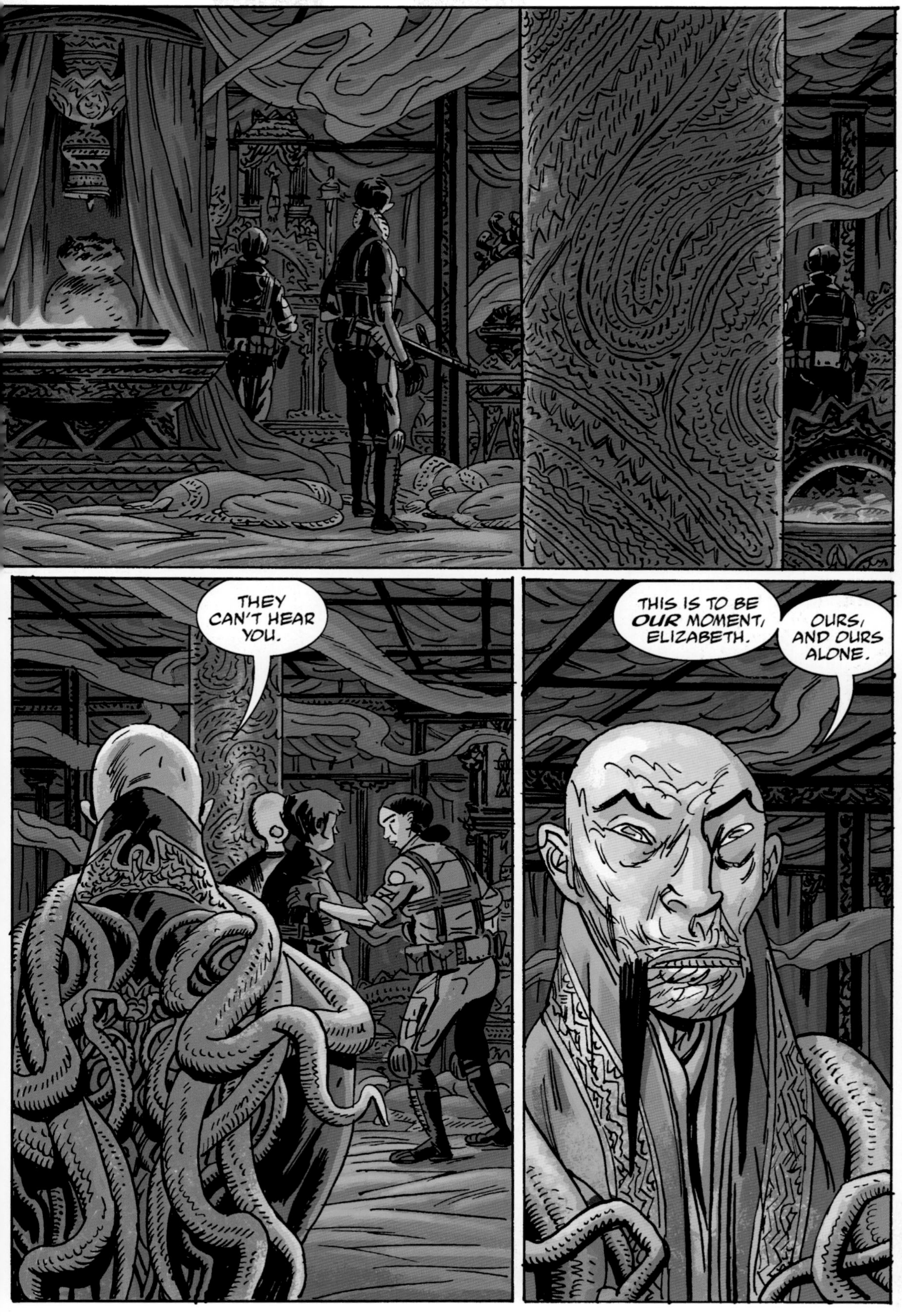
THEY CAN'T HEAR YOU.
THIS IS TO BE *OUR* MOMENT, ELIZABETH.
OURS, AND OURS ALONE.

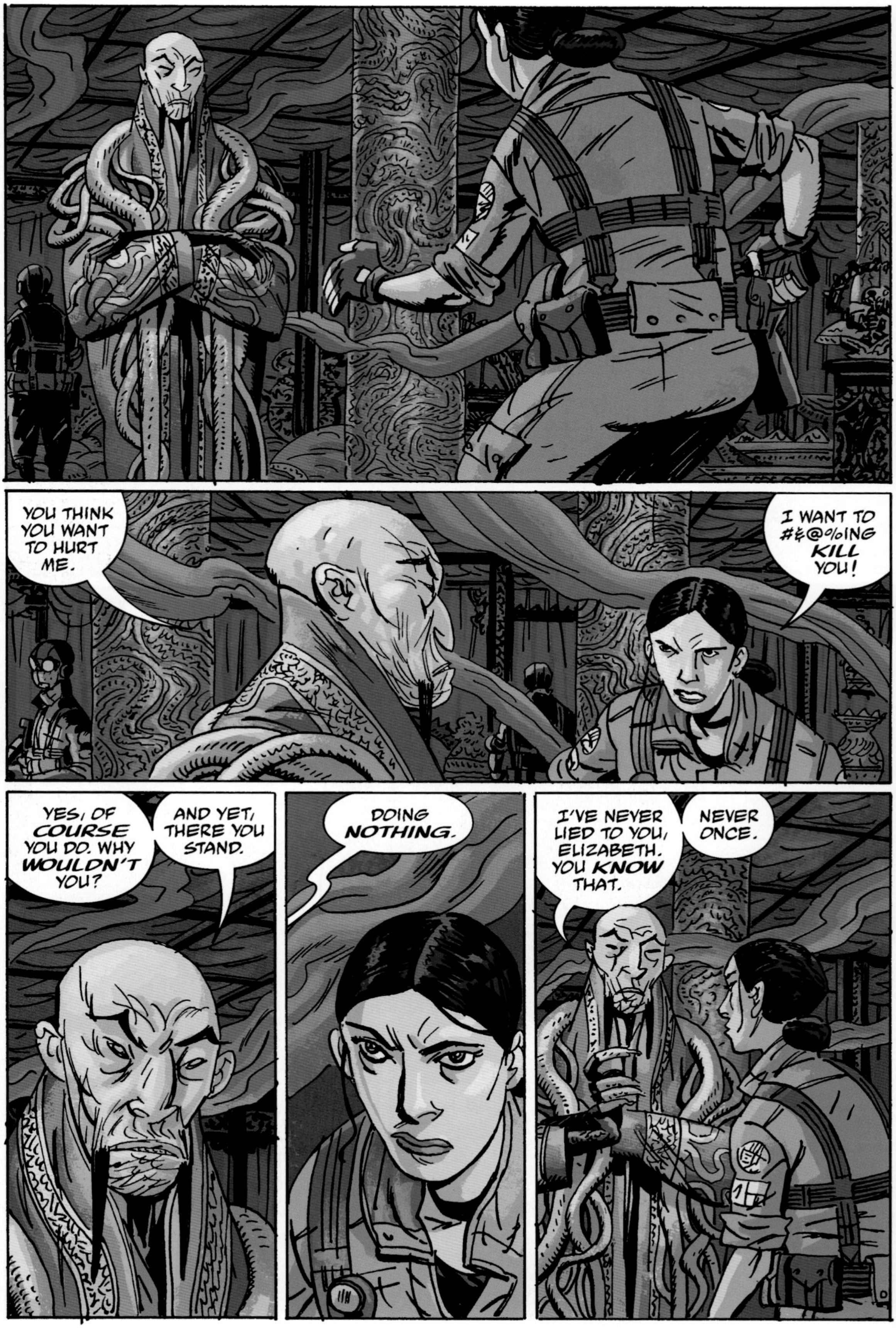
YOU THINK YOU WANT TO HURT ME.
I WANT TO #&@%ING *KILL* YOU!
YES, OF *COURSE* YOU DO. WHY *WOULDN'T* YOU?
AND YET, THERE YOU STAND.
DOING *NOTHING*.
I'VE NEVER LIED TO YOU, ELIZABETH. YOU *KNOW* THAT.
NEVER ONCE.

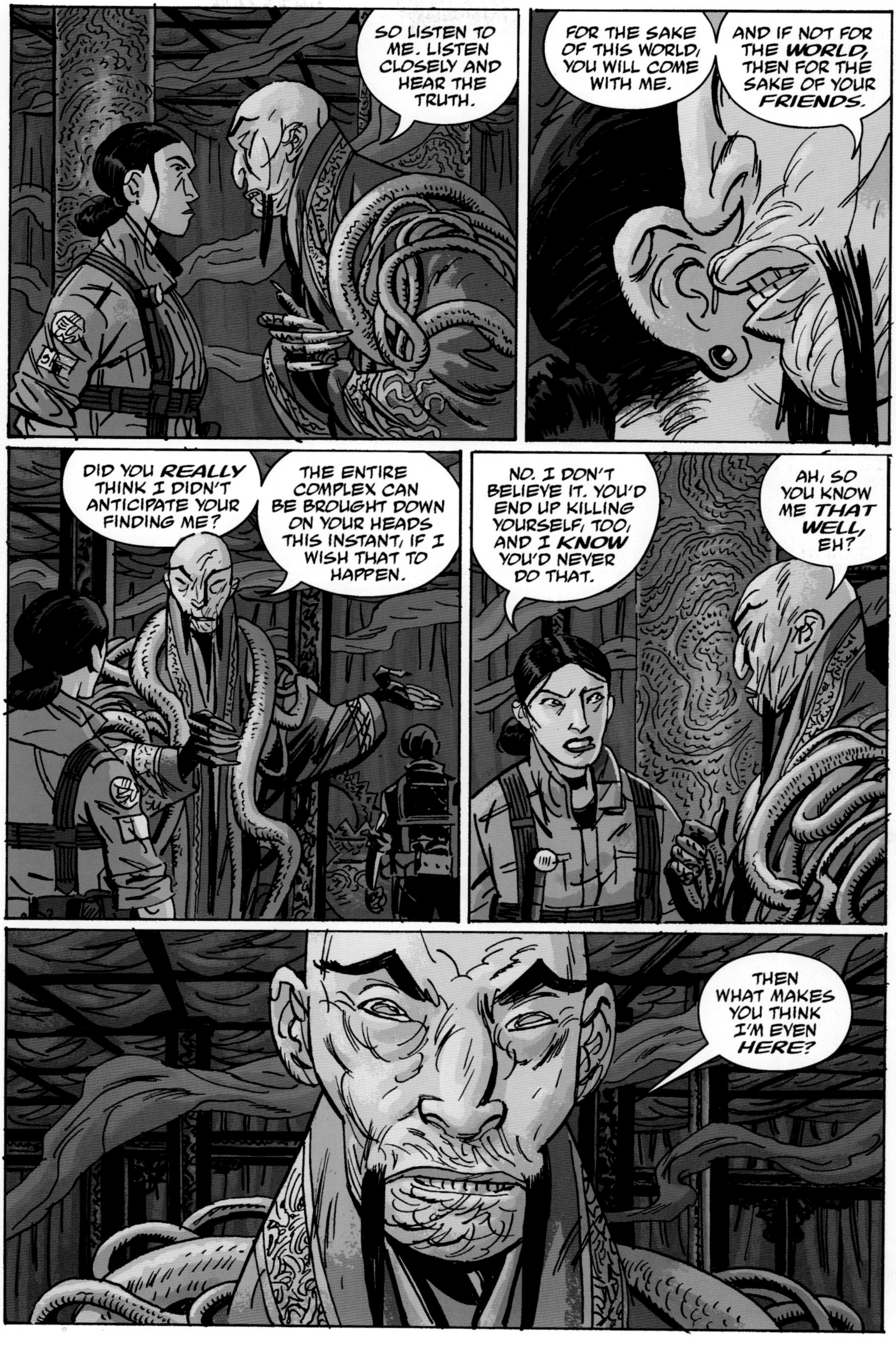

SO LISTEN TO ME. LISTEN CLOSELY AND HEAR THE TRUTH.
FOR THE SAKE OF THIS WORLD, YOU WILL COME WITH ME.
AND IF NOT FOR THE WORLD, THEN FOR THE SAKE OF YOUR FRIENDS.
DID YOU REALLY THINK I DIDN'T ANTICIPATE YOUR FINDING ME?
THE ENTIRE COMPLEX CAN BE BROUGHT DOWN ON YOUR HEADS THIS INSTANT, IF I WISH THAT TO HAPPEN.
NO. I DON'T BELIEVE IT. YOU'D END UP KILLING YOURSELF, TOO, AND I KNOW YOU'D NEVER DO THAT.
AH, SO YOU KNOW ME THAT WELL, EH?
THEN WHAT MAKES YOU THINK I'M EVEN HERE?

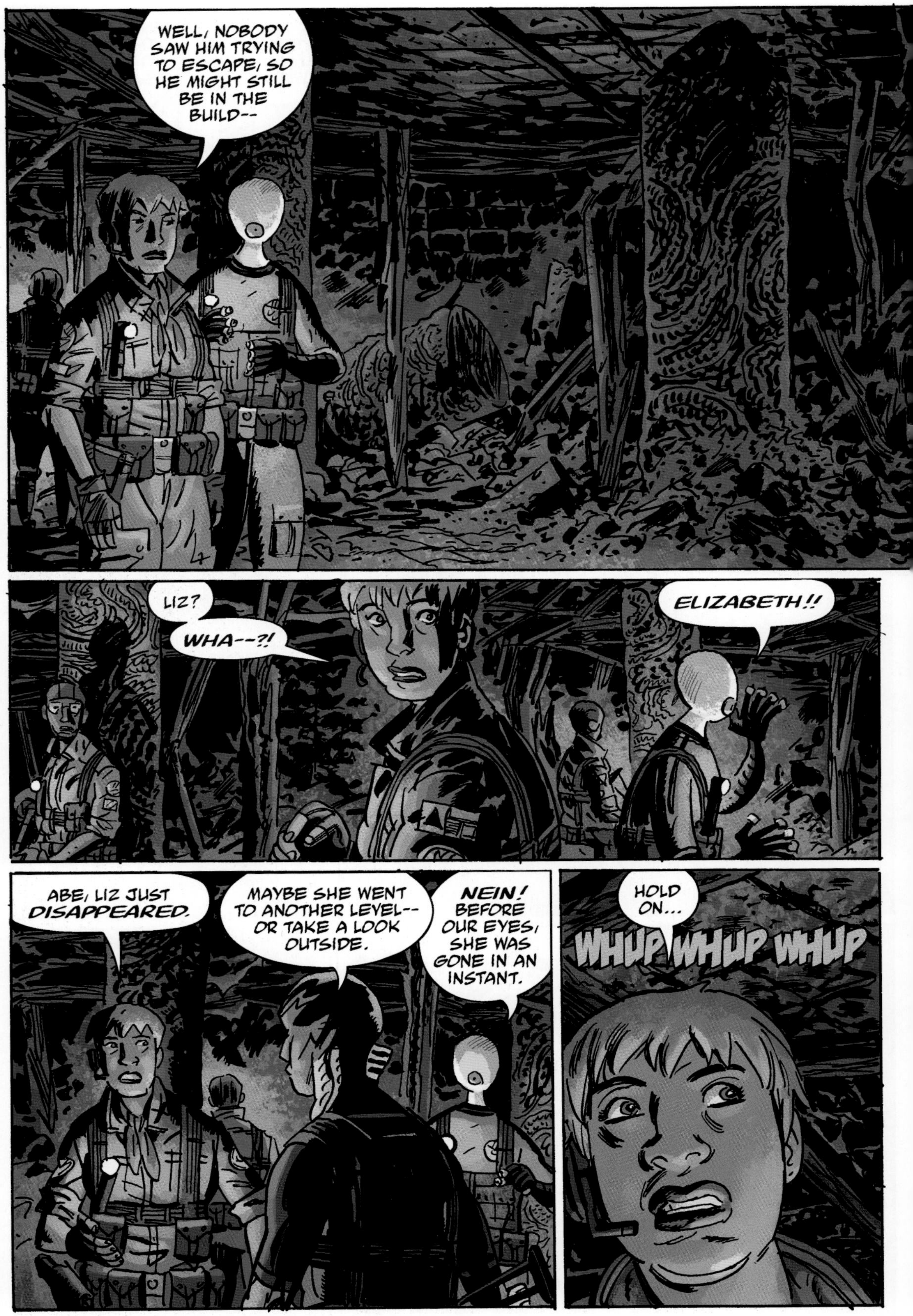

WELL, NOBODY SAW HIM TRYING TO ESCAPE, SO HE MIGHT STILL BE IN THE BUILD--
LIZ?
WHA--?!
ELIZABETH!!
ABE, LIZ JUST DISAPPEARED.
MAYBE SHE WENT TO ANOTHER LEVEL-- OR TAKE A LOOK OUTSIDE.
NEIN! BEFORE OUR EYES, SHE WAS GONE IN AN INSTANT.
HOLD ON...
WHUP WHUP WHUP

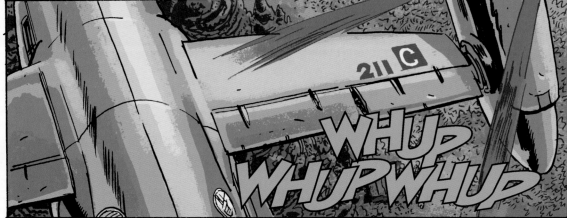

WHUP
WHUPWHUP

WHO'S FLYING THAT?

UHHHH, NONE OF *THESE* GUYS.

THEY'RE SLEEPING LIKE BABIES.

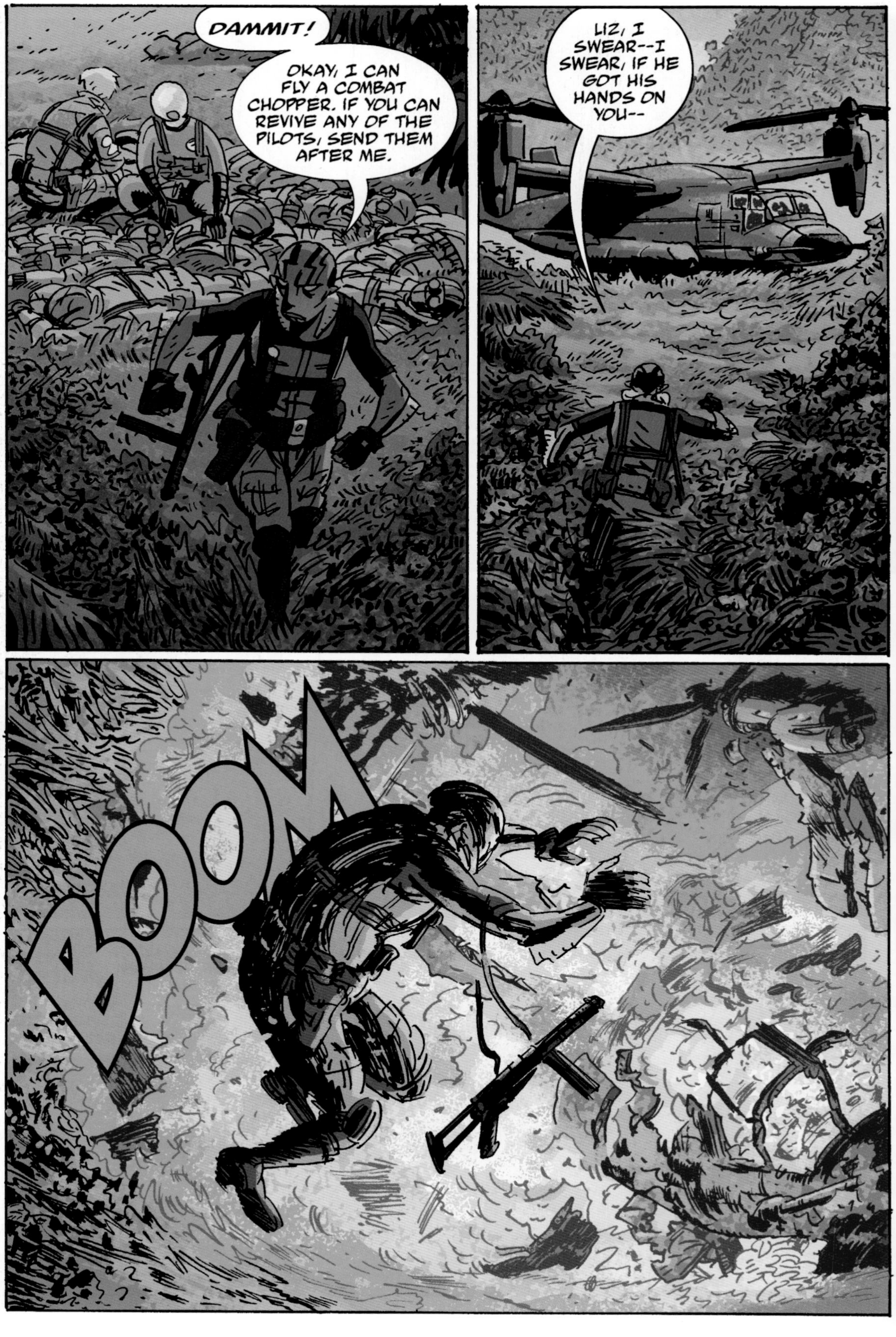
DAMMIT!
OKAY, I CAN FLY A COMBAT CHOPPER. IF YOU CAN REVIVE ANY OF THE PILOTS, SEND THEM AFTER ME.
LIZ, I SWEAR--I SWEAR, IF HE GOT HIS HANDS ON YOU--
BOOM

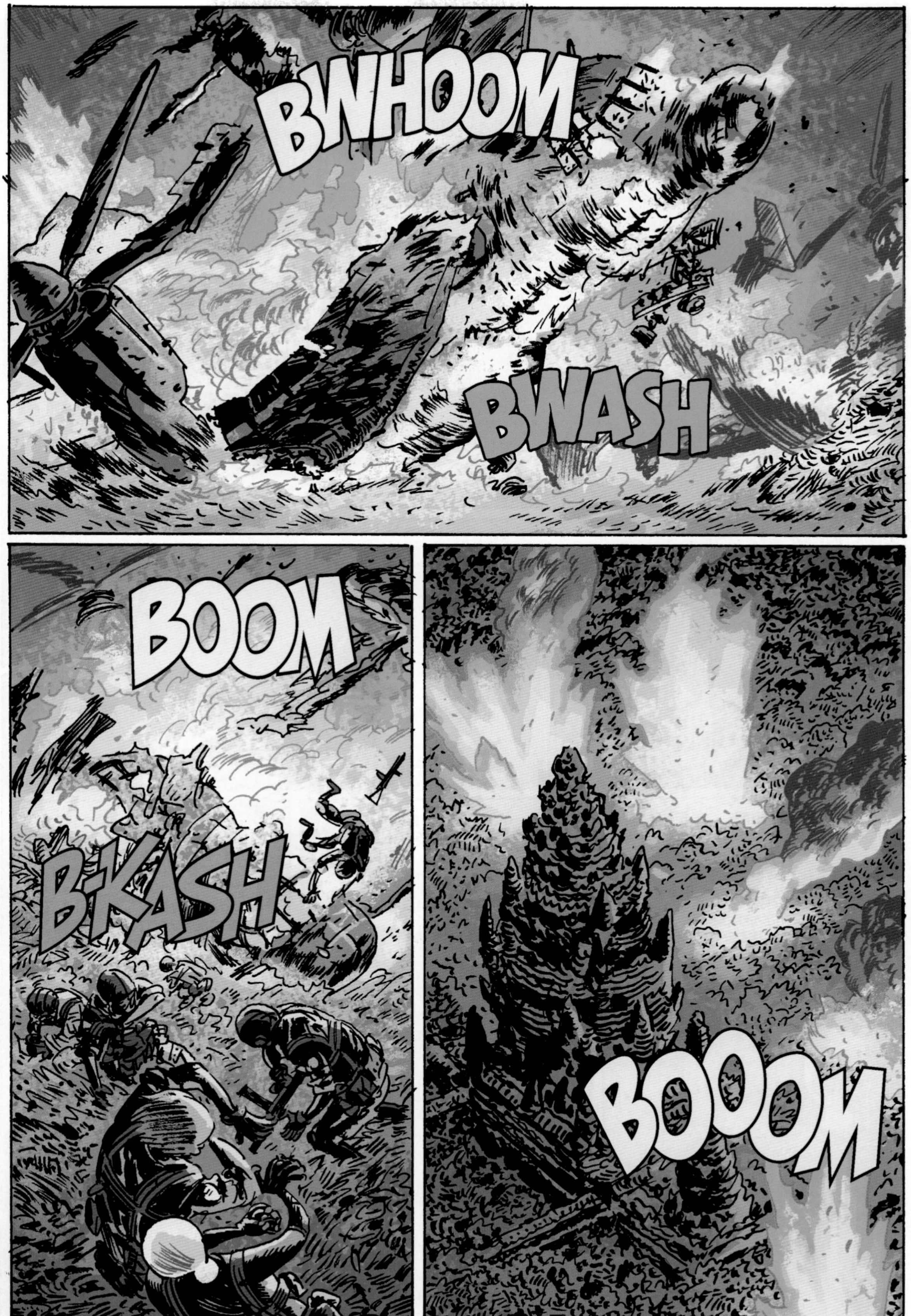
BWHOOM
BWASH
BOOM
B-KASH
BOOOM

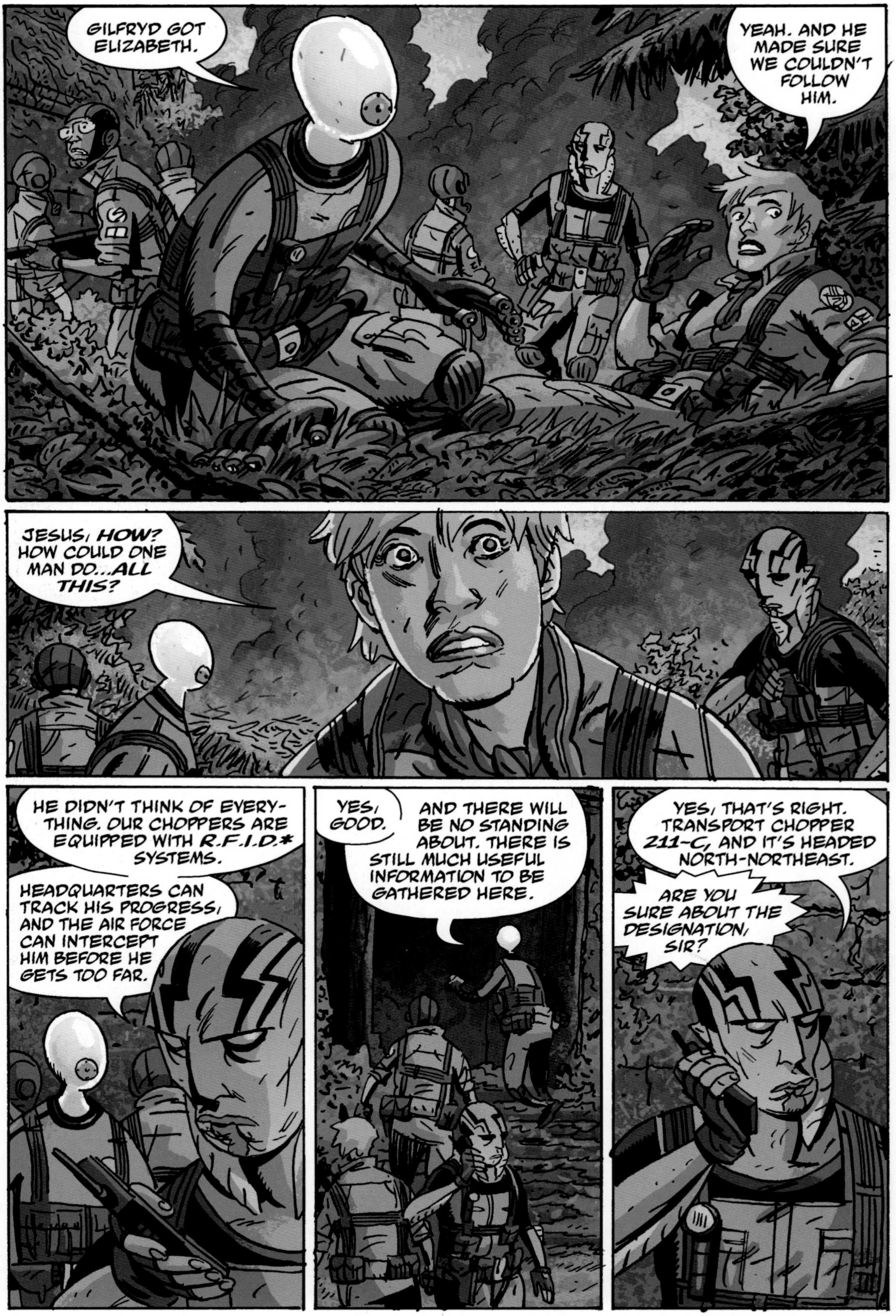
GILFRYD GOT ELIZABETH.
YEAH. AND HE MADE SURE WE COULDN'T FOLLOW HIM.
JESUS, *HOW?* HOW COULD ONE MAN DO...*ALL THIS?*
HE DIDN'T THINK OF EVERY-THING. OUR CHOPPERS ARE EQUIPPED WITH *R.F.I.D.** SYSTEMS.
HEADQUARTERS CAN TRACK HIS PROGRESS, AND THE AIR FORCE CAN INTERCEPT HIM BEFORE HE GETS TOO FAR.
YES, GOOD.
AND THERE WILL BE NO STANDING ABOUT. THERE IS STILL MUCH USEFUL INFORMATION TO BE GATHERED HERE.
YES, THAT'S RIGHT. TRANSPORT CHOPPER *211-C*, AND IT'S HEADED NORTH-NORTHEAST.
ARE YOU SURE ABOUT THE DESIGNATION, SIR?

*RADIO FREQUENCY IDENTIFICATION

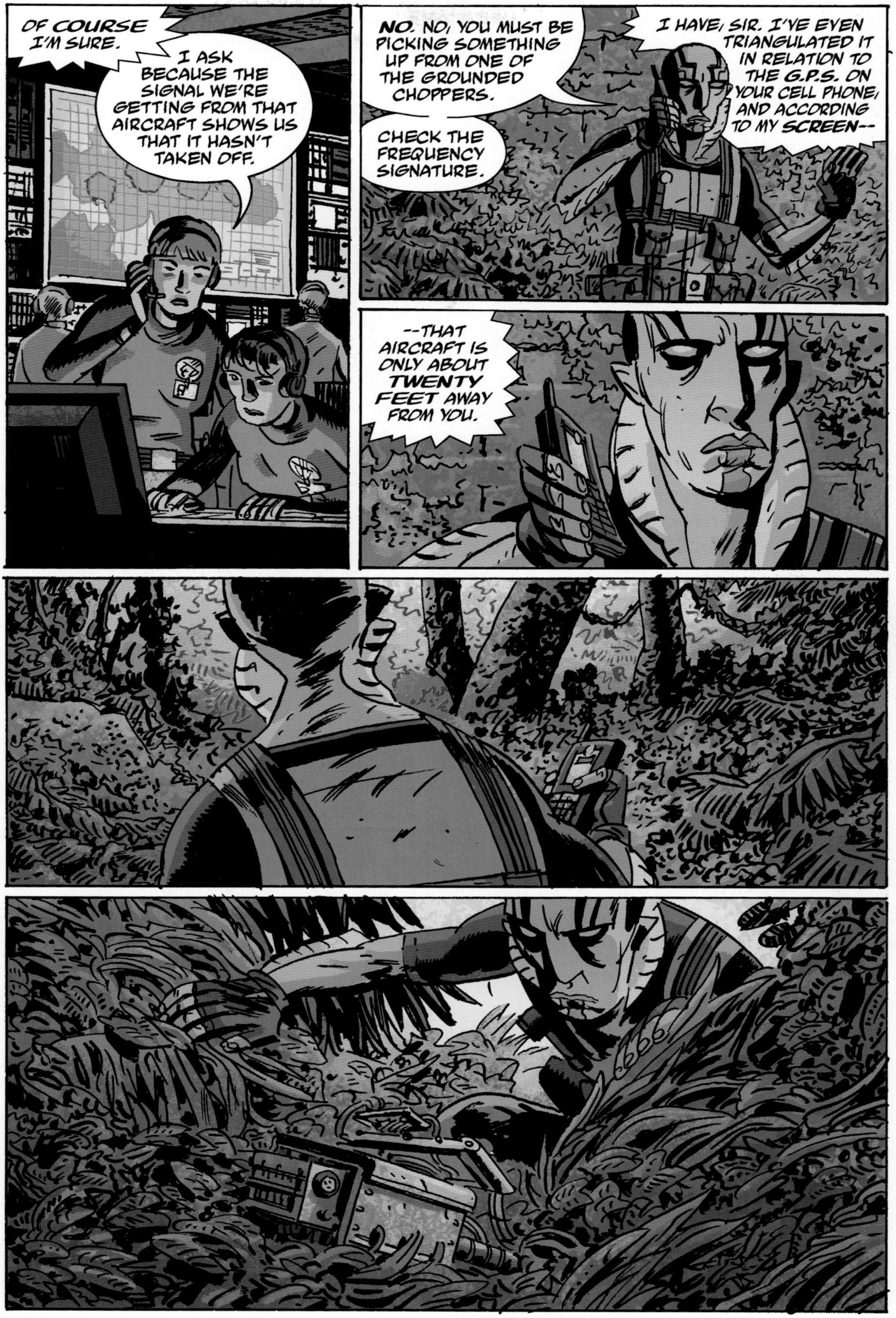
OF COURSE I'M SURE.
I ASK BECAUSE THE SIGNAL WE'RE GETTING FROM THAT AIRCRAFT SHOWS US THAT IT HASN'T TAKEN OFF.
NO. NO, YOU MUST BE PICKING SOMETHING UP FROM ONE OF THE GROUNDED CHOPPERS.
CHECK THE FREQUENCY SIGNATURE.
I HAVE, SIR. I'VE EVEN TRIANGULATED IT IN RELATION TO THE G.P.S. ON YOUR CELL PHONE, AND ACCORDING TO MY SCREEN--
--THAT AIRCRAFT IS ONLY ABOUT TWENTY FEET AWAY FROM YOU.

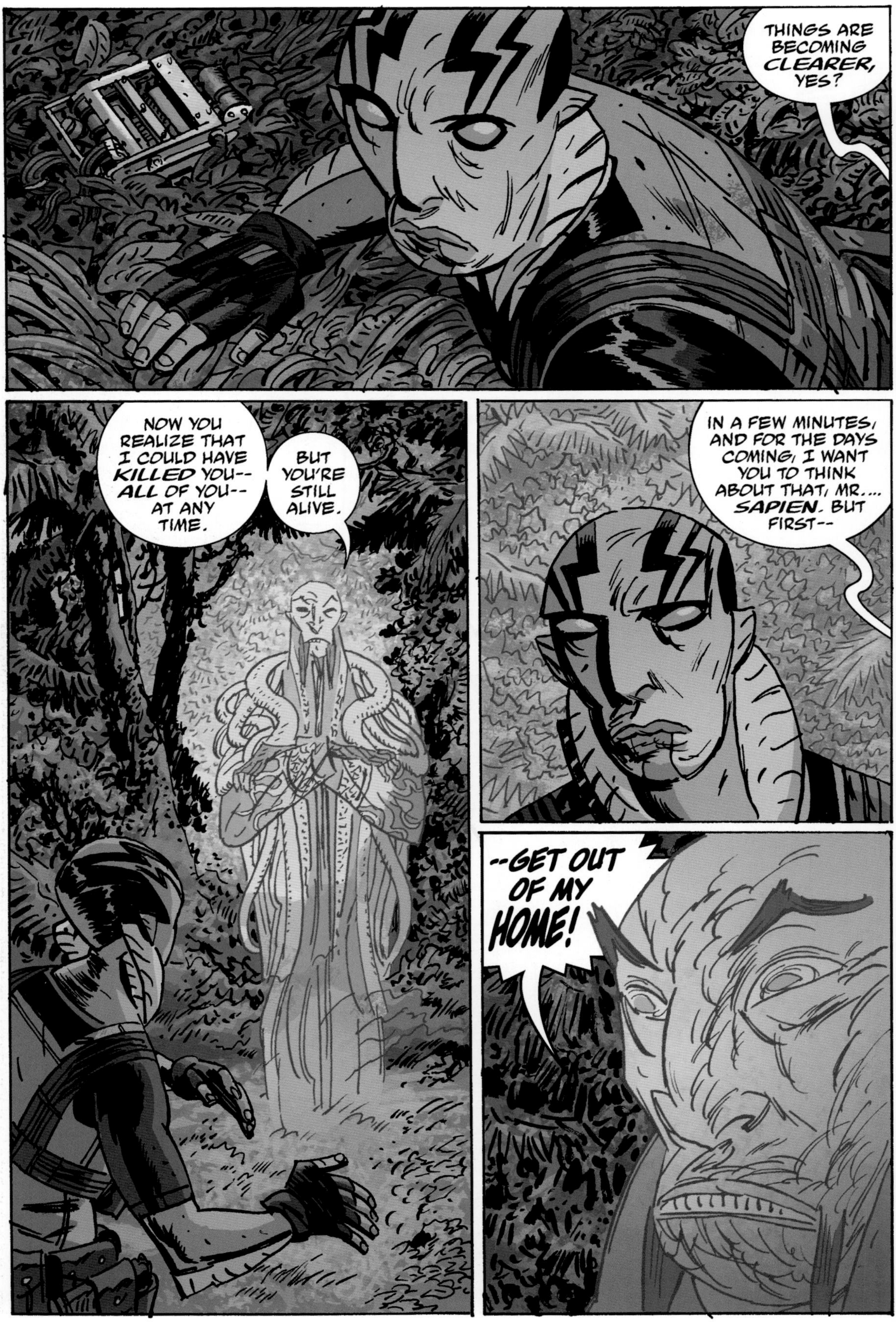
THINGS ARE BECOMING CLEARER, YES?
NOW YOU REALIZE THAT I COULD HAVE KILLED YOU-- ALL OF YOU-- AT ANY TIME.
BUT YOU'RE STILL ALIVE.
IN A FEW MINUTES, AND FOR THE DAYS COMING, I WANT YOU TO THINK ABOUT THAT, MR.... SAPIEN. BUT FIRST--
--GET OUT OF MY HOME!

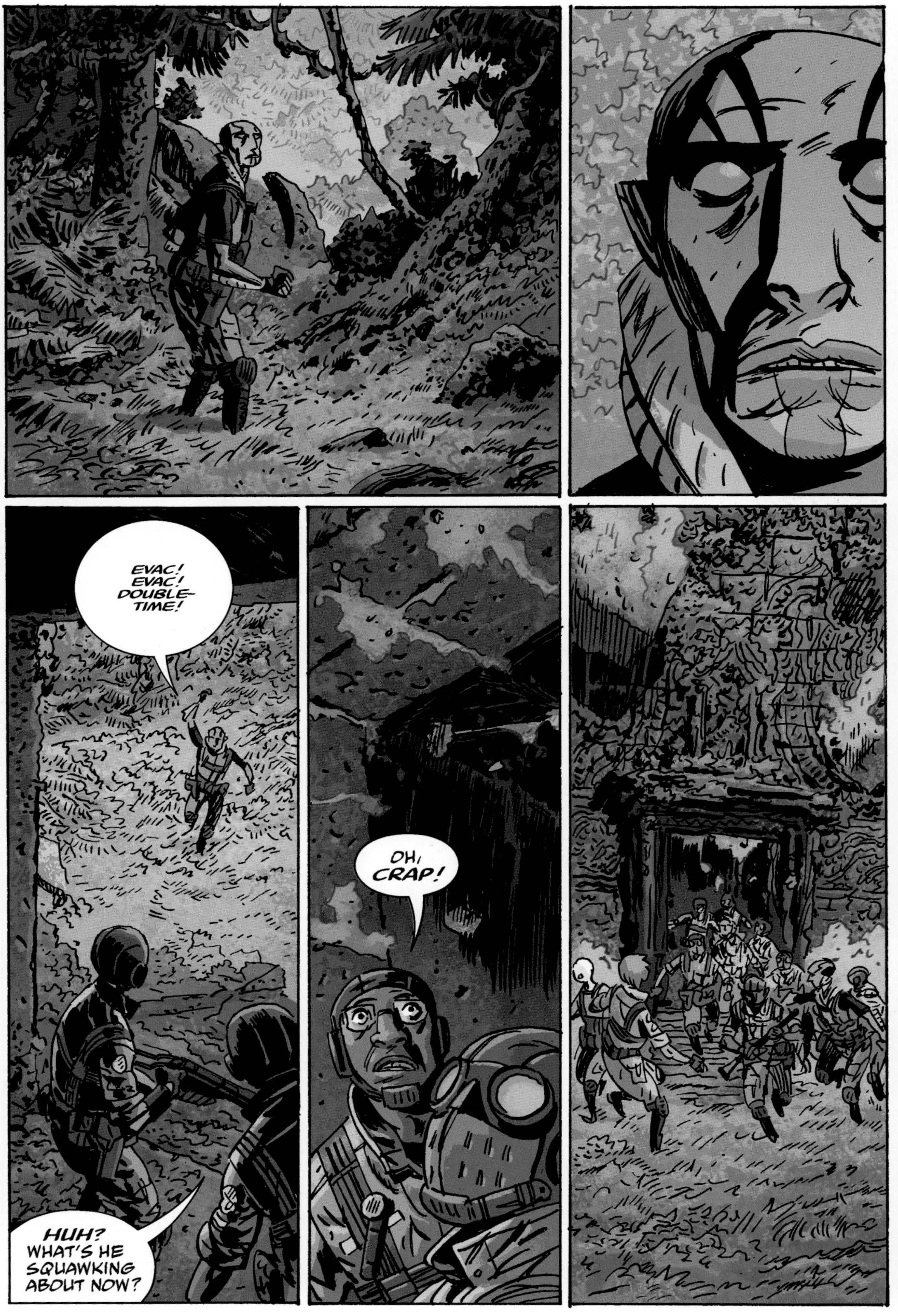
EVAC! EVAC! DOUBLE-TIME!
HUH? WHAT'S HE SQUAWKING ABOUT NOW?
OH, CRAP!

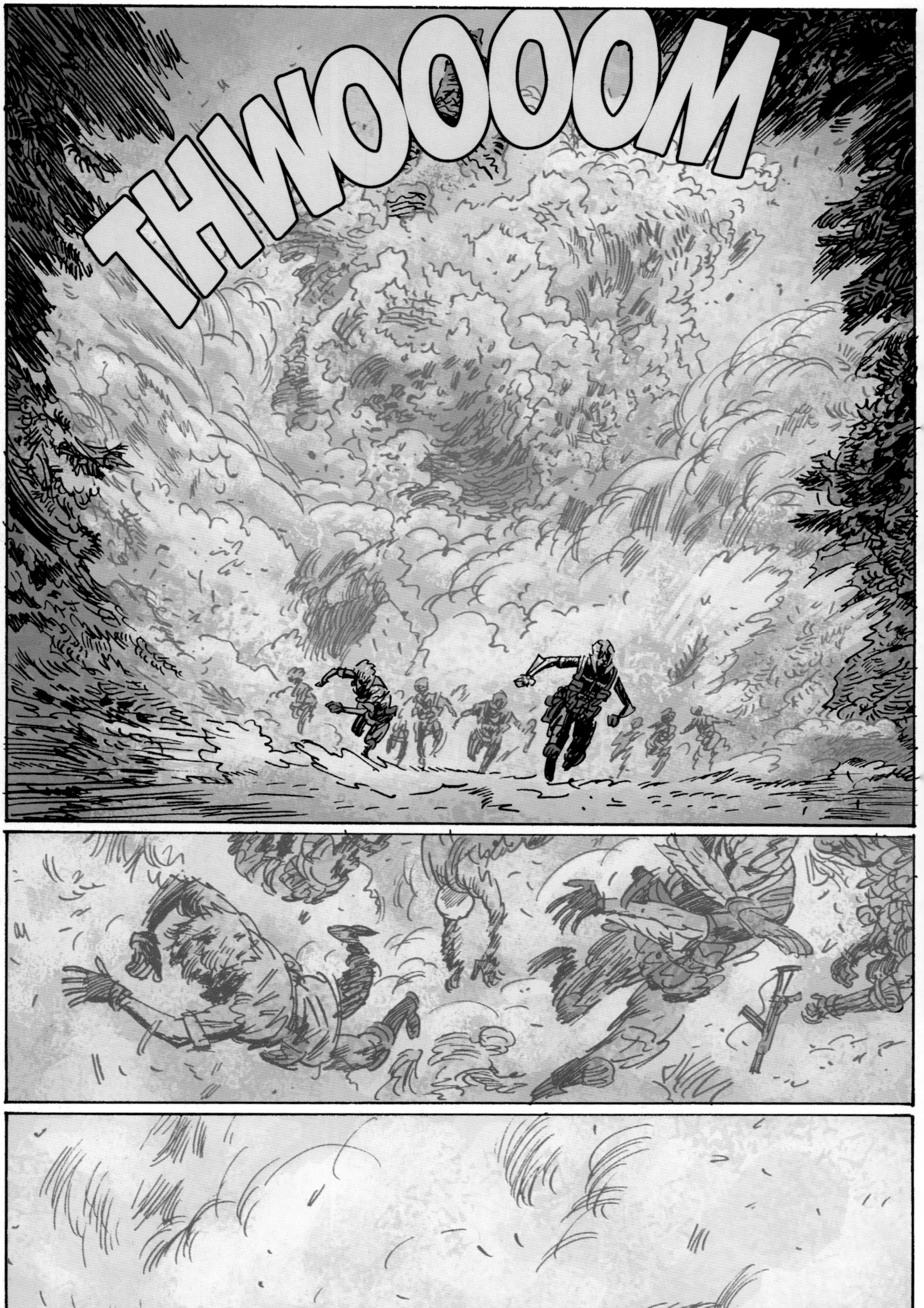
THWOOOOM

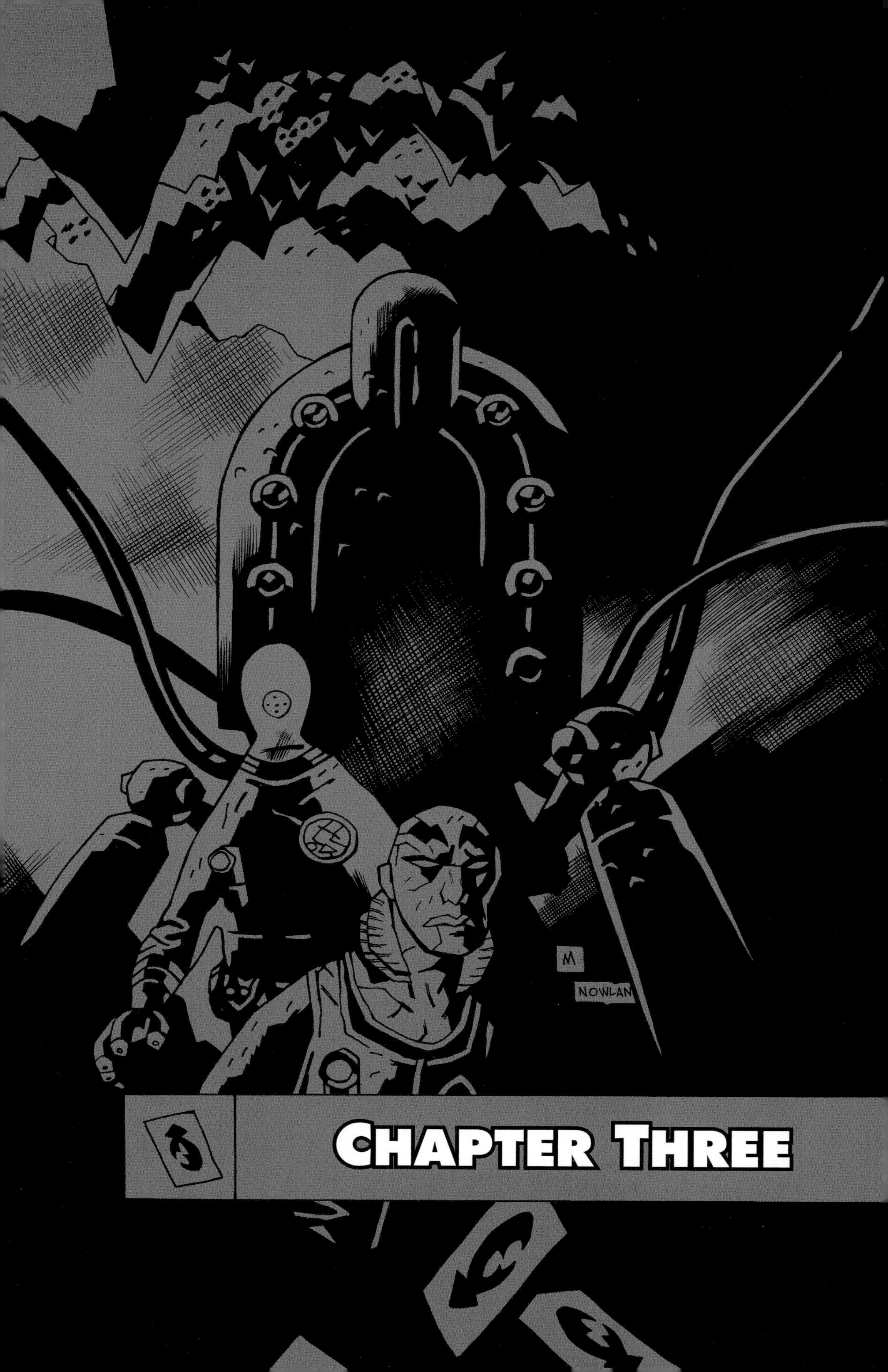
M
NOWLAN

CHAPTER THREE

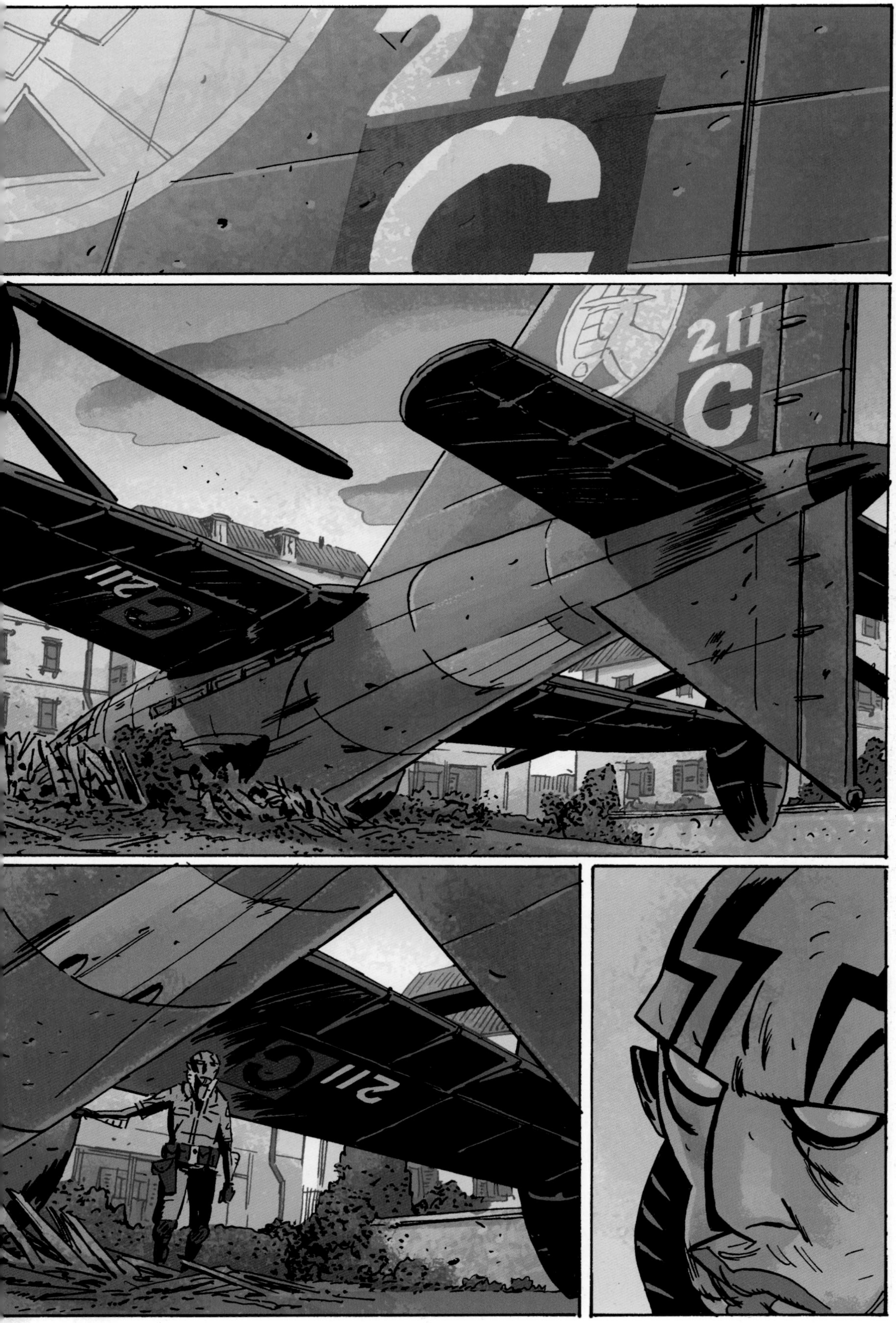
211
C

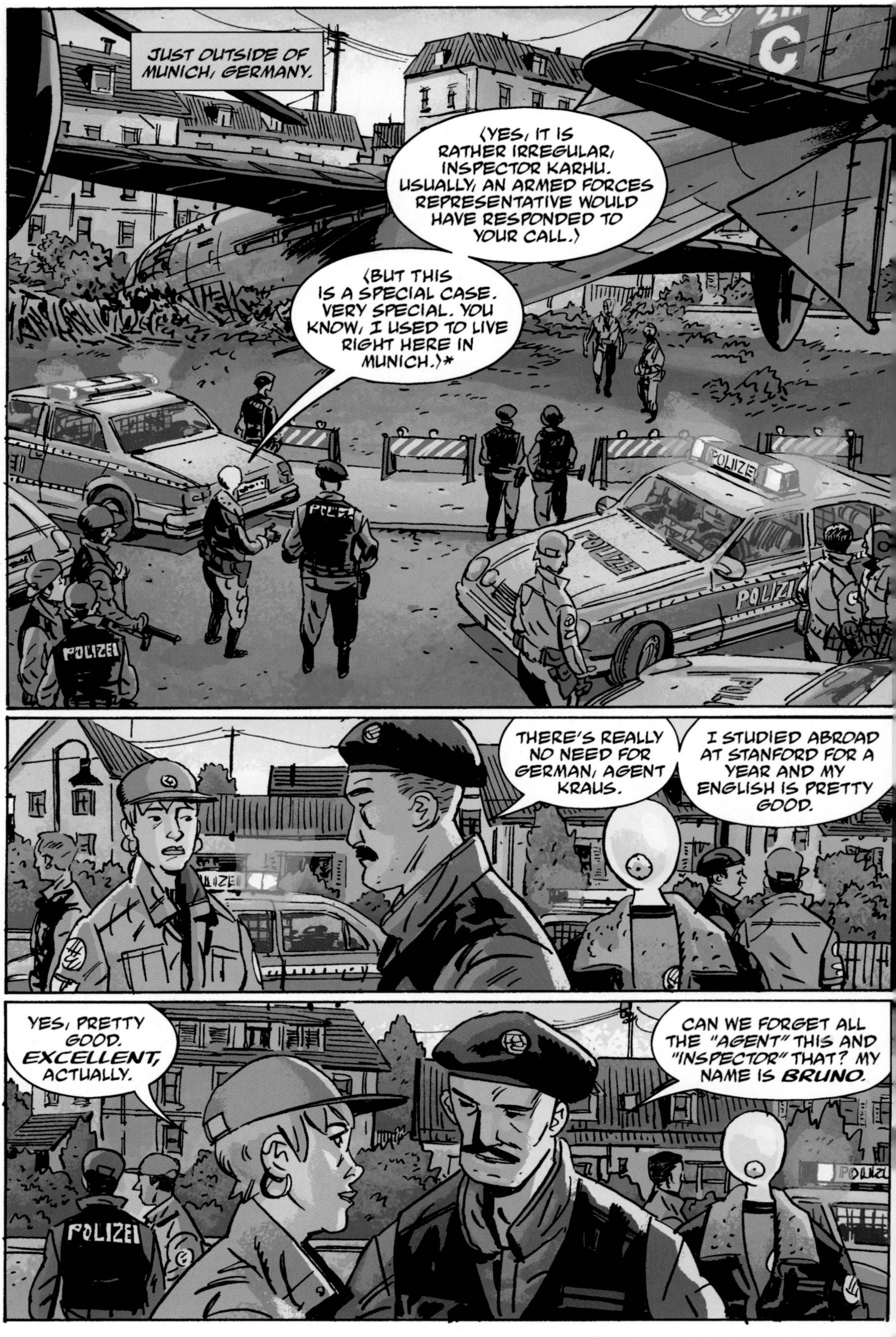
JUST OUTSIDE OF MUNICH, GERMANY.
⟨YES, IT IS RATHER IRREGULAR, INSPECTOR KARHU. USUALLY, AN ARMED FORCES REPRESENTATIVE WOULD HAVE RESPONDED TO YOUR CALL.⟩
⟨BUT THIS IS A SPECIAL CASE. VERY SPECIAL. YOU KNOW, I USED TO LIVE RIGHT HERE IN MUNICH.⟩*
POLIZEI
POLIZEI
POLIZEI
THERE'S REALLY NO NEED FOR GERMAN, AGENT KRAUS.
I STUDIED ABROAD AT STANFORD FOR A YEAR AND MY ENGLISH IS PRETTY GOOD.
YES, PRETTY GOOD. *EXCELLENT*, ACTUALLY.
CAN WE FORGET ALL THE "AGENT" THIS AND "INSPECTOR" THAT? MY NAME IS ***BRUNO***.
POLIZEI

*⟨TRANSLATED FROM THE GERMAN⟩

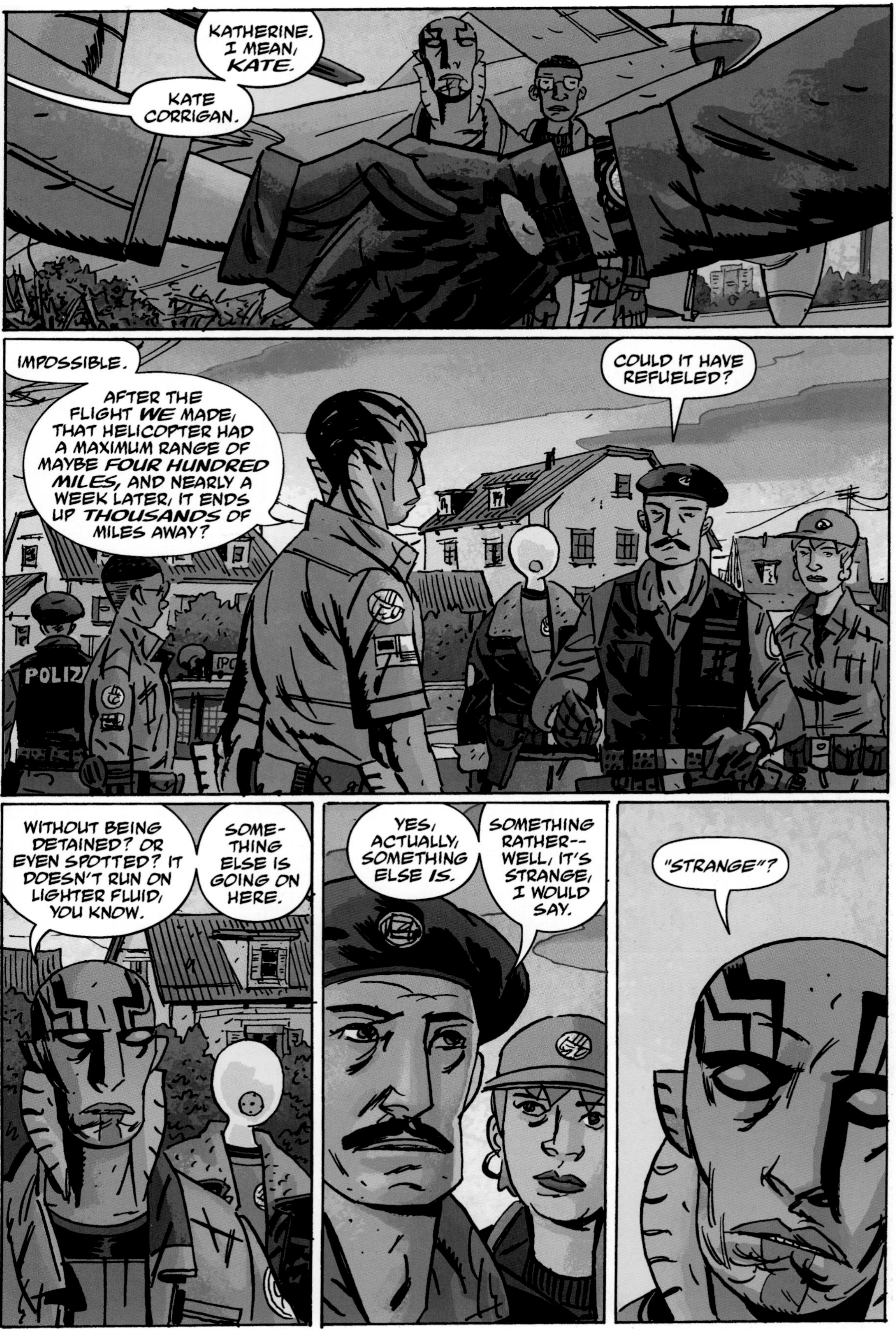
KATHERINE. I MEAN, KATE.
KATE CORRIGAN.
IMPOSSIBLE.
AFTER THE FLIGHT WE MADE, THAT HELICOPTER HAD A MAXIMUM RANGE OF MAYBE FOUR HUNDRED MILES, AND NEARLY A WEEK LATER, IT ENDS UP THOUSANDS OF MILES AWAY?
COULD IT HAVE REFUELED?
POLIZ
WITHOUT BEING DETAINED? OR EVEN SPOTTED? IT DOESN'T RUN ON LIGHTER FLUID, YOU KNOW.
SOMETHING ELSE IS GOING ON HERE.
YES, ACTUALLY, SOMETHING ELSE IS.
SOMETHING RATHER-- WELL, IT'S STRANGE, I WOULD SAY.
"STRANGE"?

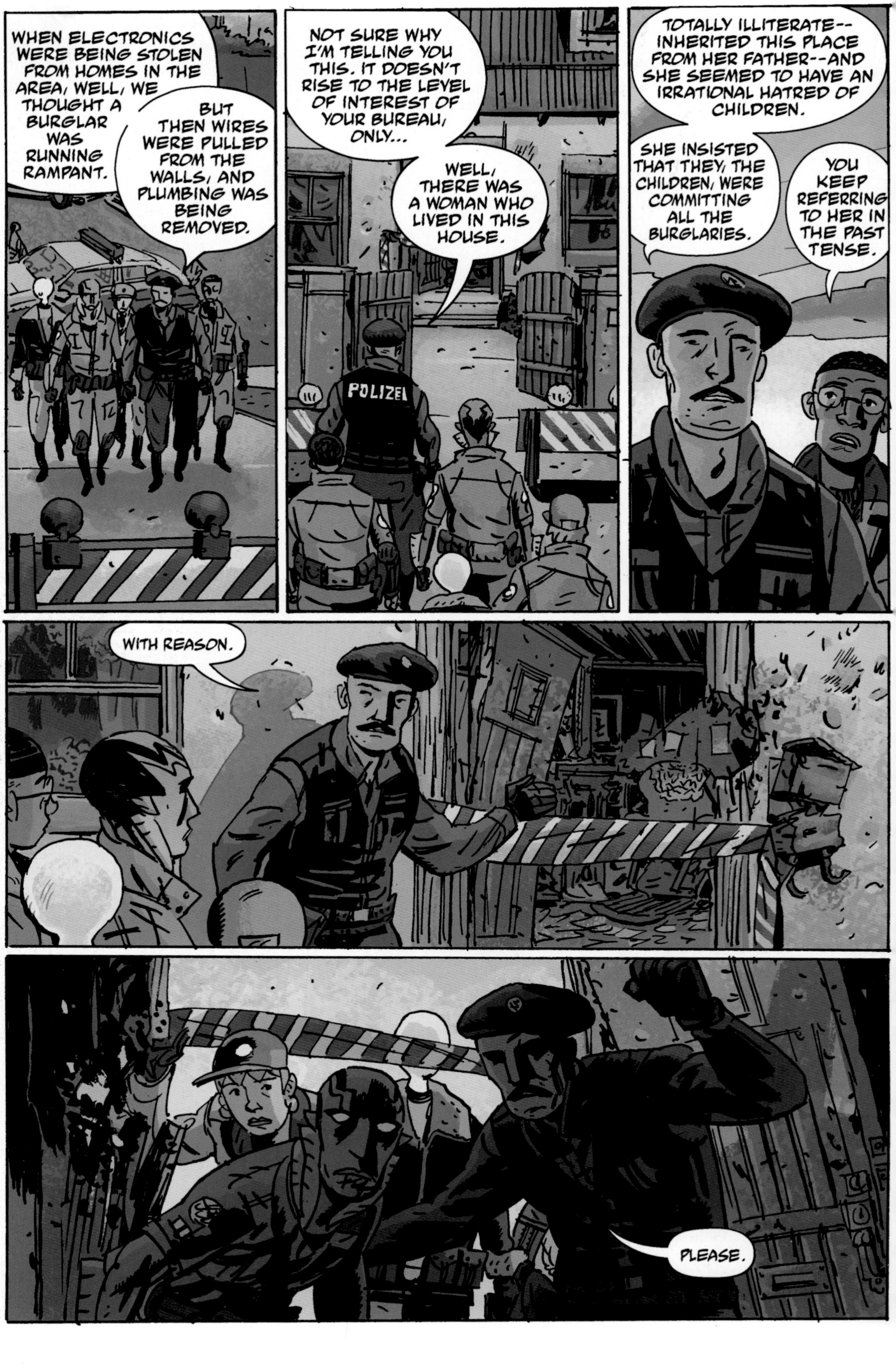
WHEN ELECTRONICS WERE BEING STOLEN FROM HOMES IN THE AREA, WELL, WE THOUGHT A BURGLAR WAS RUNNING RAMPANT.
BUT THEN WIRES WERE PULLED FROM THE WALLS, AND PLUMBING WAS BEING REMOVED.
NOT SURE WHY I'M TELLING YOU THIS. IT DOESN'T RISE TO THE LEVEL OF INTEREST OF YOUR BUREAU, ONLY...
WELL, THERE WAS A WOMAN WHO LIVED IN THIS HOUSE.
POLIZEI
TOTALLY ILLITERATE-- INHERITED THIS PLACE FROM HER FATHER--AND SHE SEEMED TO HAVE AN IRRATIONAL HATRED OF CHILDREN.
SHE INSISTED THAT THEY, THE CHILDREN, WERE COMMITTING ALL THE BURGLARIES.
YOU KEEP REFERRING TO HER IN THE PAST TENSE.
WITH REASON.
PLEASE.

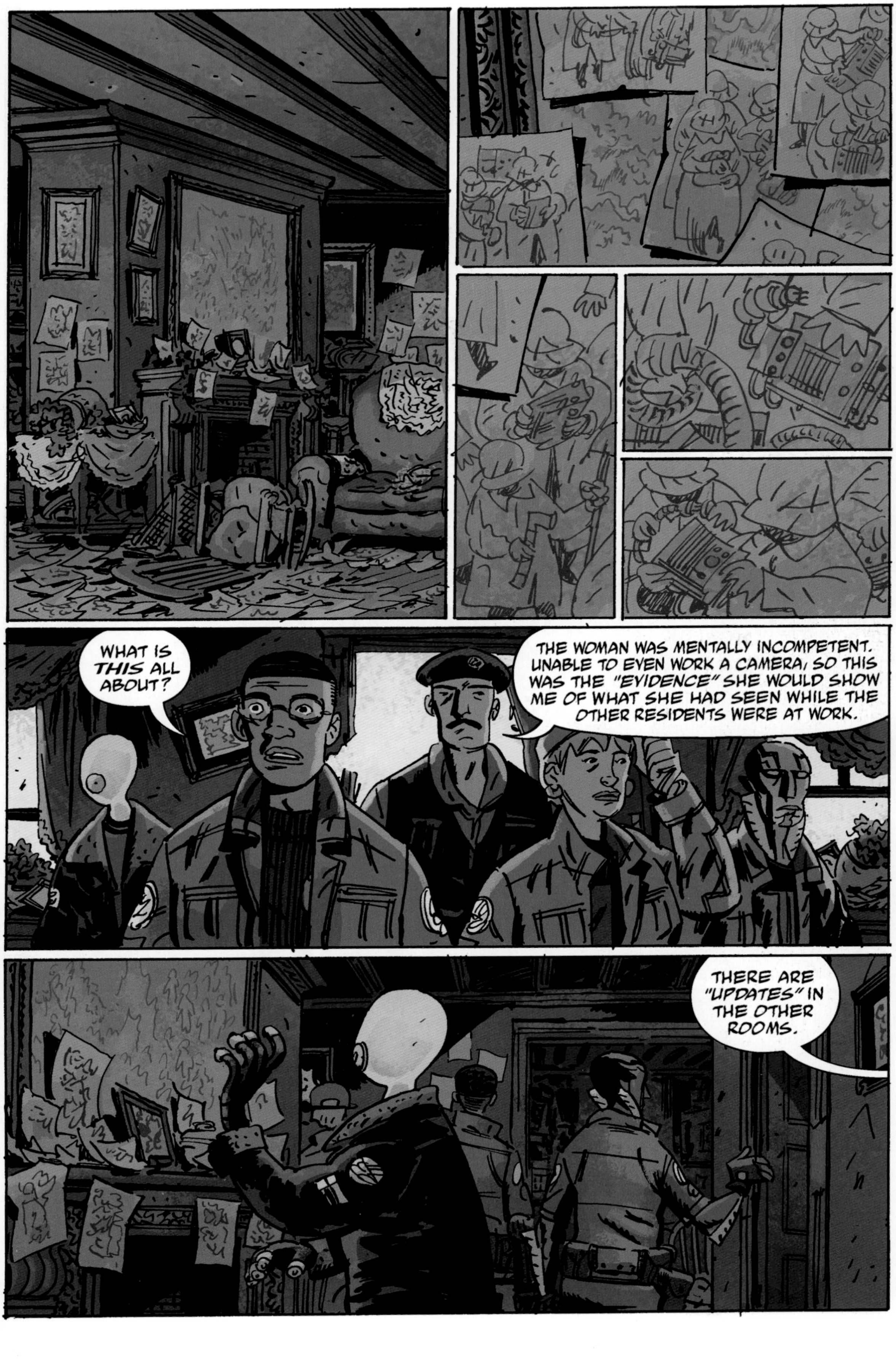
WHAT IS THIS ALL ABOUT?
THE WOMAN WAS MENTALLY INCOMPETENT. UNABLE TO EVEN WORK A CAMERA, SO THIS WAS THE "EVIDENCE" SHE WOULD SHOW ME OF WHAT SHE HAD SEEN WHILE THE OTHER RESIDENTS WERE AT WORK.
THERE ARE "UPDATES" IN THE OTHER ROOMS.

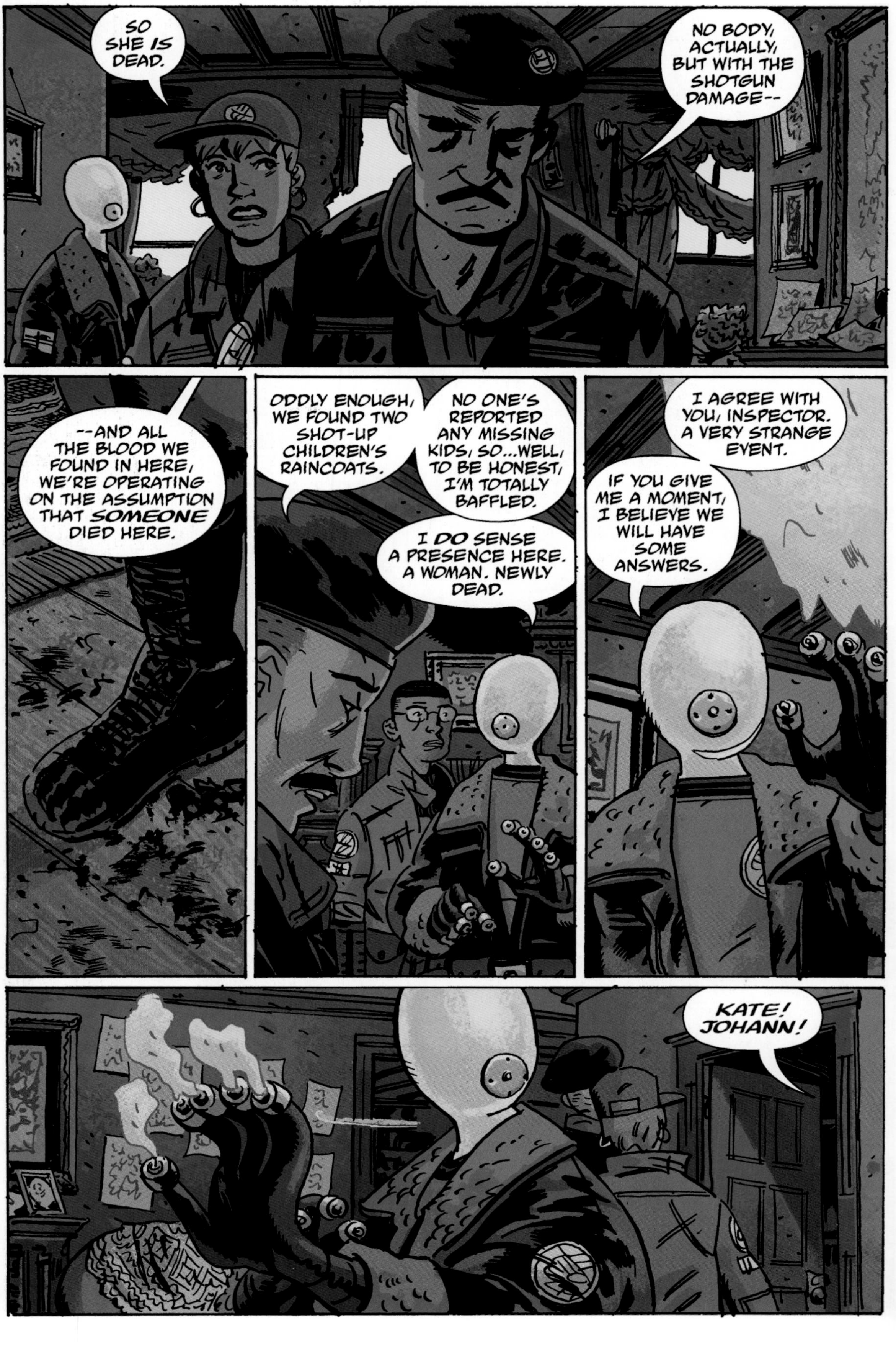
SO SHE IS DEAD.
NO BODY, ACTUALLY, BUT WITH THE SHOTGUN DAMAGE--
--AND ALL THE BLOOD WE FOUND IN HERE, WE'RE OPERATING ON THE ASSUMPTION THAT SOMEONE DIED HERE.
ODDLY ENOUGH, WE FOUND TWO SHOT-UP CHILDREN'S RAINCOATS.
NO ONE'S REPORTED ANY MISSING KIDS, SO...WELL, TO BE HONEST, I'M TOTALLY BAFFLED.
I DO SENSE A PRESENCE HERE. A WOMAN. NEWLY DEAD.
I AGREE WITH YOU, INSPECTOR. A VERY STRANGE EVENT.
IF YOU GIVE ME A MOMENT, I BELIEVE WE WILL HAVE SOME ANSWERS.
KATE! JOHANN!

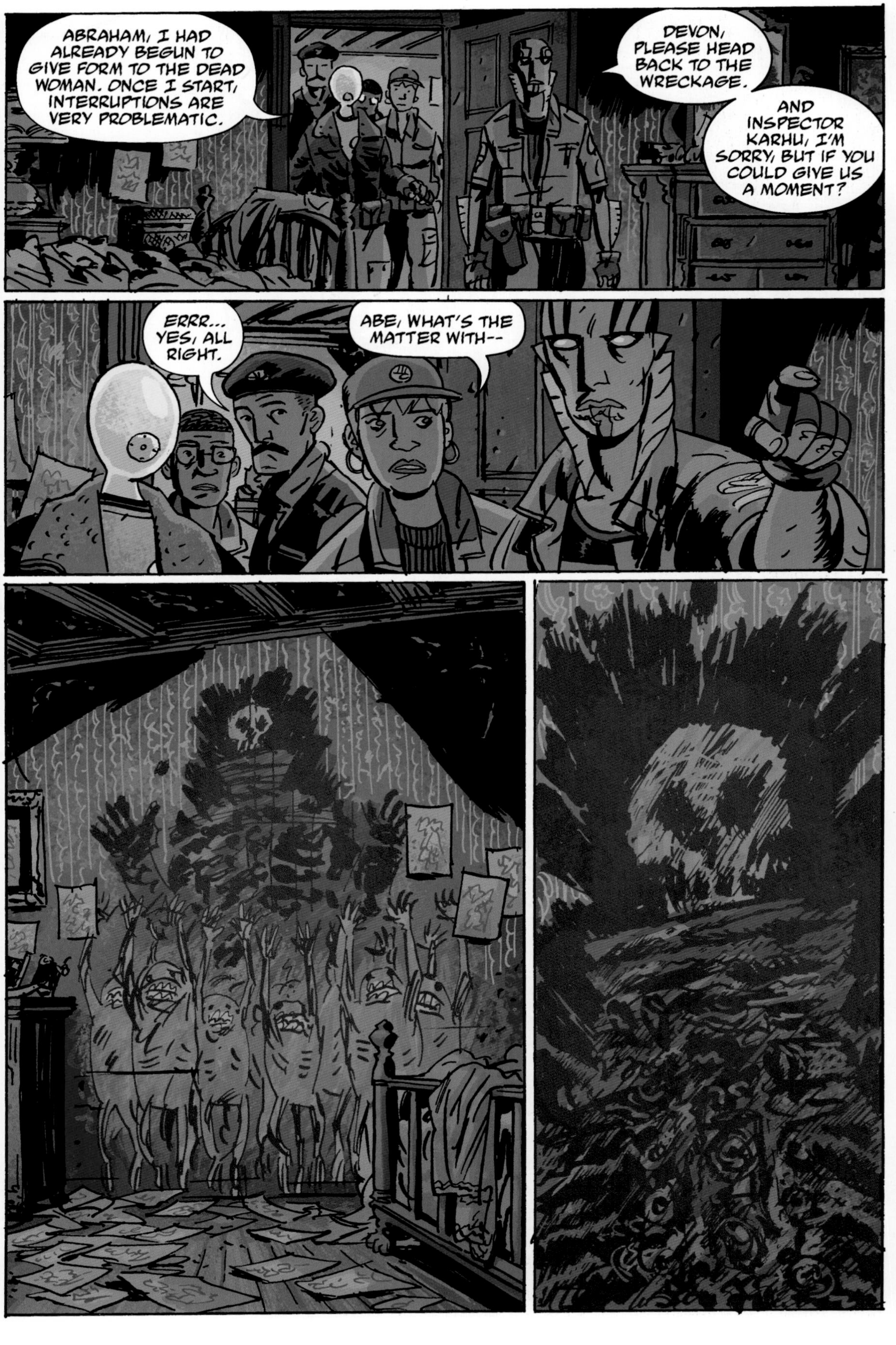

ABRAHAM, I HAD ALREADY BEGUN TO GIVE FORM TO THE DEAD WOMAN. ONCE I START, INTERRUPTIONS ARE VERY PROBLEMATIC.
DEVON, PLEASE HEAD BACK TO THE WRECKAGE.
AND INSPECTOR KARHU, I'M SORRY, BUT IF YOU COULD GIVE US A MOMENT?
ERRR... YES, ALL RIGHT.
ABE, WHAT'S THE MATTER WITH--

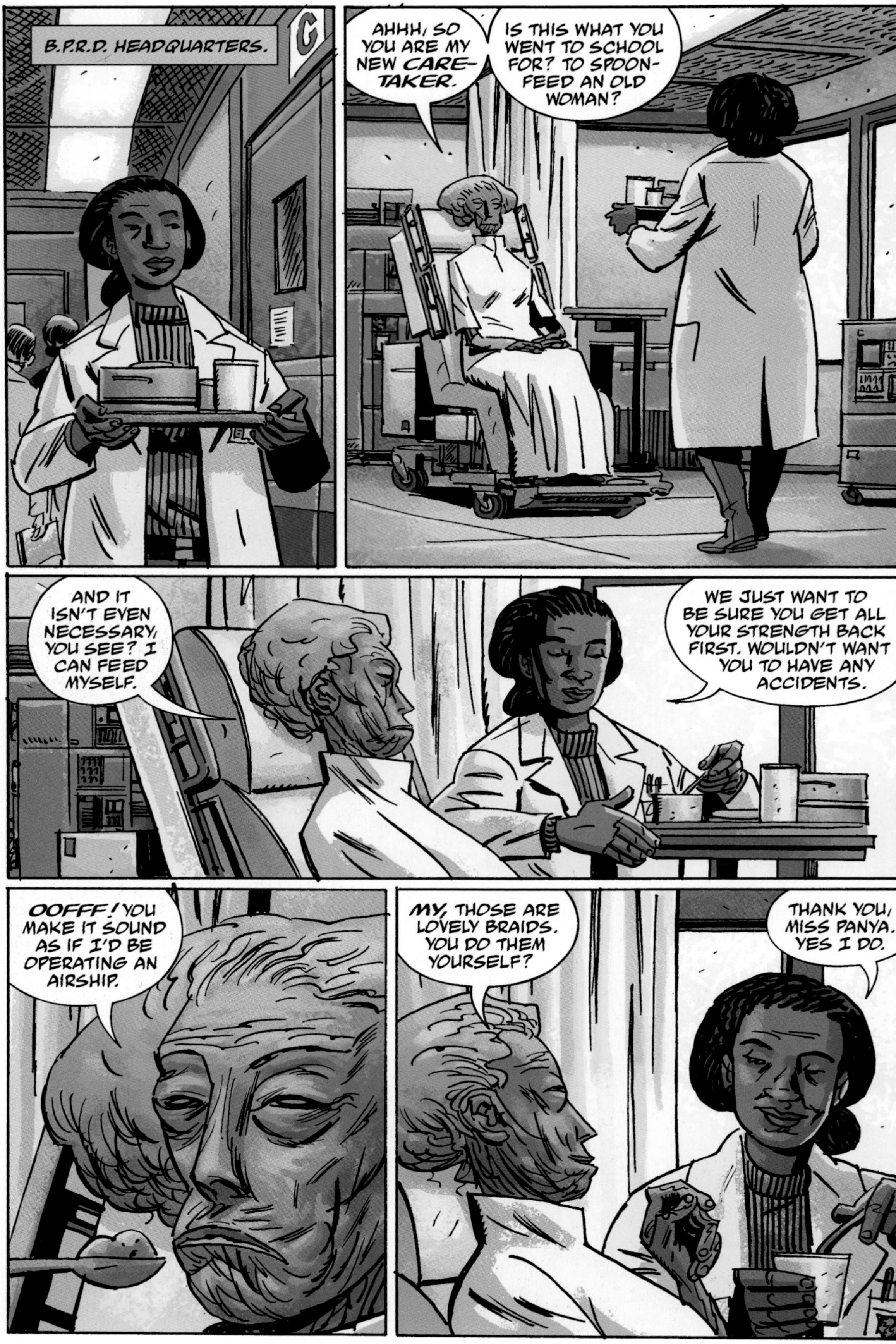

B.P.R.D. HEADQUARTERS.
AHHH, SO YOU ARE MY NEW CARE-TAKER.
IS THIS WHAT YOU WENT TO SCHOOL FOR? TO SPOON-FEED AN OLD WOMAN?
AND IT ISN'T EVEN NECESSARY, YOU SEE? I CAN FEED MYSELF.
WE JUST WANT TO BE SURE YOU GET ALL YOUR STRENGTH BACK FIRST. WOULDN'T WANT YOU TO HAVE ANY ACCIDENTS.
OOFFF! YOU MAKE IT SOUND AS IF I'D BE OPERATING AN AIRSHIP.
MY, THOSE ARE LOVELY BRAIDS. YOU DO THEM YOURSELF?
THANK YOU, MISS PANYA. YES I DO.

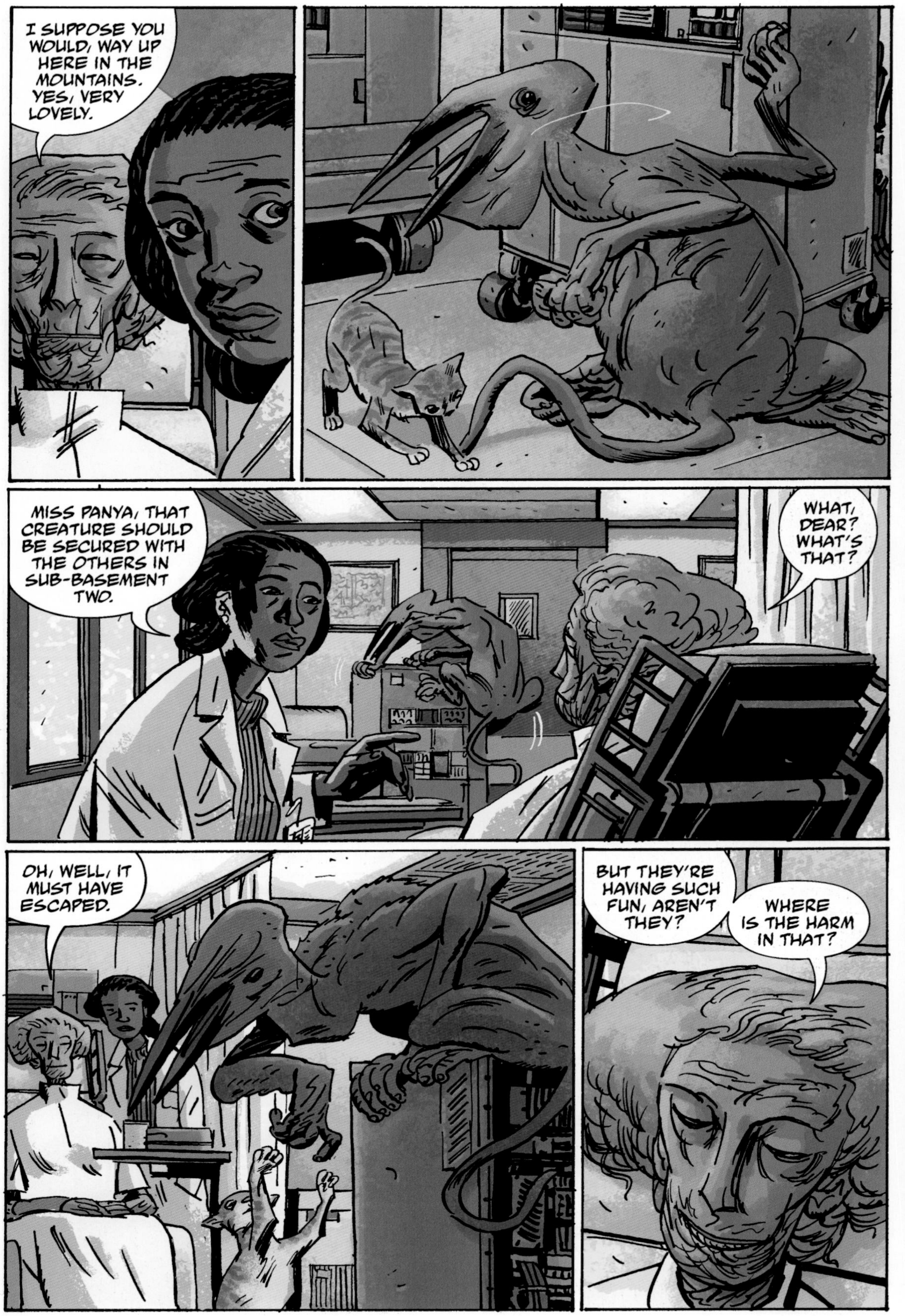
I SUPPOSE YOU WOULD, WAY UP HERE IN THE MOUNTAINS. YES, VERY LOVELY.
MISS PANYA, THAT CREATURE SHOULD BE SECURED WITH THE OTHERS IN SUB-BASEMENT TWO.
WHAT, DEAR? WHAT'S THAT?
OH, WELL, IT MUST HAVE ESCAPED.
BUT THEY'RE HAVING SUCH FUN, AREN'T THEY?
WHERE IS THE HARM IN THAT?

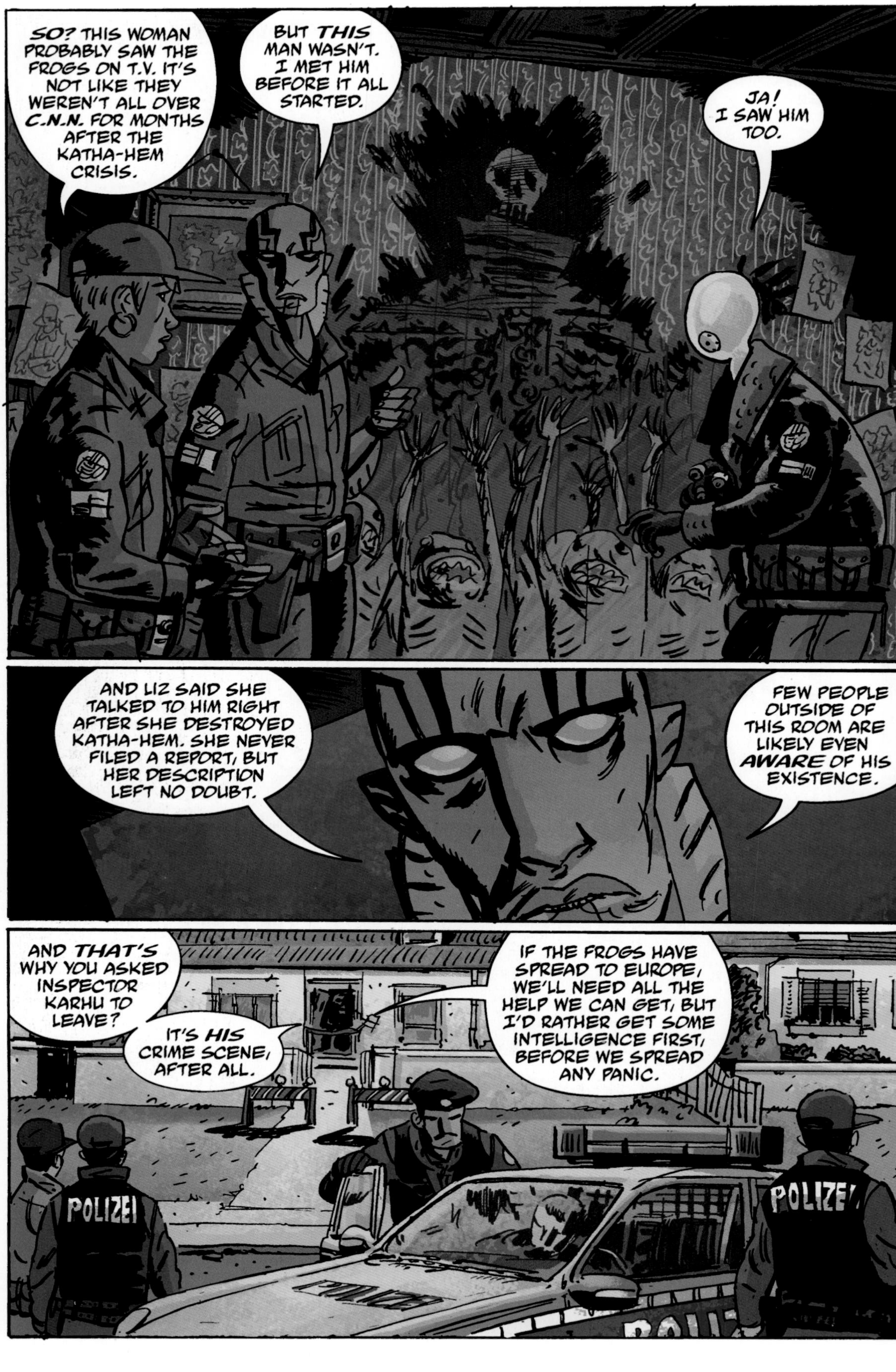
SO? THIS WOMAN PROBABLY SAW THE FROGS ON T.V. IT'S NOT LIKE THEY WEREN'T ALL OVER C.N.N. FOR MONTHS AFTER THE KATHA-HEM CRISIS.
BUT THIS MAN WASN'T. I MET HIM BEFORE IT ALL STARTED.
JA! I SAW HIM TOO.
AND LIZ SAID SHE TALKED TO HIM RIGHT AFTER SHE DESTROYED KATHA-HEM. SHE NEVER FILED A REPORT, BUT HER DESCRIPTION LEFT NO DOUBT.
FEW PEOPLE OUTSIDE OF THIS ROOM ARE LIKELY EVEN AWARE OF HIS EXISTENCE.
AND THAT'S WHY YOU ASKED INSPECTOR KARHU TO LEAVE?
IT'S HIS CRIME SCENE, AFTER ALL.
IF THE FROGS HAVE SPREAD TO EUROPE, WE'LL NEED ALL THE HELP WE CAN GET, BUT I'D RATHER GET SOME INTELLIGENCE FIRST, BEFORE WE SPREAD ANY PANIC.
POLIZEI
POLIZEI

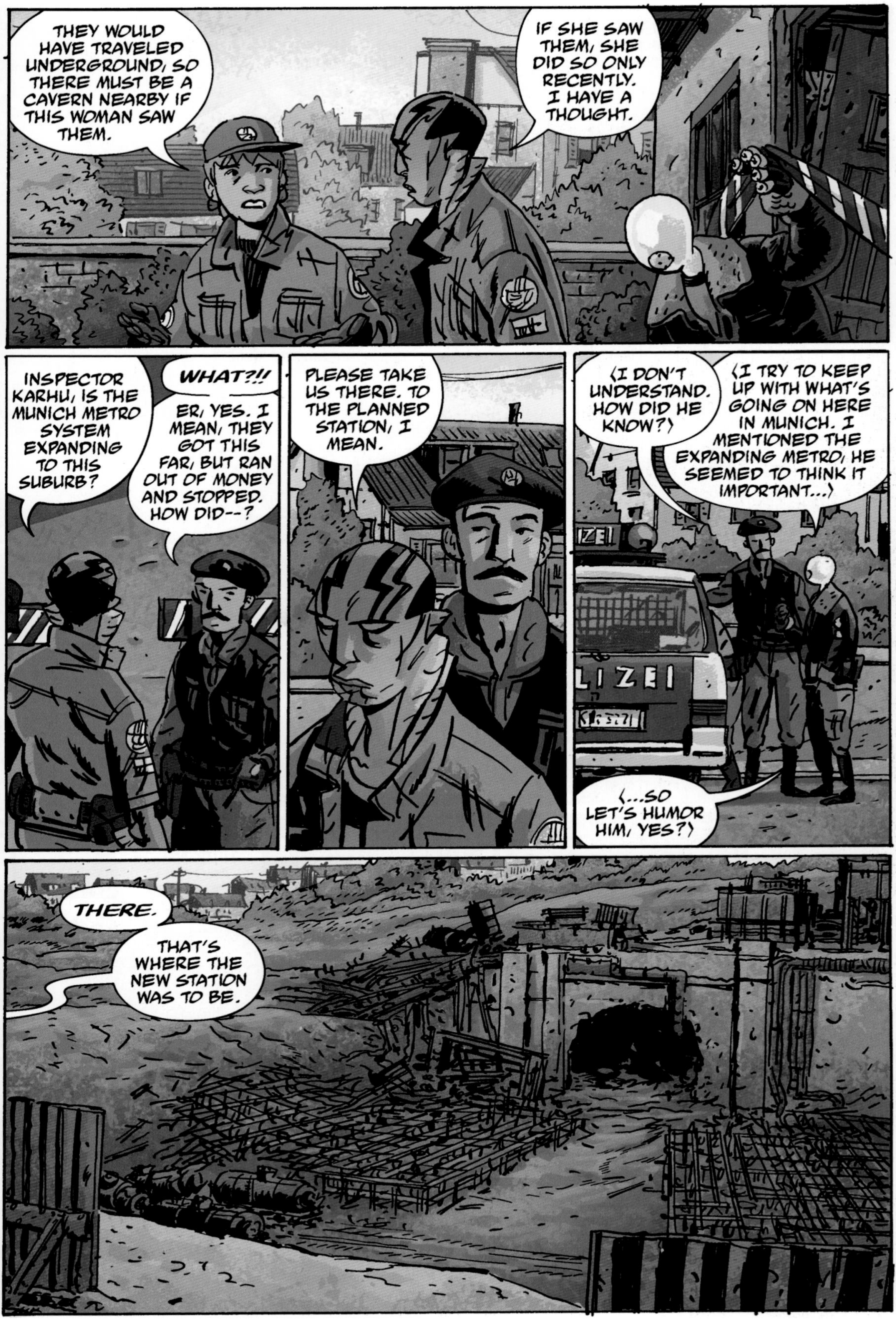
THEY WOULD HAVE TRAVELED UNDERGROUND, SO THERE MUST BE A CAVERN NEARBY IF THIS WOMAN SAW THEM.
IF SHE SAW THEM, SHE DID SO ONLY RECENTLY. I HAVE A THOUGHT.
INSPECTOR KARHU, IS THE MUNICH METRO SYSTEM EXPANDING TO THIS SUBURB?
WHAT?!!
ER, YES. I MEAN, THEY GOT THIS FAR, BUT RAN OUT OF MONEY AND STOPPED. HOW DID--?
PLEASE TAKE US THERE. TO THE PLANNED STATION, I MEAN.
‹I DON'T UNDERSTAND. HOW DID HE KNOW?›
‹I TRY TO KEEP UP WITH WHAT'S GOING ON HERE IN MUNICH. I MENTIONED THE EXPANDING METRO, HE SEEMED TO THINK IT IMPORTANT...›
‹...SO LET'S HUMOR HIM, YES?›
LIZEI
THERE.
THAT'S WHERE THE NEW STATION WAS TO BE.

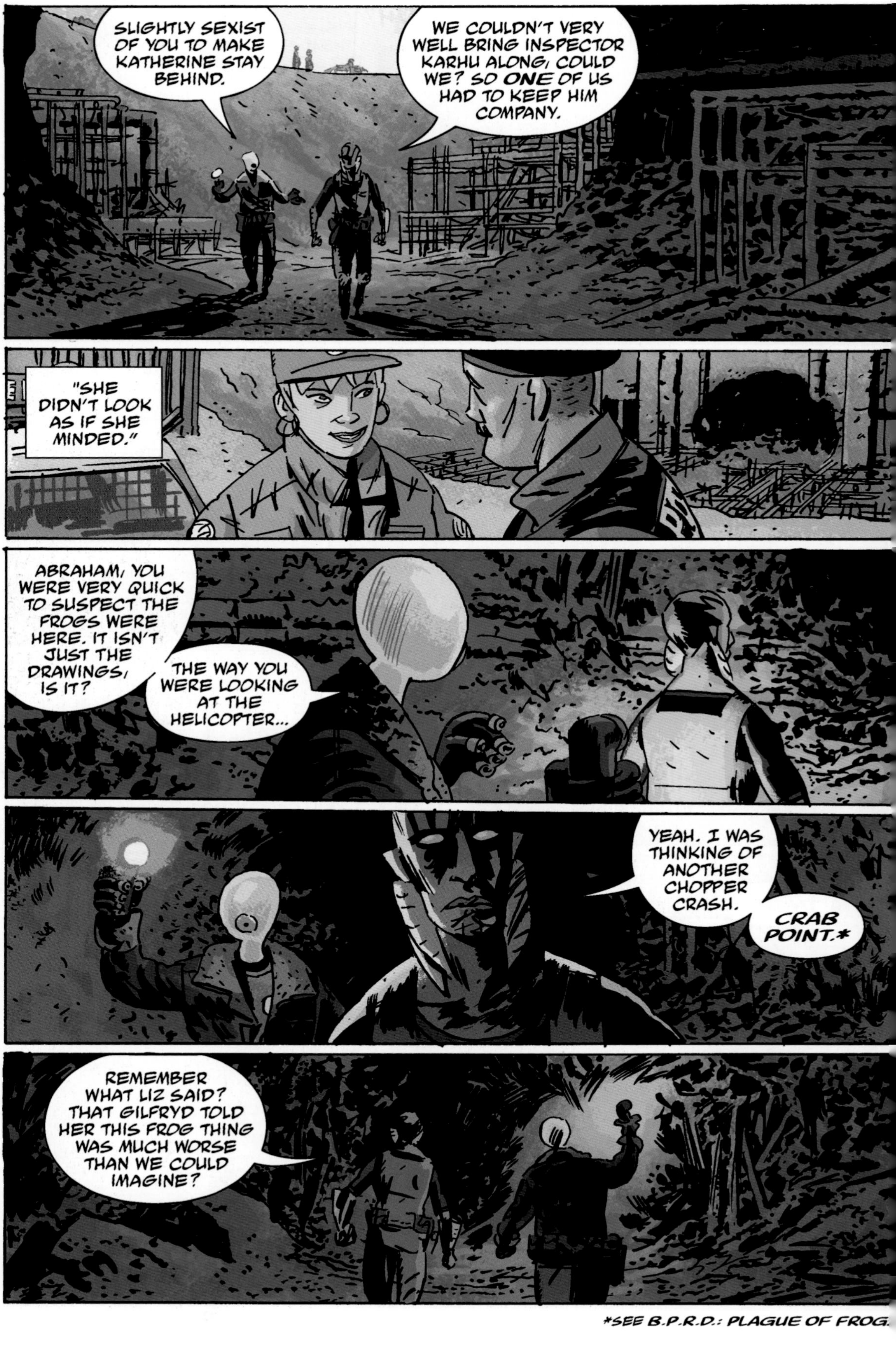
SLIGHTLY SEXIST OF YOU TO MAKE KATHERINE STAY BEHIND.
WE COULDN'T VERY WELL BRING INSPECTOR KARHU ALONG, COULD WE? SO ONE OF US HAD TO KEEP HIM COMPANY.
"SHE DIDN'T LOOK AS IF SHE MINDED."
ABRAHAM, YOU WERE VERY QUICK TO SUSPECT THE FROGS WERE HERE. IT ISN'T JUST THE DRAWINGS, IS IT?
THE WAY YOU WERE LOOKING AT THE HELICOPTER...
YEAH. I WAS THINKING OF ANOTHER CHOPPER CRASH.
CRAB POINT.*
REMEMBER WHAT LIZ SAID? THAT GILFRYD TOLD HER THIS FROG THING WAS MUCH WORSE THAN WE COULD IMAGINE?

*SEE B.P.R.D.: PLAGUE OF FROG

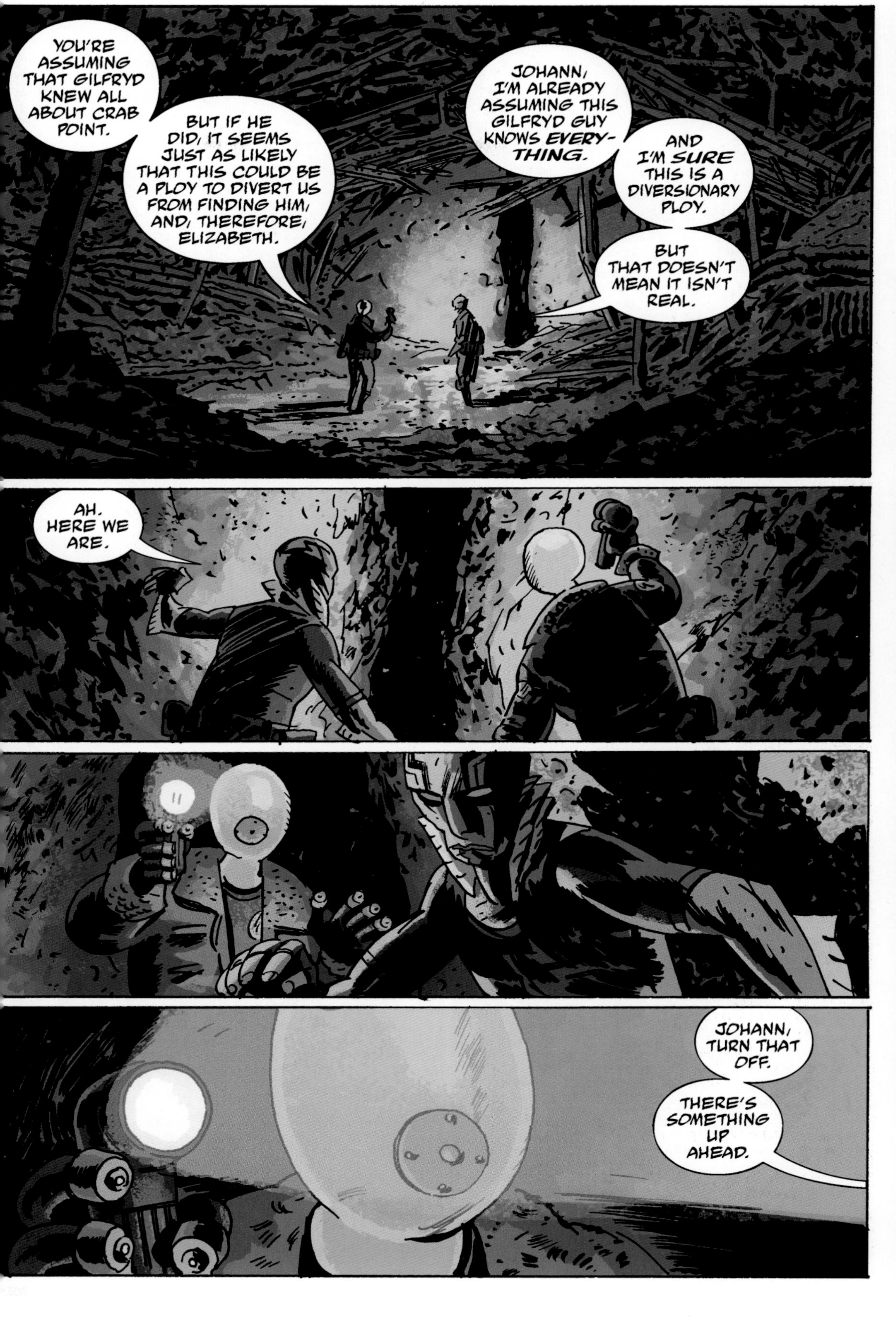
YOU'RE ASSUMING THAT GILFRYD KNEW ALL ABOUT CRAB POINT.
BUT IF HE DID, IT SEEMS JUST AS LIKELY THAT THIS COULD BE A PLOY TO DIVERT US FROM FINDING HIM, AND, THEREFORE, ELIZABETH.
JOHANN, I'M ALREADY ASSUMING THIS GILFRYD GUY KNOWS *EVERYTHING*.
AND I'M *SURE* THIS IS A DIVERSIONARY PLOY.
BUT THAT DOESN'T MEAN IT ISN'T REAL.
AH. HERE WE ARE.
JOHANN, TURN THAT OFF.
THERE'S SOMETHING UP AHEAD.

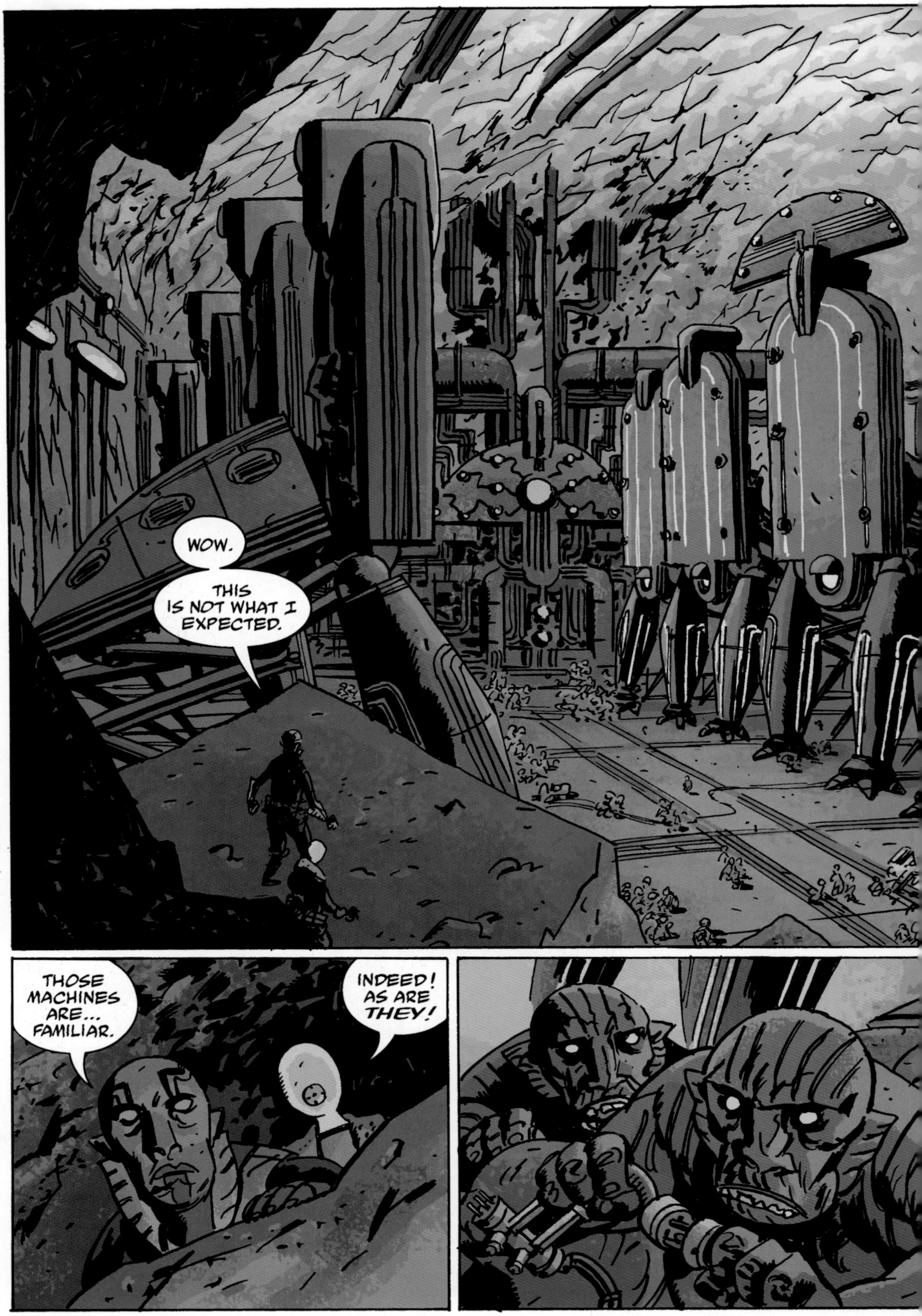
WOW.
THIS IS NOT WHAT I EXPECTED.
THOSE MACHINES ARE... FAMILIAR.
INDEED! AS ARE *THEY*!

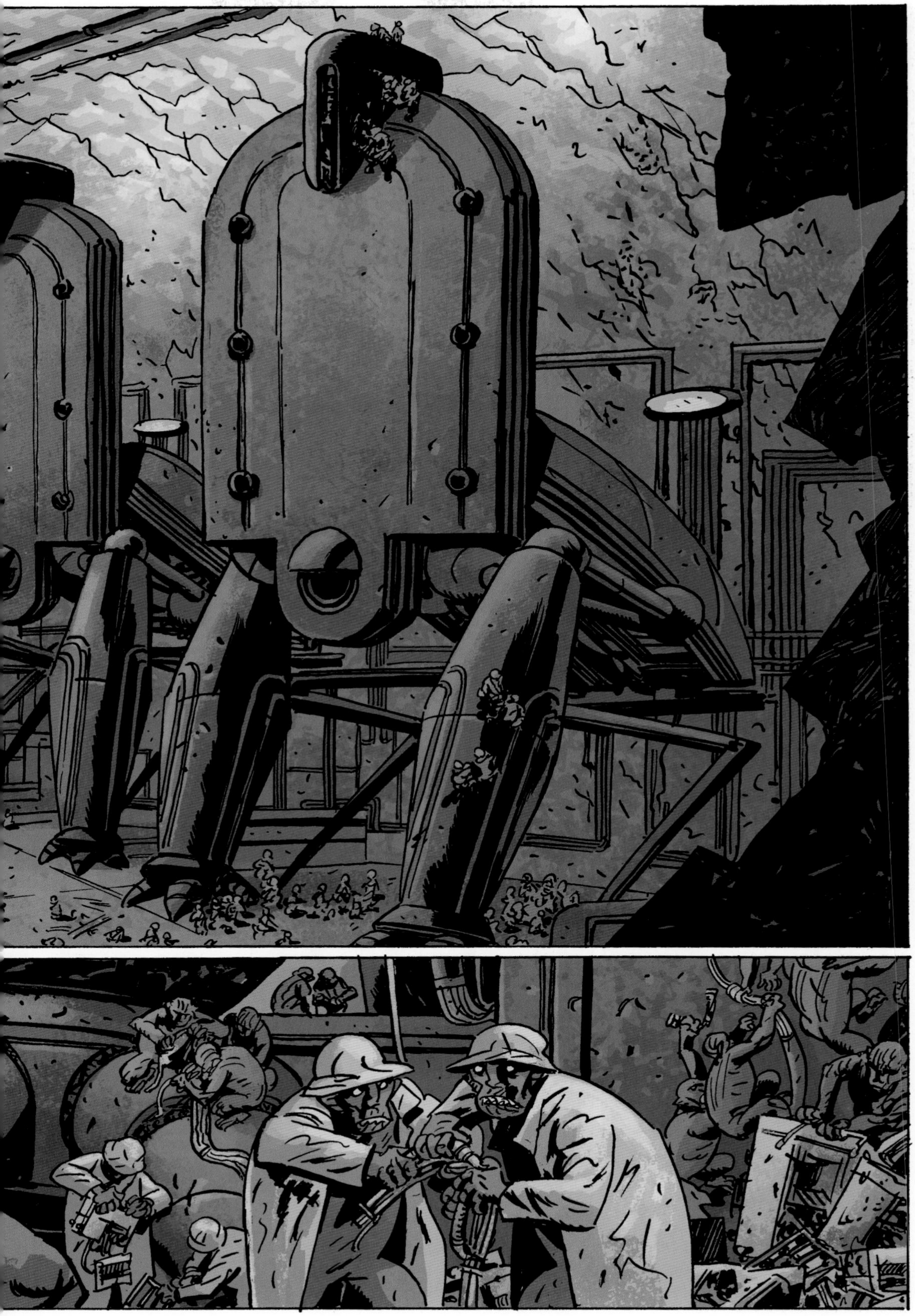

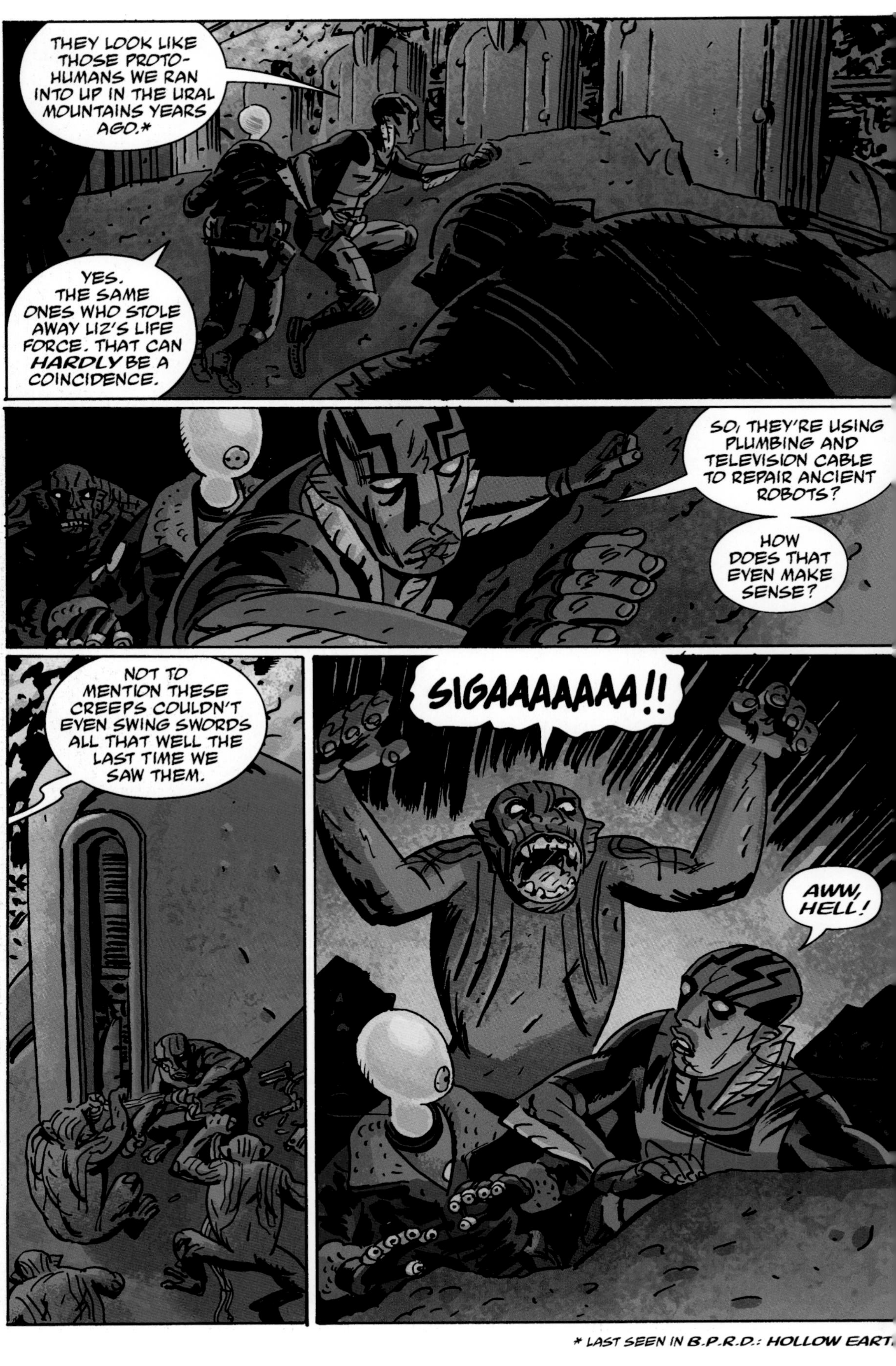
THEY LOOK LIKE THOSE PROTO-HUMANS WE RAN INTO UP IN THE URAL MOUNTAINS YEARS AGO.*
YES. THE SAME ONES WHO STOLE AWAY LIZ'S LIFE FORCE. THAT CAN HARDLY BE A COINCIDENCE.
SO, THEY'RE USING PLUMBING AND TELEVISION CABLE TO REPAIR ANCIENT ROBOTS?
HOW DOES THAT EVEN MAKE SENSE?
NOT TO MENTION THESE CREEPS COULDN'T EVEN SWING SWORDS ALL THAT WELL THE LAST TIME WE SAW THEM.
SIGAAAAAAA!!
AWW, HELL!

* LAST SEEN IN *B.P.R.D.: HOLLOW EART*

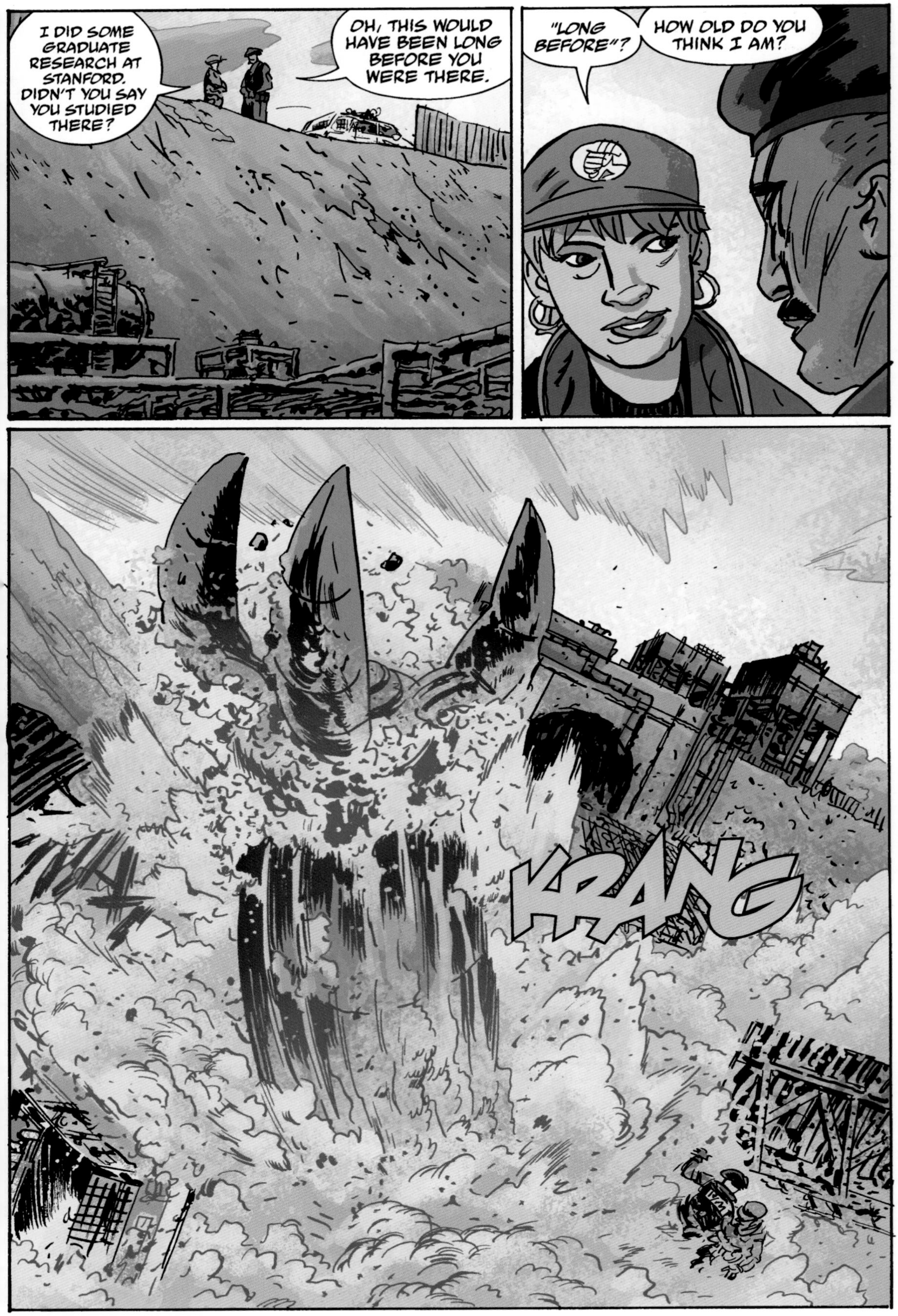
I DID SOME GRADUATE RESEARCH AT STANFORD. DIDN'T YOU SAY YOU STUDIED THERE?
OH, THIS WOULD HAVE BEEN LONG BEFORE YOU WERE THERE.
"LONG BEFORE"?
HOW OLD DO YOU THINK I AM?
KRANG

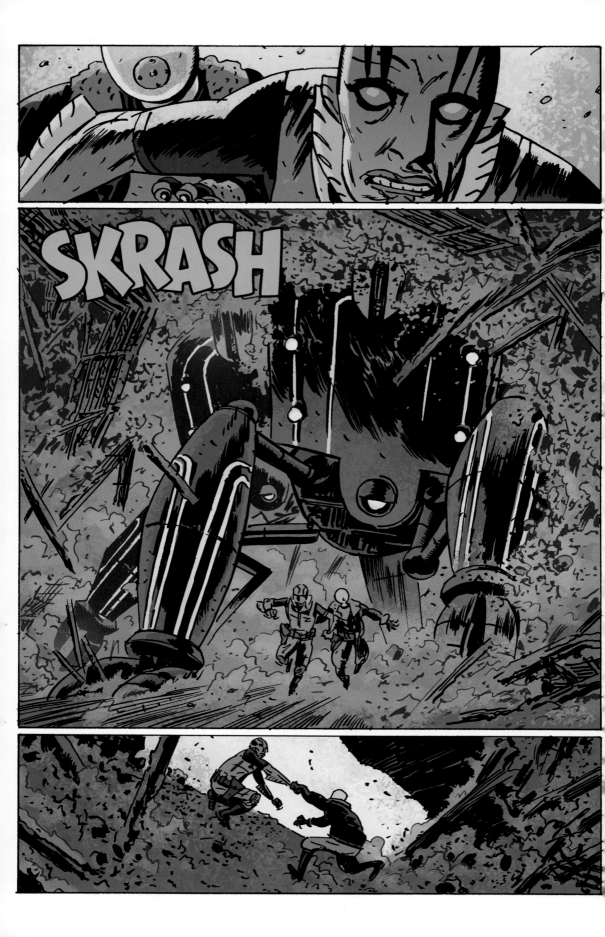

SKRASH

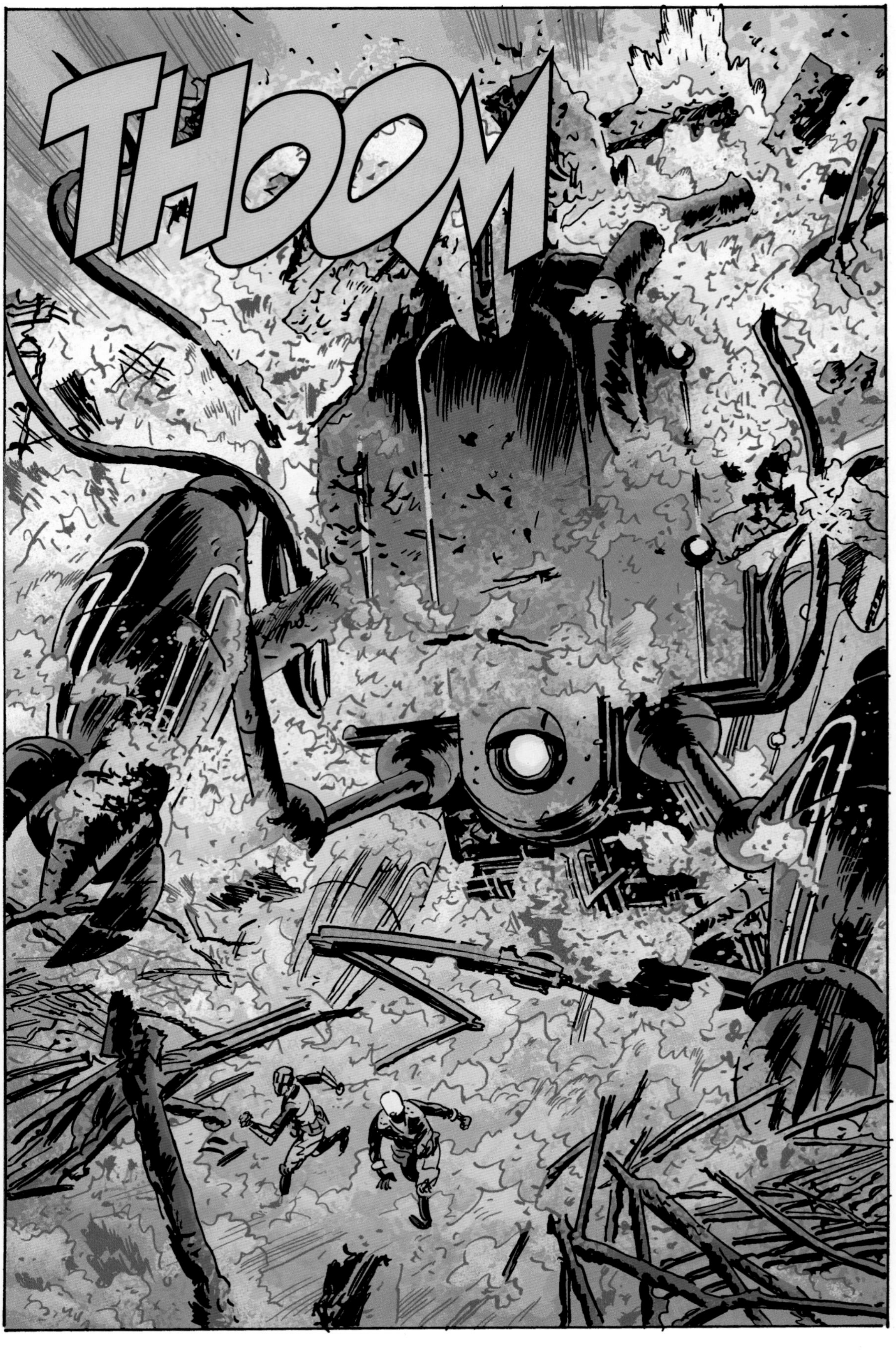
THOOM

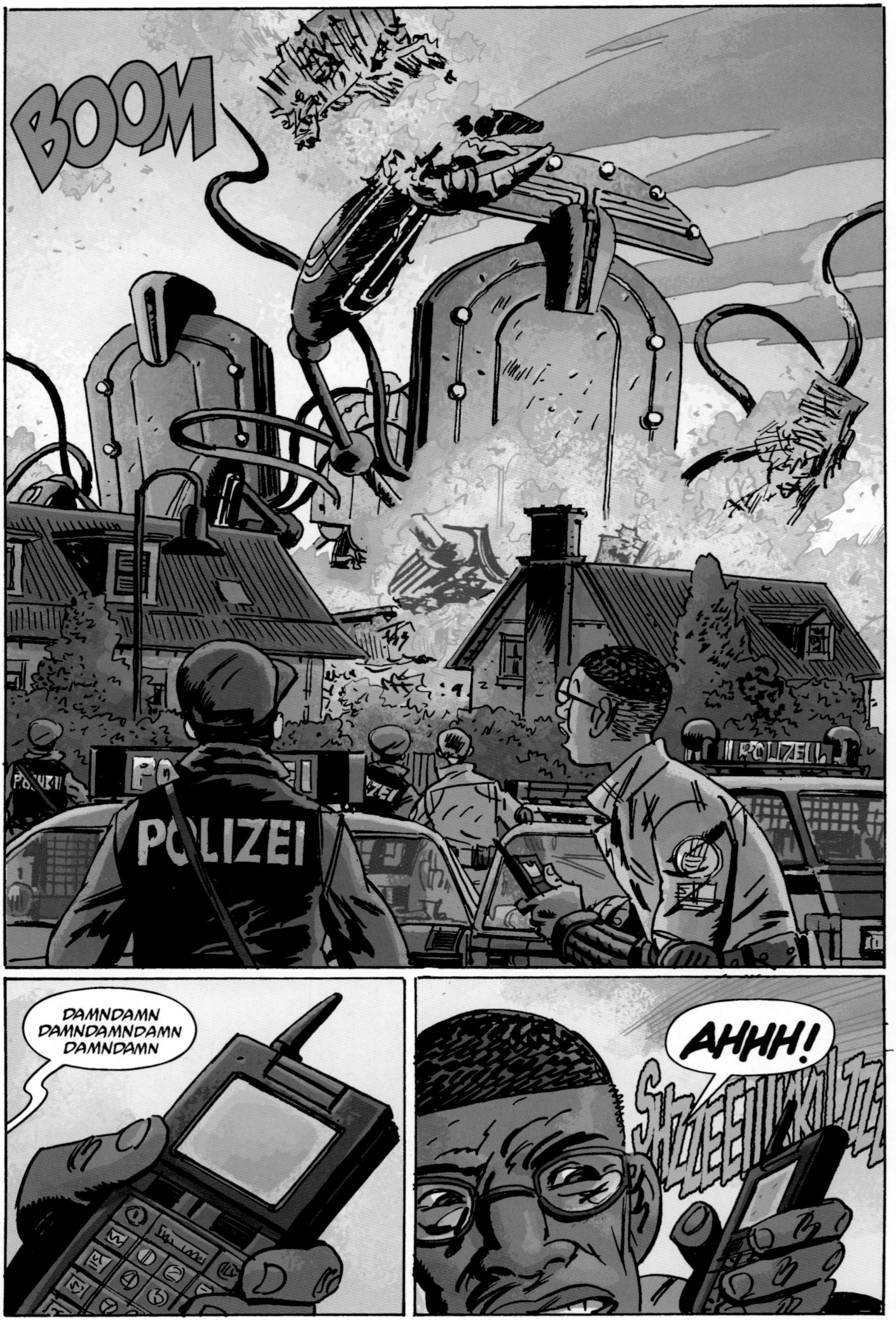
BOOM
POLIZEI
POLIZEI
DAMNDAMN DAMNDAMNDAMN DAMNDAMN
AHHH!

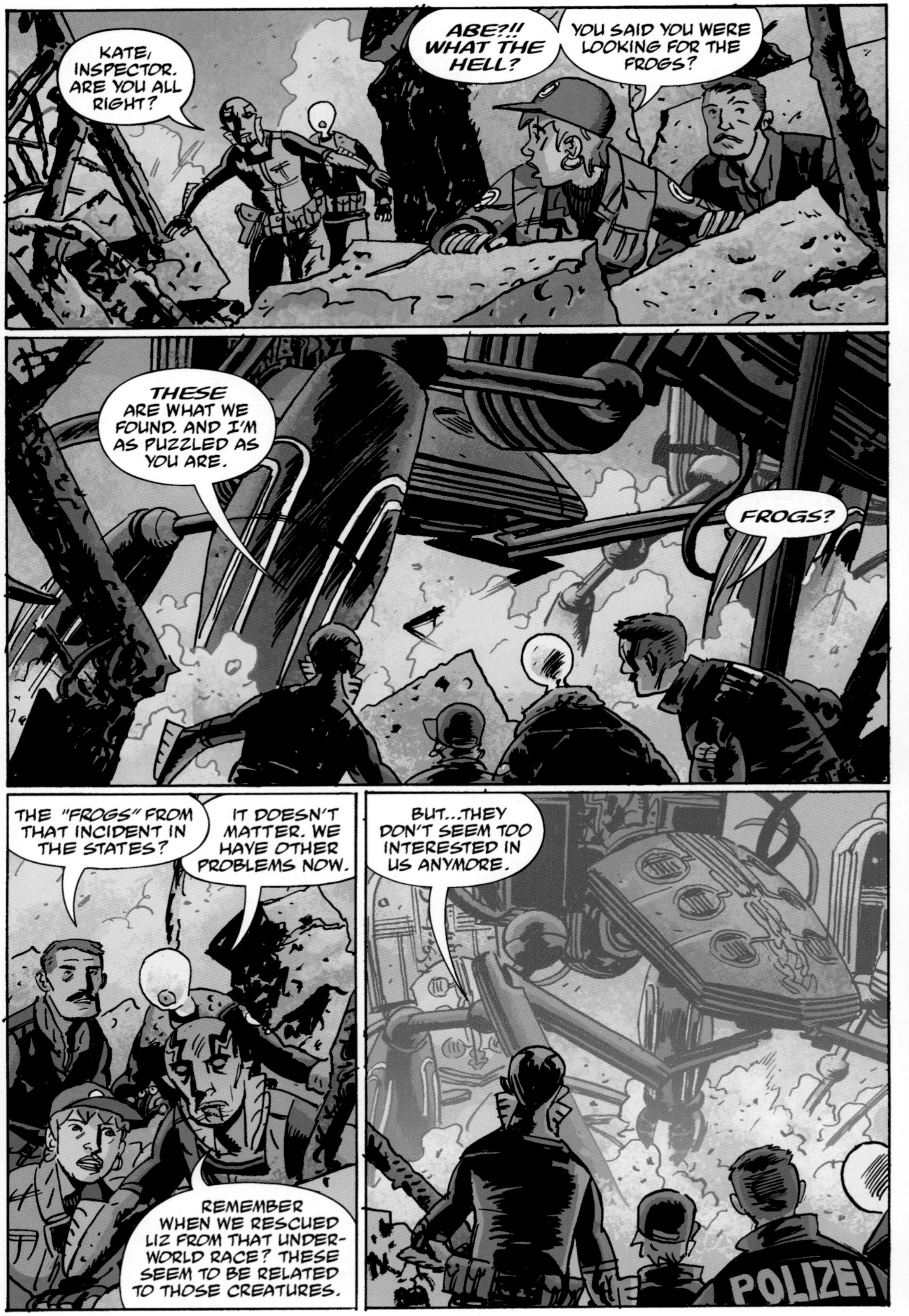
KATE, INSPECTOR. ARE YOU ALL RIGHT?
ABE?!! WHAT THE HELL?
YOU SAID YOU WERE LOOKING FOR THE FROGS?
THESE ARE WHAT WE FOUND. AND I'M AS PUZZLED AS YOU ARE.
FROGS?
THE "FROGS" FROM THAT INCIDENT IN THE STATES?
IT DOESN'T MATTER. WE HAVE OTHER PROBLEMS NOW.
REMEMBER WHEN WE RESCUED LIZ FROM THAT UNDER-WORLD RACE? THESE SEEM TO BE RELATED TO THOSE CREATURES.
BUT...THEY DON'T SEEM TOO INTERESTED IN US ANYMORE.
POLIZEI

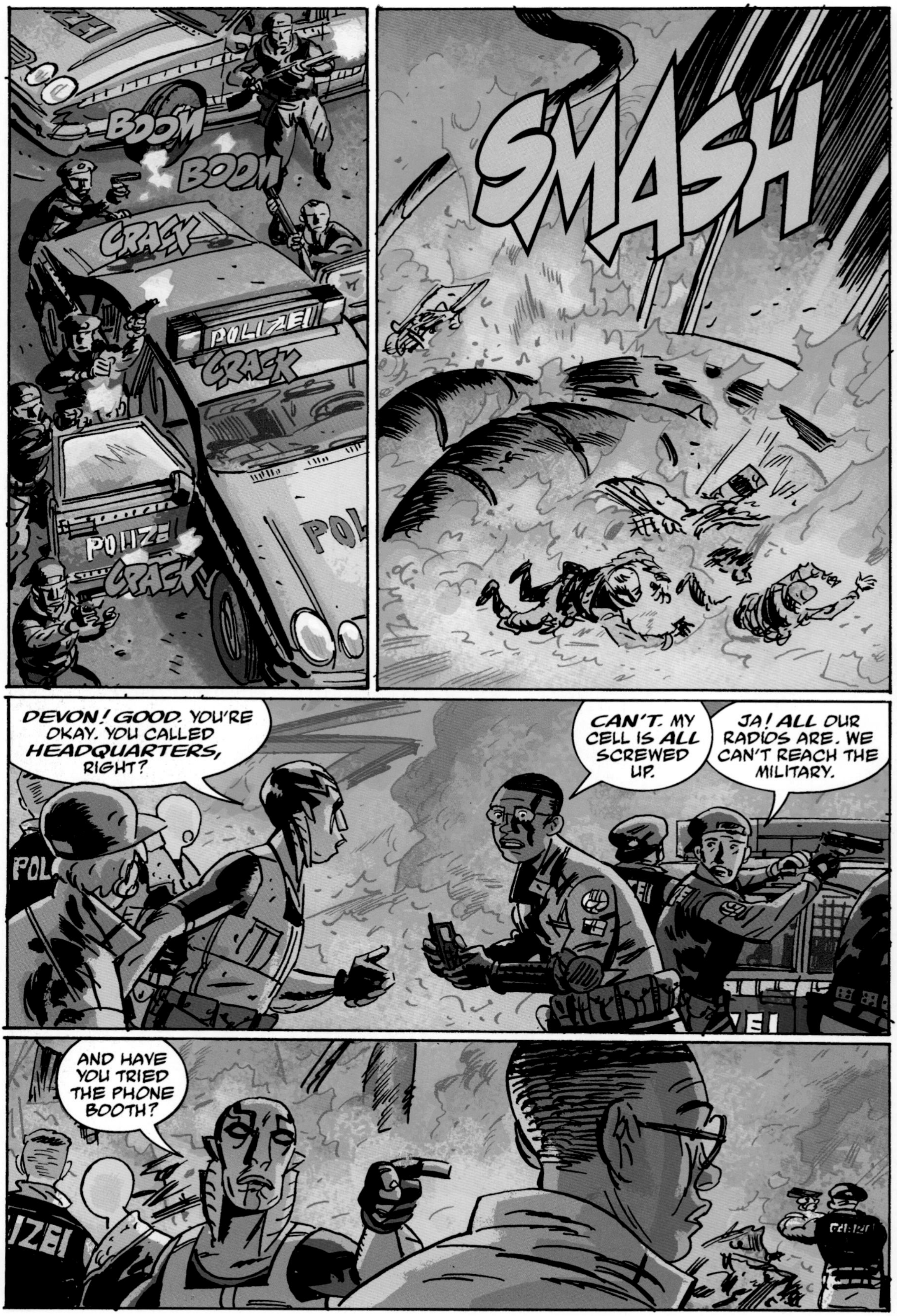
BOOM
BOOM
CRACK
POLIZEI
CRACK
POLIZEI
CRACK
SMASH
DEVON! GOOD. YOU'RE OKAY. YOU CALLED HEADQUARTERS, RIGHT?
CAN'T. MY CELL IS ALL SCREWED UP.
JA! ALL OUR RADIOS ARE. WE CAN'T REACH THE MILITARY.
AND HAVE YOU TRIED THE PHONE BOOTH?

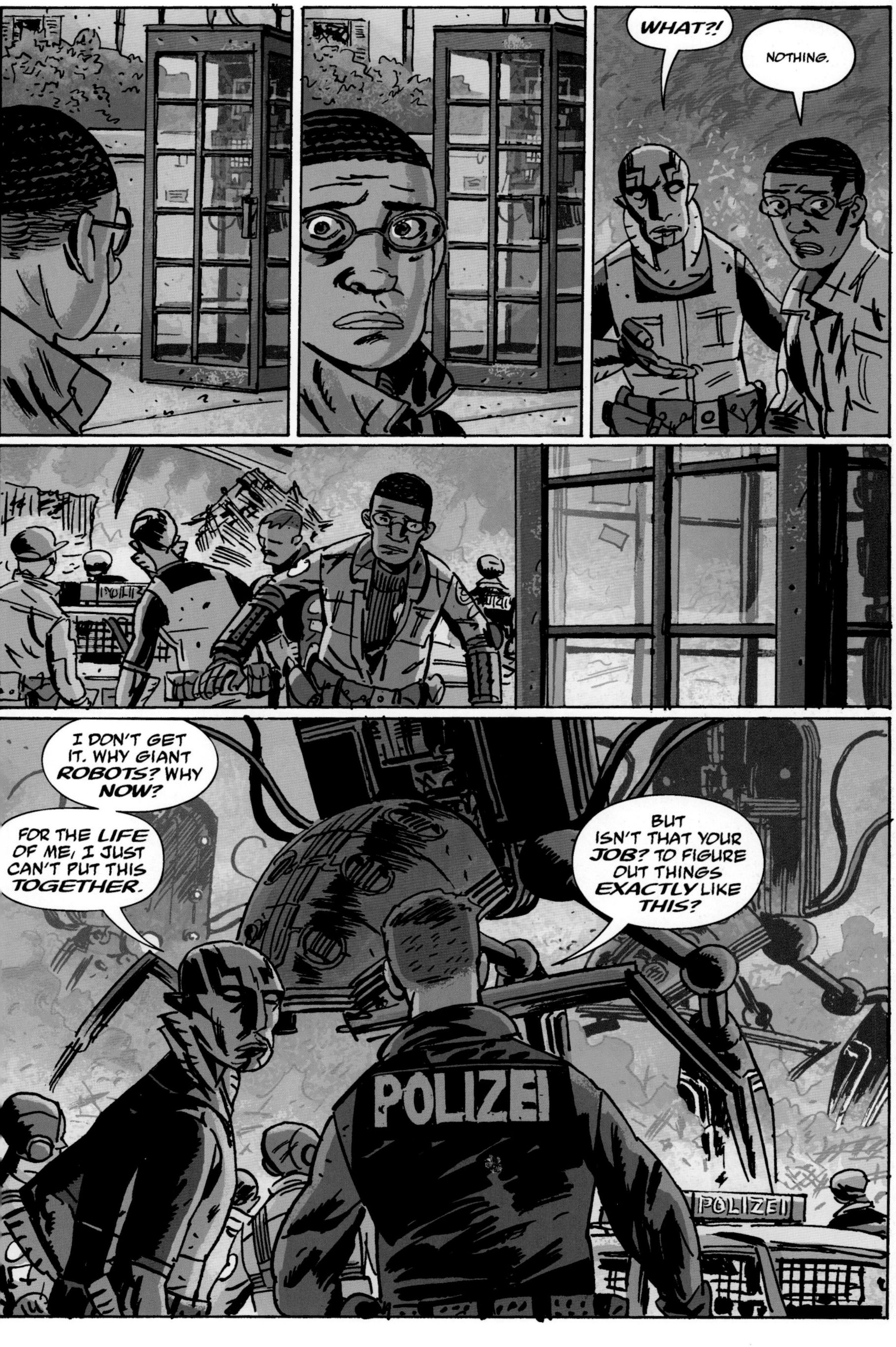
WHAT?!
NOTHING.
POLIZEI
I DON'T GET IT. WHY GIANT ROBOTS? WHY NOW?
FOR THE LIFE OF ME, I JUST CAN'T PUT THIS TOGETHER.
BUT ISN'T THAT YOUR JOB? TO FIGURE OUT THINGS EXACTLY LIKE THIS?
POLIZEI
POLIZEI

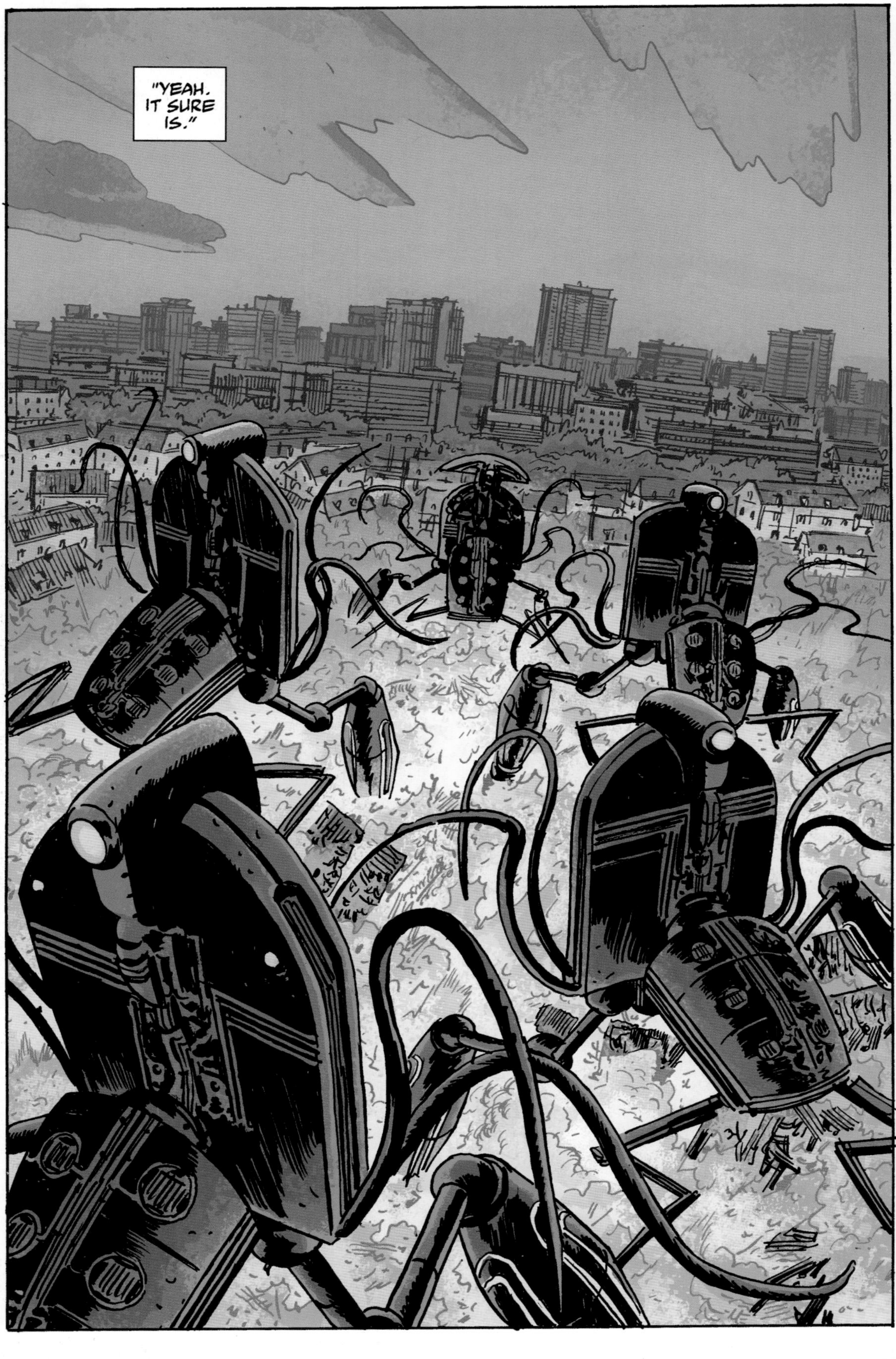
"YEAH. IT SURE IS."

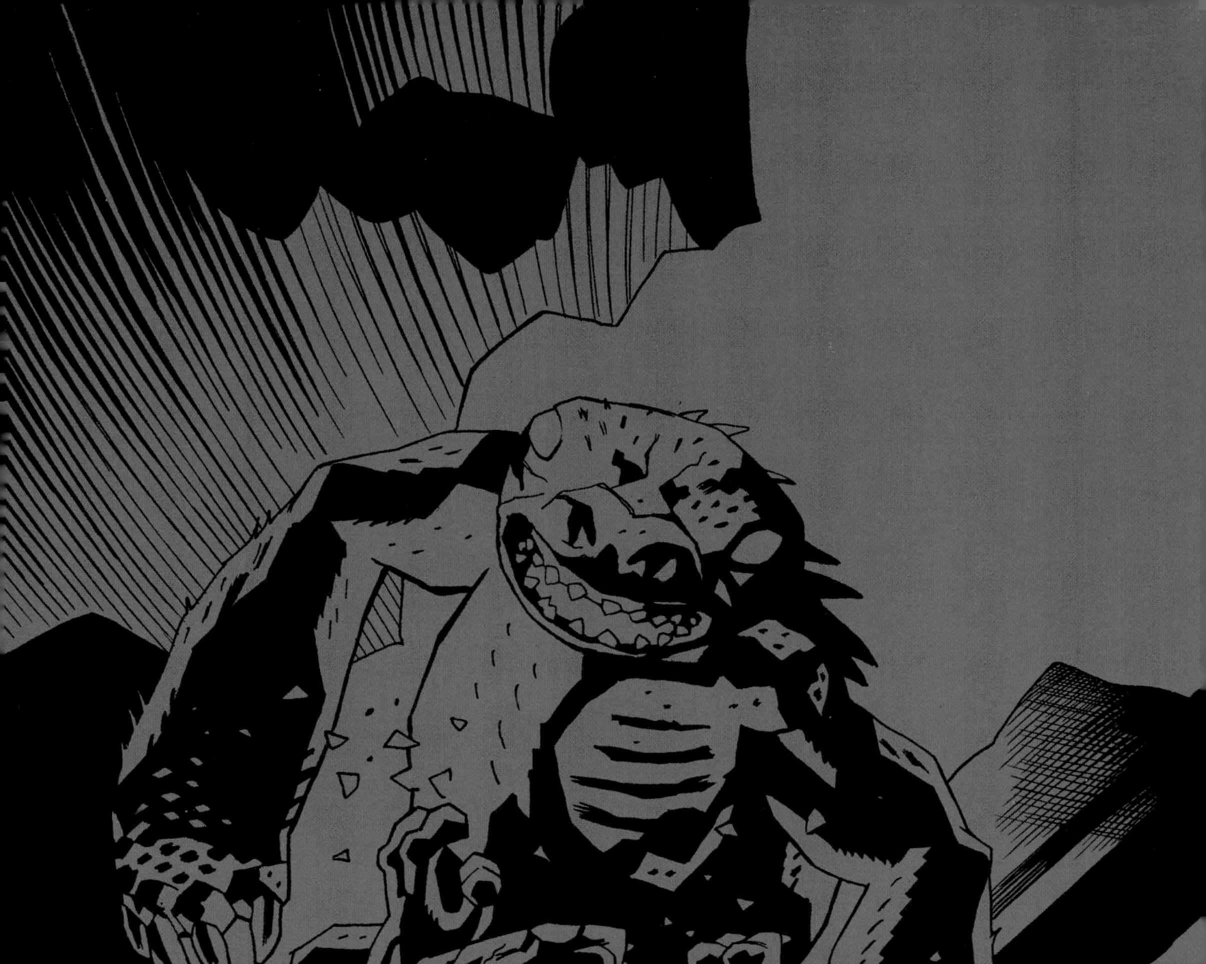
HELLO
M
NOWLAN

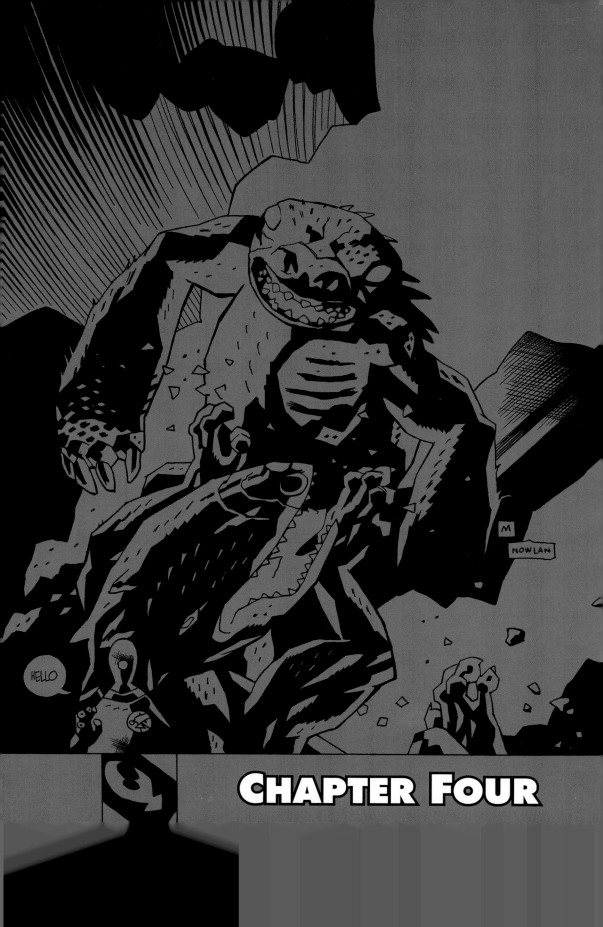

CHAPTER FOUR

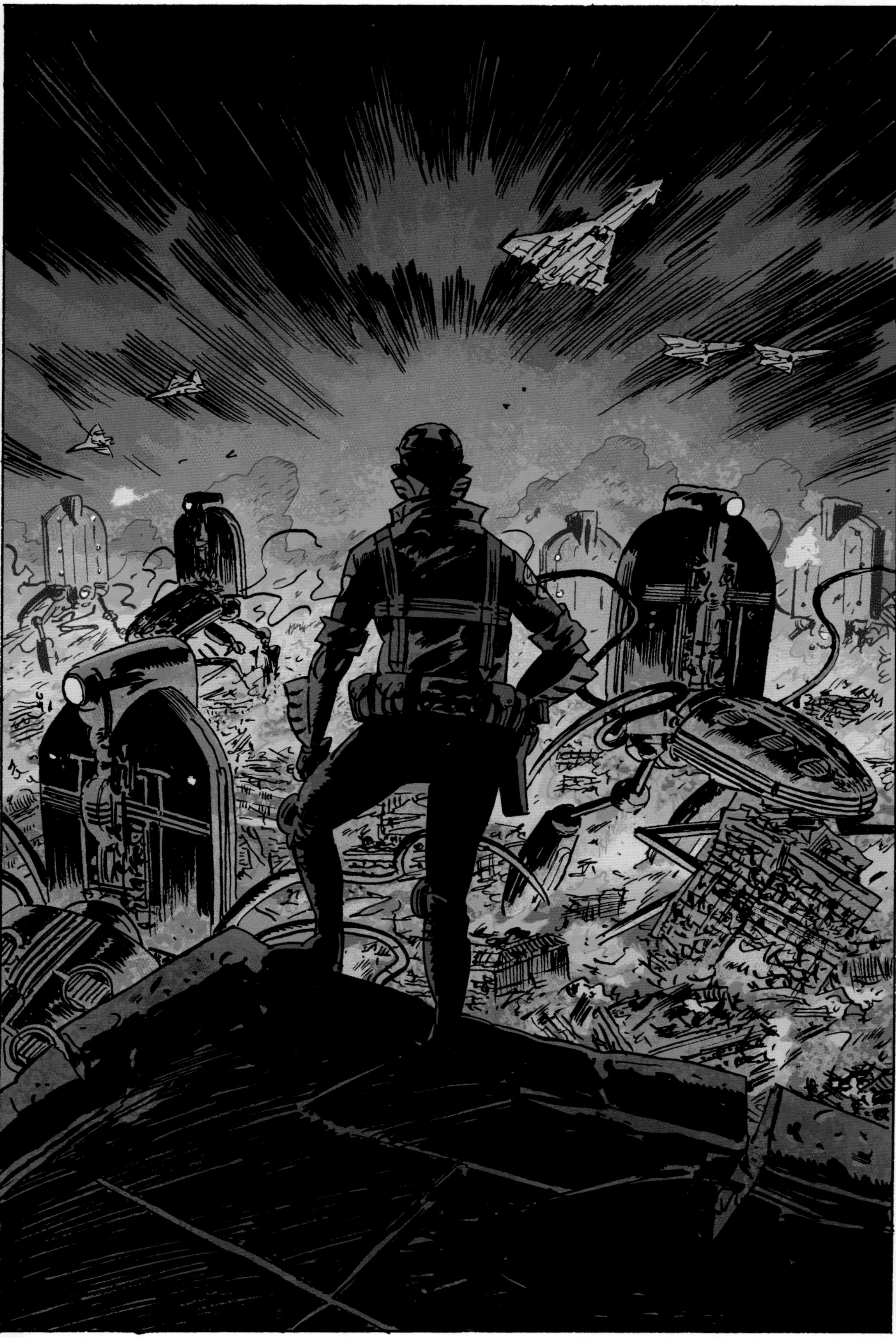

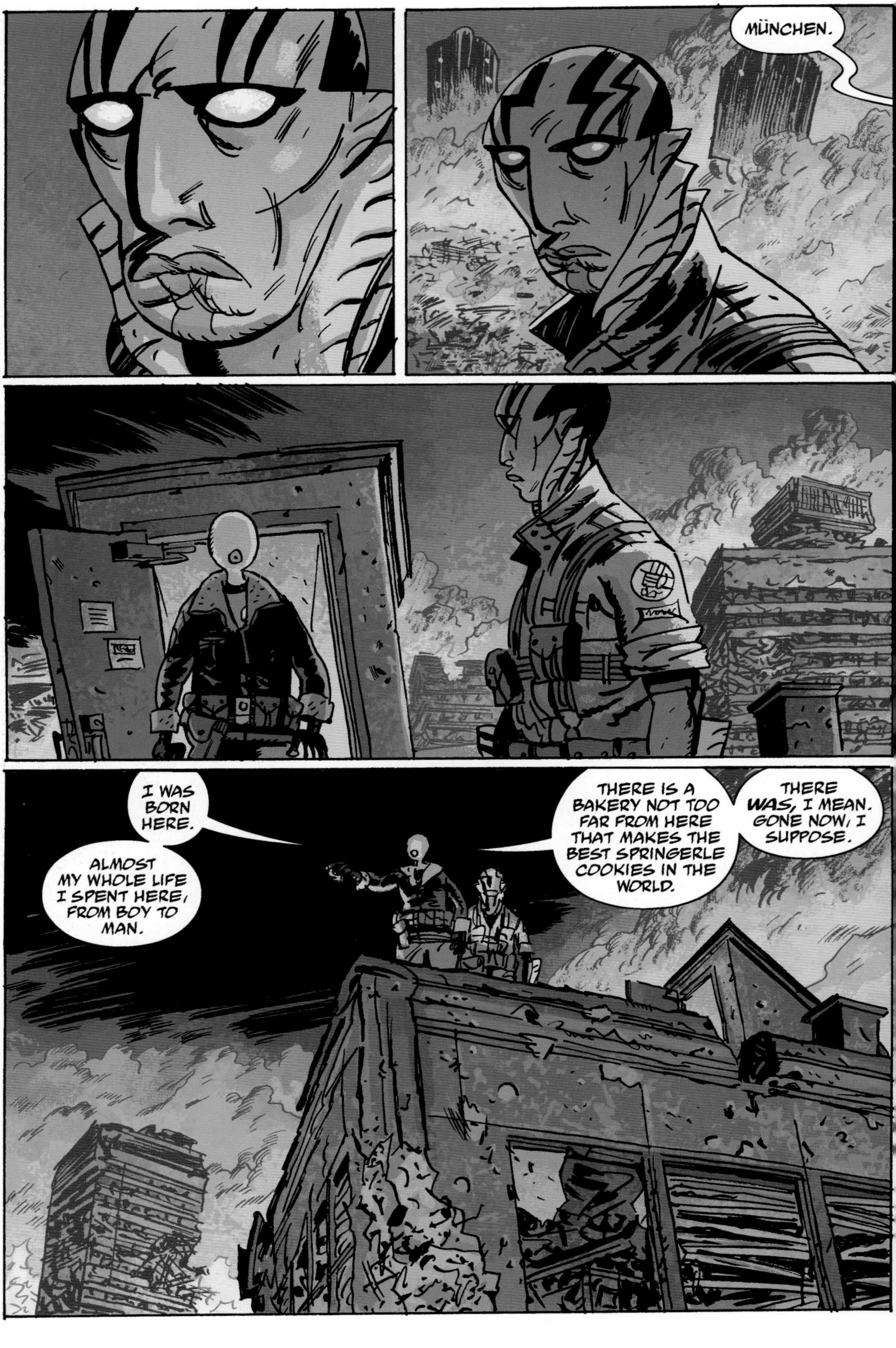
MÜNCHEN.
I WAS BORN HERE.
ALMOST MY WHOLE LIFE I SPENT HERE, FROM BOY TO MAN.
THERE IS A BAKERY NOT TOO FAR FROM HERE THAT MAKES THE BEST SPRINGERLE COOKIES IN THE WORLD.
THERE *WAS*, I MEAN. GONE NOW, I SUPPOSE.

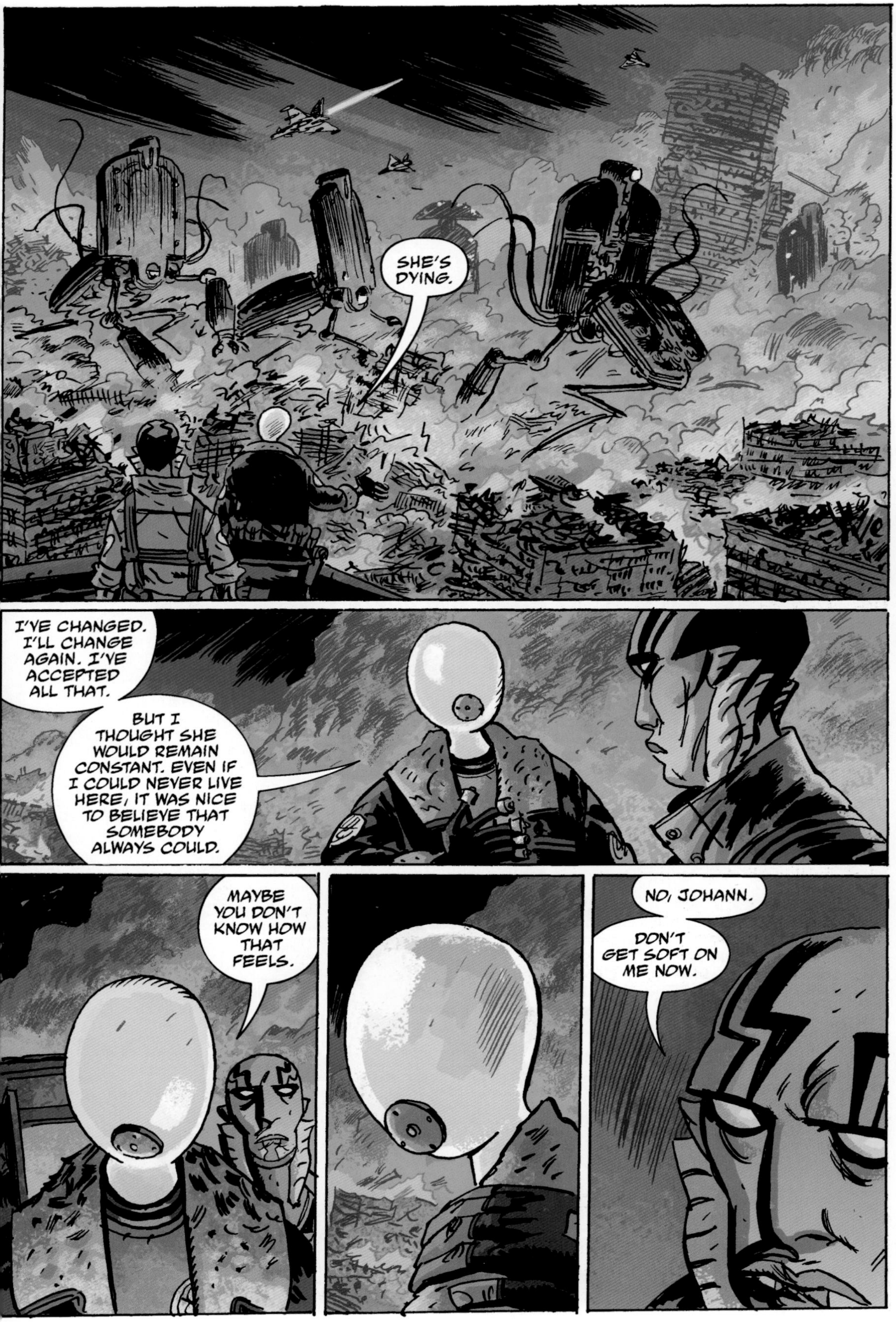
SHE'S DYING.
I'VE CHANGED. I'LL CHANGE AGAIN. I'VE ACCEPTED ALL THAT.
BUT I THOUGHT SHE WOULD REMAIN CONSTANT. EVEN IF I COULD NEVER LIVE HERE, IT WAS NICE TO BELIEVE THAT SOMEBODY ALWAYS COULD.
MAYBE YOU DON'T KNOW HOW THAT FEELS.
NO, JOHANN.
DON'T GET SOFT ON ME NOW.

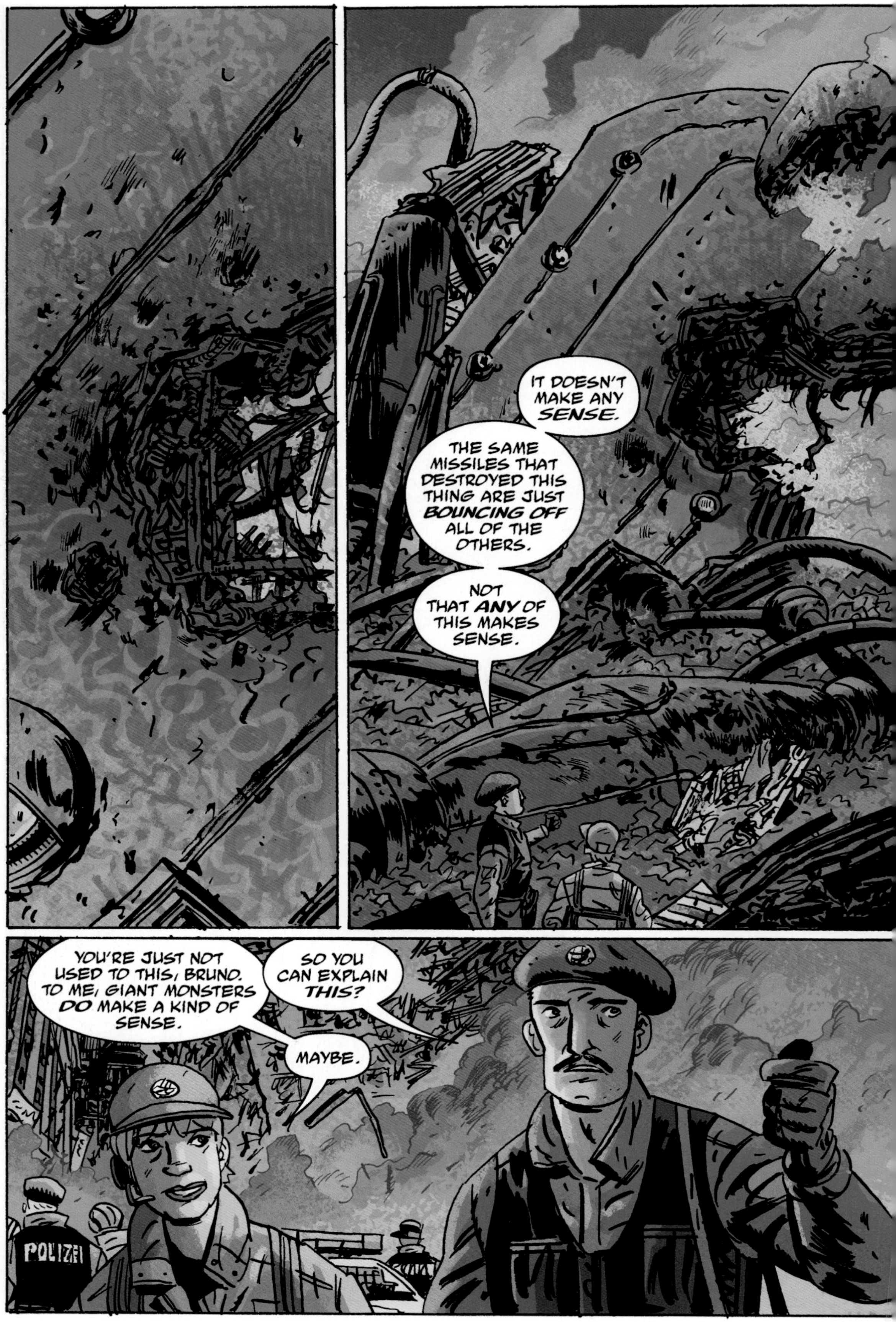
IT DOESN'T MAKE ANY SENSE.
THE SAME MISSILES THAT DESTROYED THIS THING ARE JUST BOUNCING OFF ALL OF THE OTHERS.
NOT THAT ANY OF THIS MAKES SENSE.
YOU'RE JUST NOT USED TO THIS, BRUNO. TO ME, GIANT MONSTERS DO MAKE A KIND OF SENSE.
SO YOU CAN EXPLAIN THIS?
MAYBE.
POLIZEI

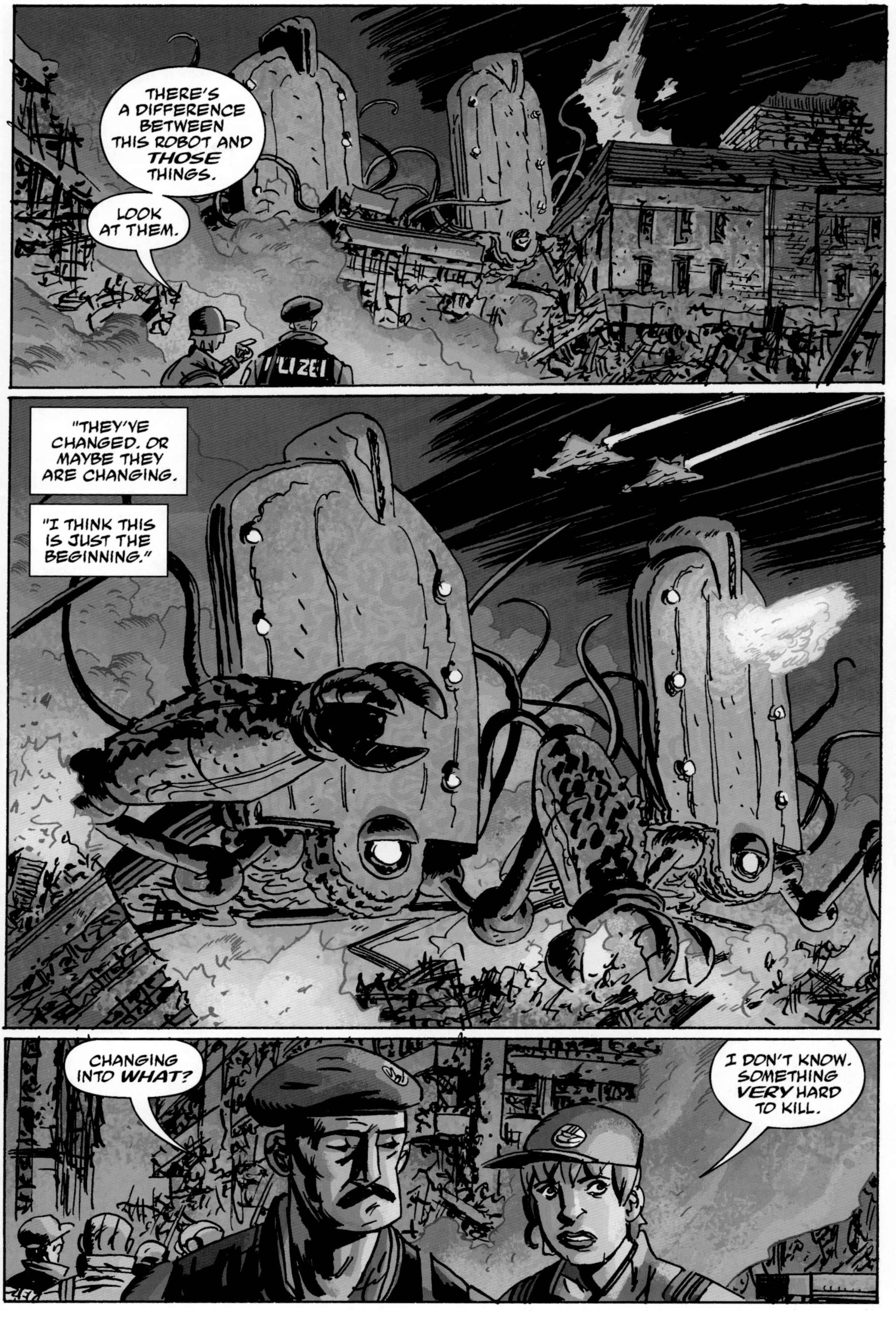
THERE'S A DIFFERENCE BETWEEN THIS ROBOT AND THOSE THINGS.
LOOK AT THEM.
LIZEI
"THEY'VE CHANGED. OR MAYBE THEY ARE CHANGING.
"I THINK THIS IS JUST THE BEGINNING."
CHANGING INTO WHAT?
I DON'T KNOW. SOMETHING VERY HARD TO KILL.

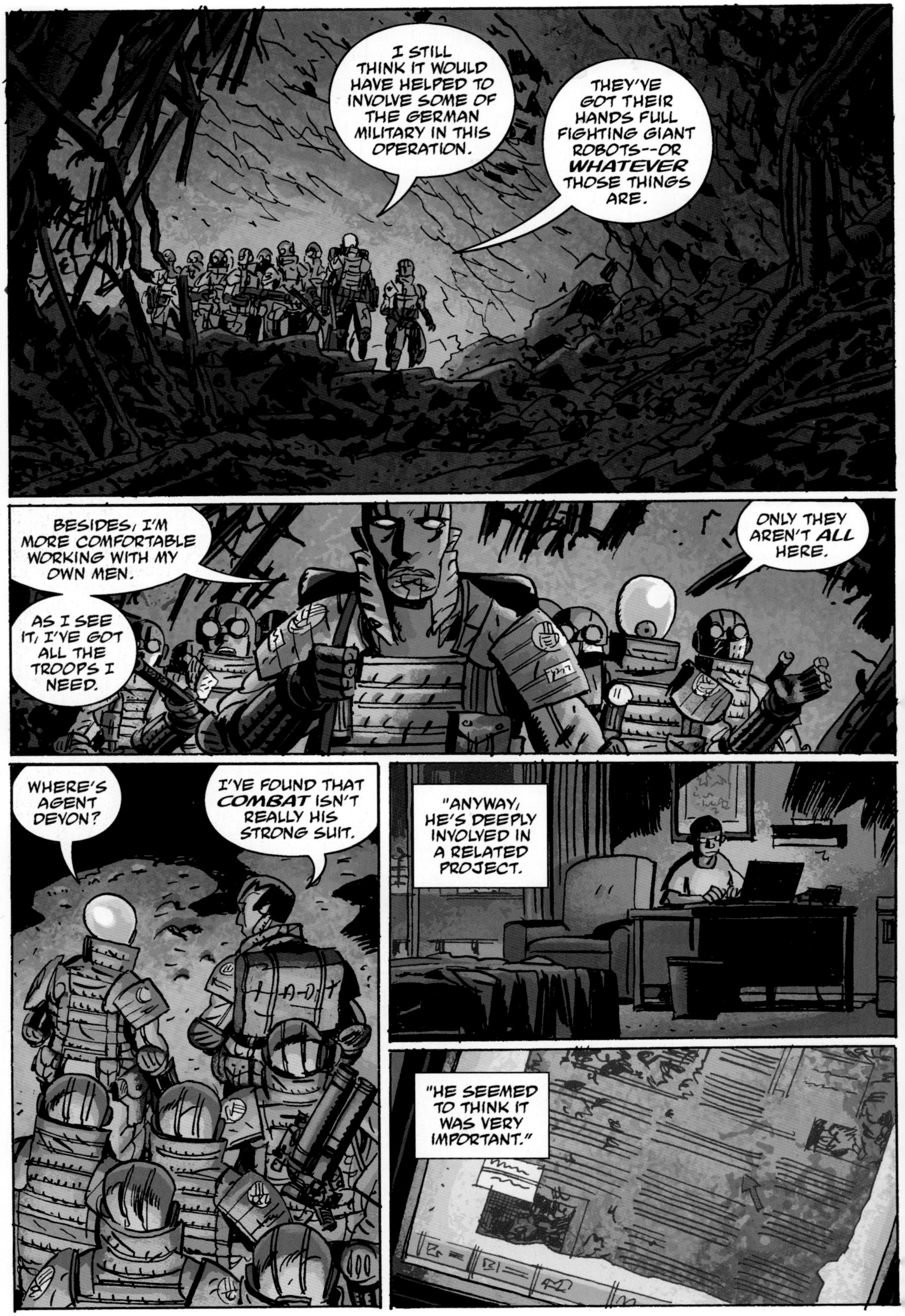
I STILL THINK IT WOULD HAVE HELPED TO INVOLVE SOME OF THE GERMAN MILITARY IN THIS OPERATION.
THEY'VE GOT THEIR HANDS FULL FIGHTING GIANT ROBOTS--OR WHATEVER THOSE THINGS ARE.
BESIDES, I'M MORE COMFORTABLE WORKING WITH MY OWN MEN.
AS I SEE IT, I'VE GOT ALL THE TROOPS I NEED.
ONLY THEY AREN'T ALL HERE.
WHERE'S AGENT DEVON?
I'VE FOUND THAT COMBAT ISN'T REALLY HIS STRONG SUIT.
"ANYWAY, HE'S DEEPLY INVOLVED IN A RELATED PROJECT.
"HE SEEMED TO THINK IT WAS VERY IMPORTANT."

AND **OUR** PROJECT. WHAT IS THAT? EXACTLY?

THE DUFFEL BAG, FOR INSTANCE.

C-4. PLASTIC EXPLOSIVES. ABOUT THREE HUNDRED POUNDS.

THAT SEEMS LIKE A LOT.

FOR OUR PURPOSES, I THINK WE'LL NEED A LOT.

YES, AGAIN, **WHAT** PURPOSE?

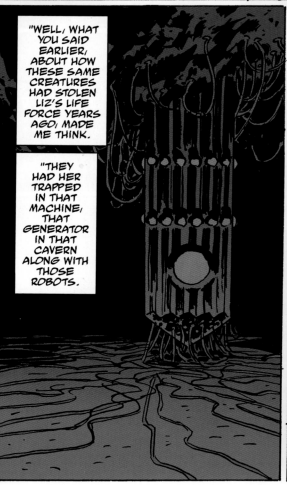

"WELL, WHAT YOU SAID EARLIER, ABOUT HOW THESE SAME CREATURES HAD STOLEN LIZ'S LIFE FORCE YEARS AGO, MADE ME THINK.

"THEY HAD HER TRAPPED IN THAT MACHINE, THAT GENERATOR IN THAT CAVERN ALONG WITH THOSE ROBOTS.

"THAT STRANGE CREATURE--THE LEADER, I THINK, OF THE OTHERS-- HE WANTED LIZ. WANTED TO SQUEEZE THE ENERGY FROM HER. REMEMBER?"

101

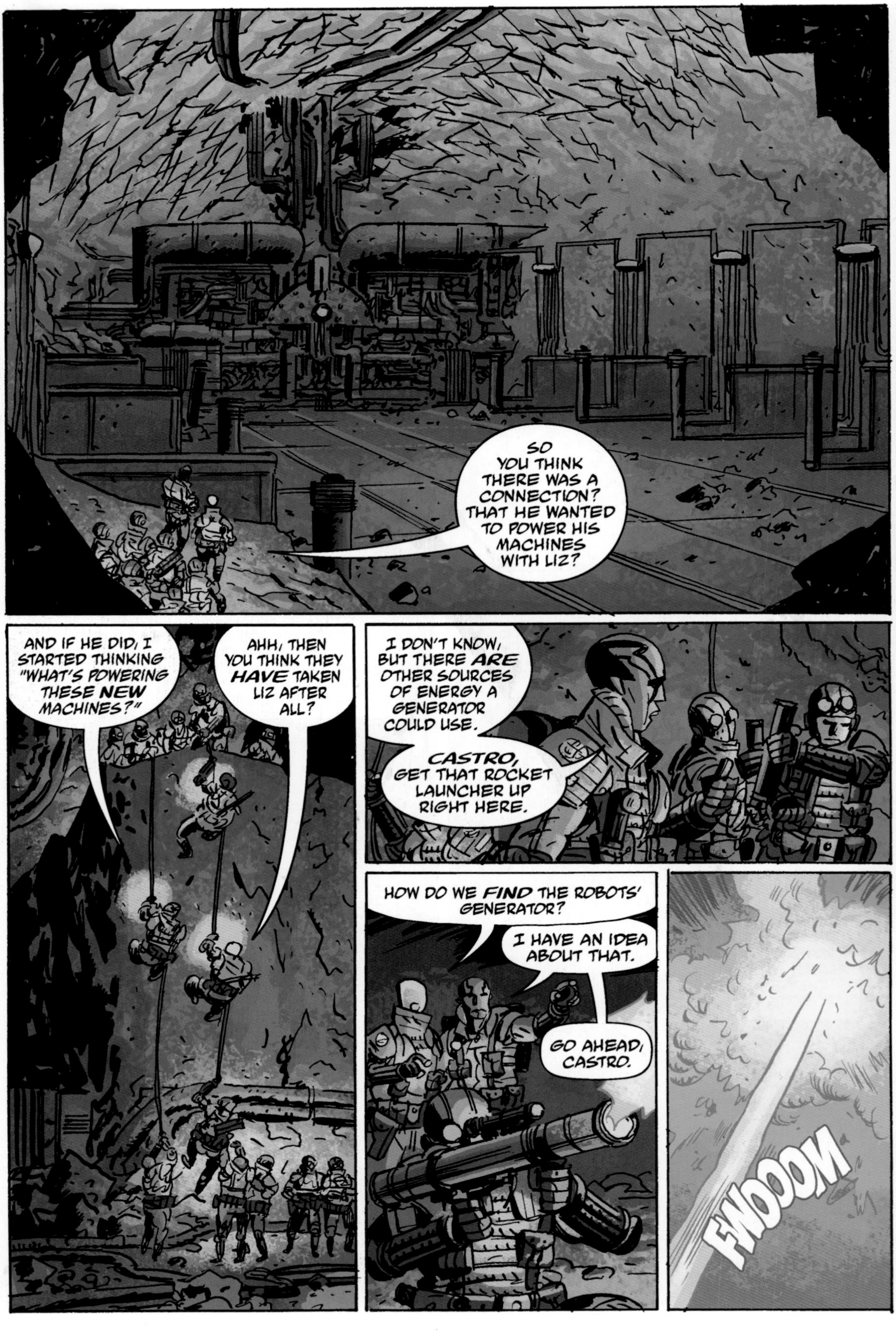
SO YOU THINK THERE WAS A CONNECTION? THAT HE WANTED TO POWER HIS MACHINES WITH LIZ?
AND IF HE DID, I STARTED THINKING "WHAT'S POWERING THESE NEW MACHINES?"
AHH, THEN YOU THINK THEY HAVE TAKEN LIZ AFTER ALL?
I DON'T KNOW, BUT THERE ARE OTHER SOURCES OF ENERGY A GENERATOR COULD USE.
CASTRO, GET THAT ROCKET LAUNCHER UP RIGHT HERE.
HOW DO WE FIND THE ROBOTS' GENERATOR?
I HAVE AN IDEA ABOUT THAT.
GO AHEAD, CASTRO.
FWOOOM

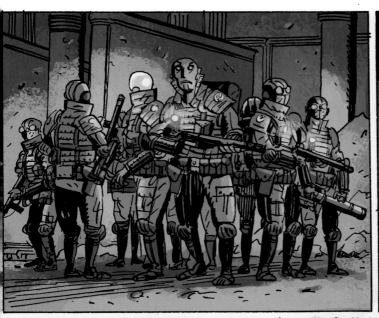

ALL RIGHT, EVERY-BODY.

LOCK AND LOAD.

BLAM BLAM BLAM

BLAM

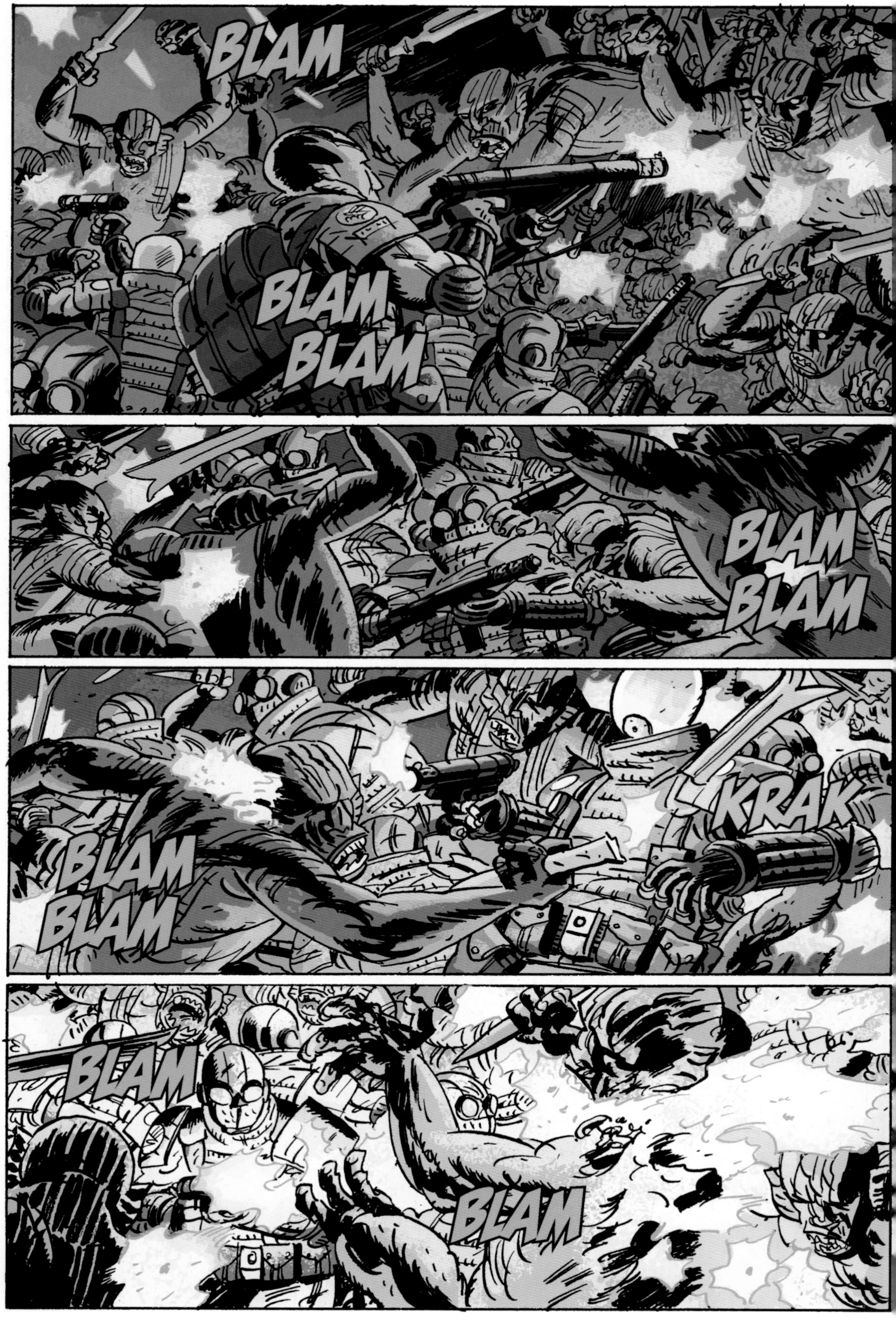
BLAM
BLAM
BLAM
BLAM
BLAM
KRAK
BLAM
BLAM
BLAM
BLAM

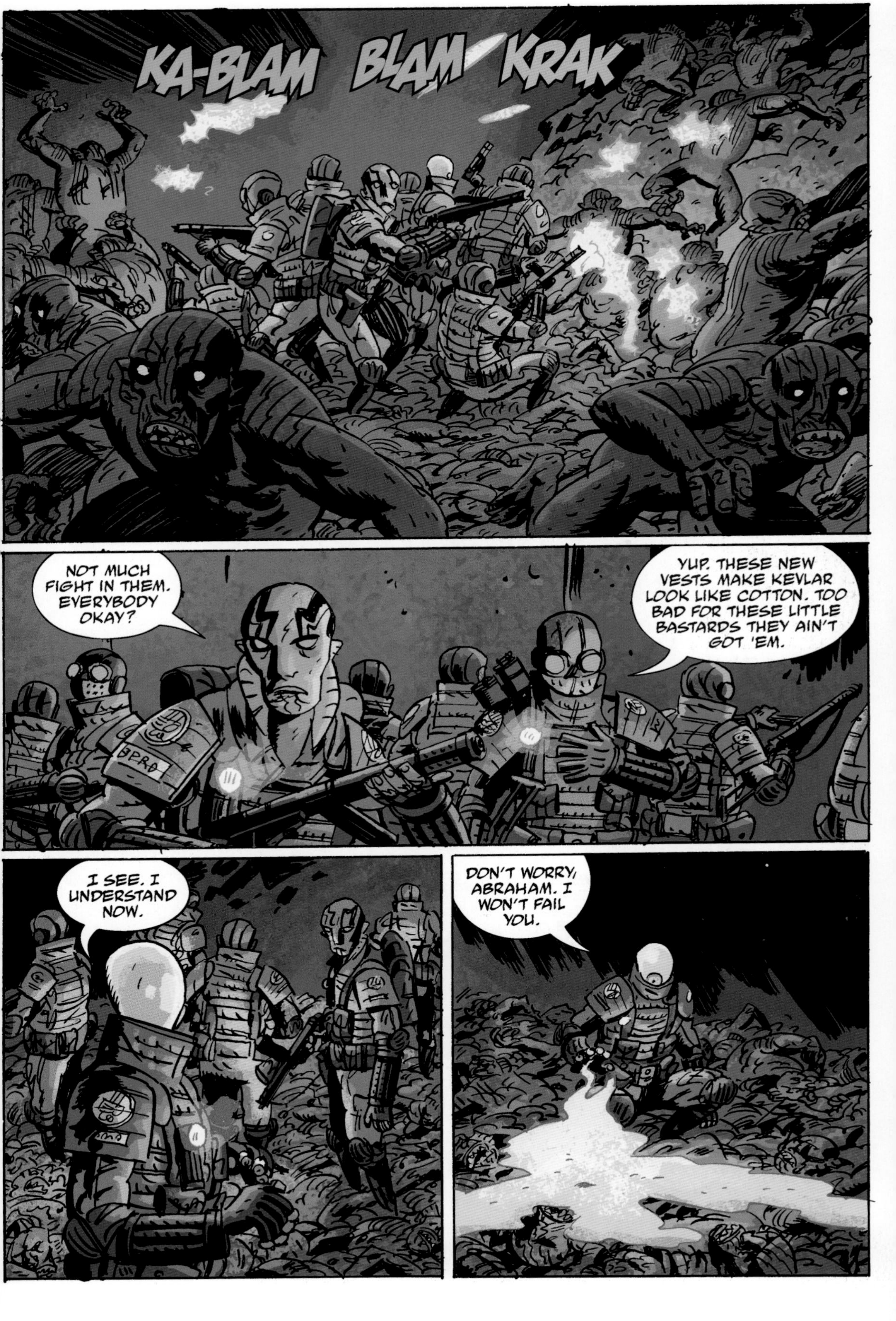
KA-BLAM BLAM KRAK
NOT MUCH FIGHT IN THEM. EVERYBODY OKAY?
YUP. THESE NEW VESTS MAKE KEVLAR LOOK LIKE COTTON. TOO BAD FOR THESE LITTLE BASTARDS THEY AIN'T GOT 'EM.
I SEE. I UNDERSTAND NOW.
DON'T WORRY, ABRAHAM. I WON'T FAIL YOU.

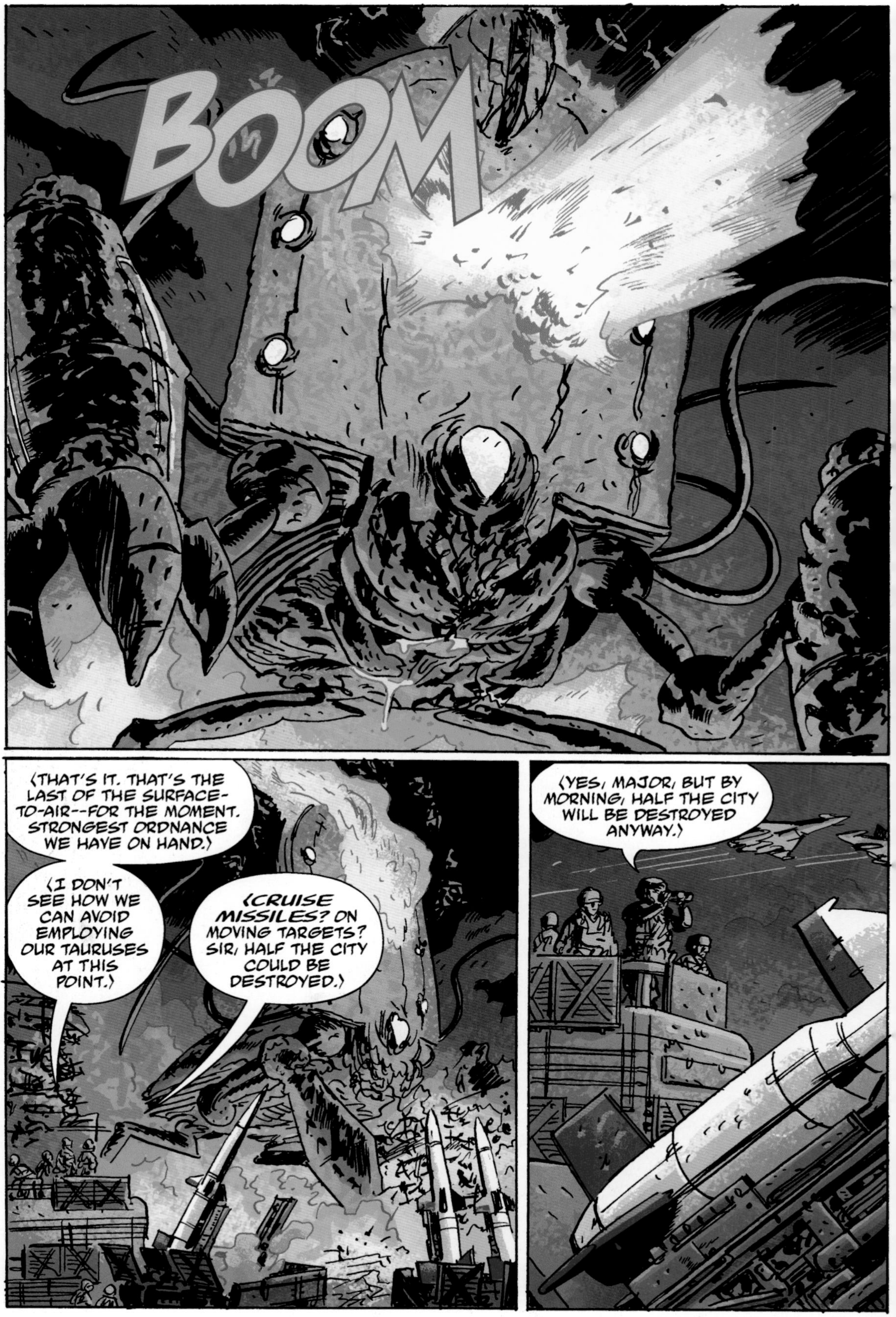
BOOM
⟨THAT'S IT. THAT'S THE LAST OF THE SURFACE-TO-AIR--FOR THE MOMENT. STRONGEST ORDNANCE WE HAVE ON HAND.⟩
⟨I DON'T SEE HOW WE CAN AVOID EMPLOYING OUR TAURUSES AT THIS POINT.⟩
⟨*CRUISE MISSILES?* ON MOVING TARGETS? SIR, HALF THE CITY COULD BE DESTROYED.⟩
⟨YES, MAJOR, BUT BY MORNING, HALF THE CITY WILL BE DESTROYED ANYWAY.⟩

⟨TRANSLATED FROM GERMAN⟩

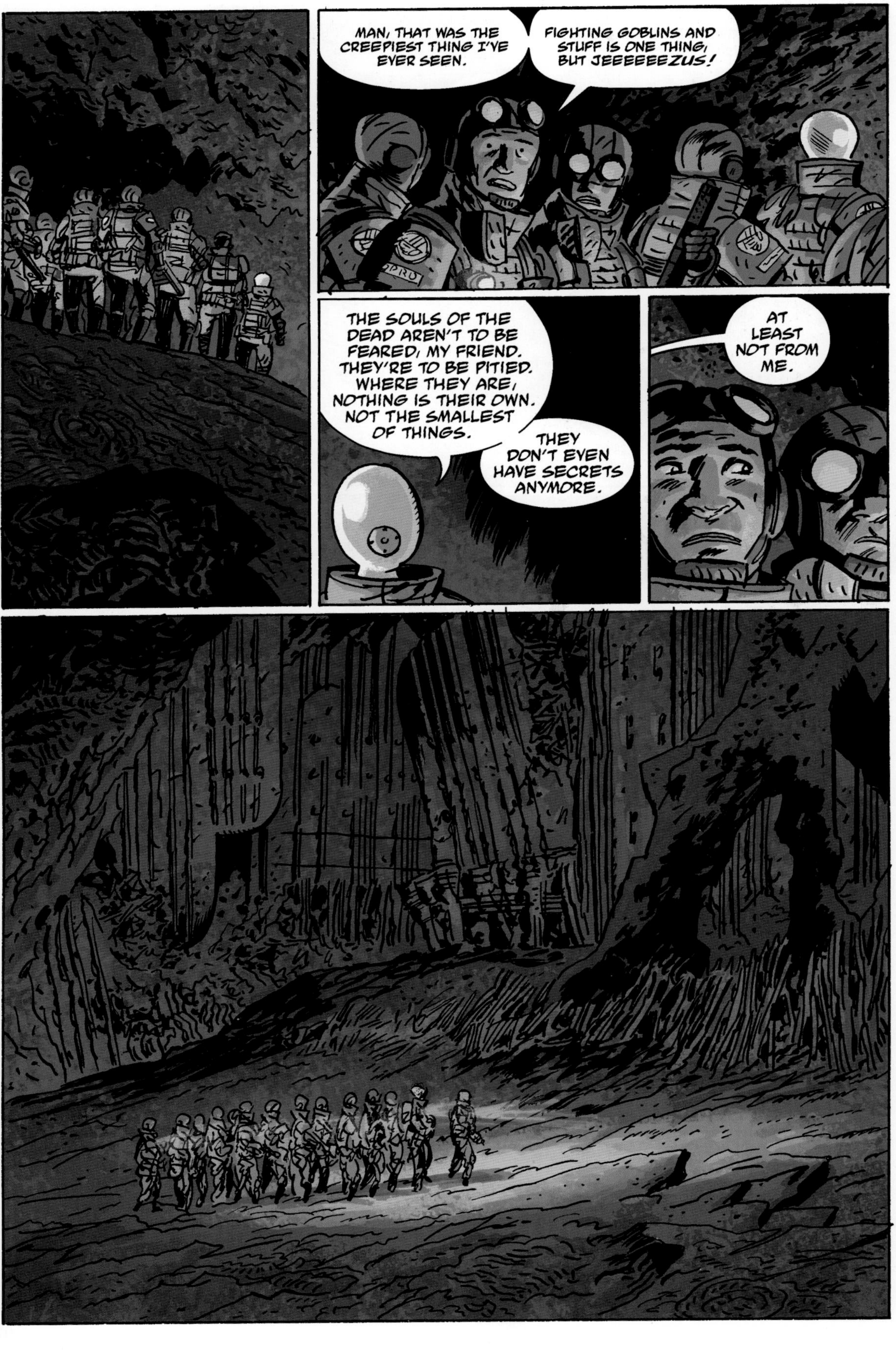
MAN, THAT WAS THE CREEPIEST THING I'VE EVER SEEN.
FIGHTING GOBLINS AND STUFF IS ONE THING, BUT JEEEEEEZUS!
THE SOULS OF THE DEAD AREN'T TO BE FEARED, MY FRIEND. THEY'RE TO BE PITIED. WHERE THEY ARE, NOTHING IS THEIR OWN. NOT THE SMALLEST OF THINGS.
THEY DON'T EVEN HAVE SECRETS ANYMORE.
AT LEAST NOT FROM ME.

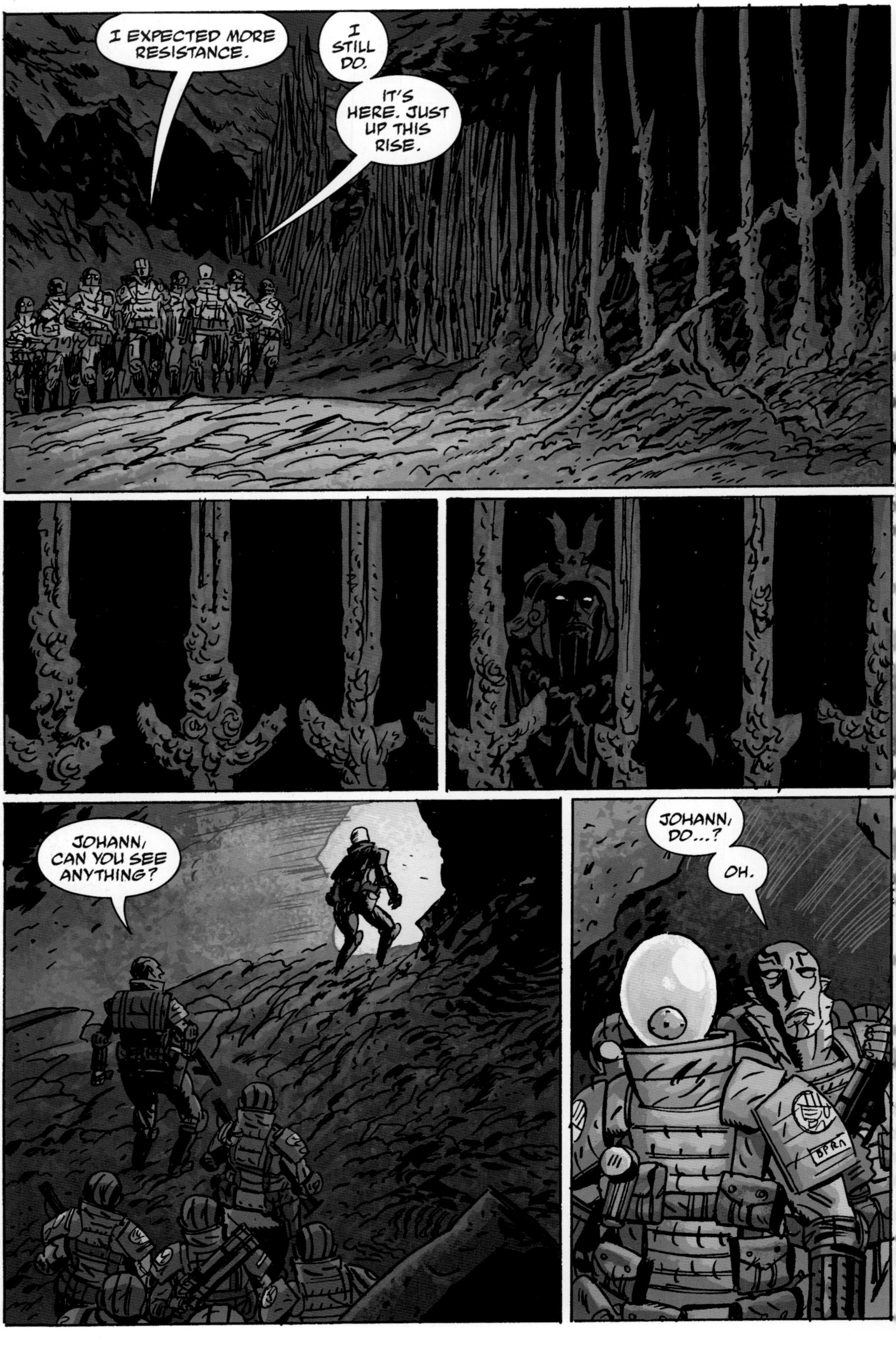
I EXPECTED MORE RESISTANCE.
I STILL DO.
IT'S HERE. JUST UP THIS RISE.
JOHANN, CAN YOU SEE ANYTHING?
JOHANN, DO...?
OH.
BPRD

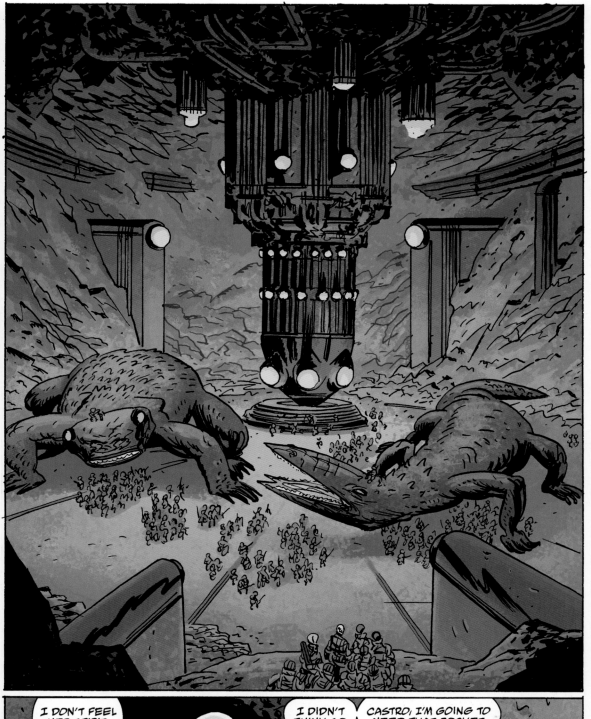

I DON'T FEEL HER SPIRIT. LIZ IS NOT HERE.

I DIDN'T THINK SO.

CASTRO, I'M GOING TO NEED THAT ROCKET LAUNCHER.

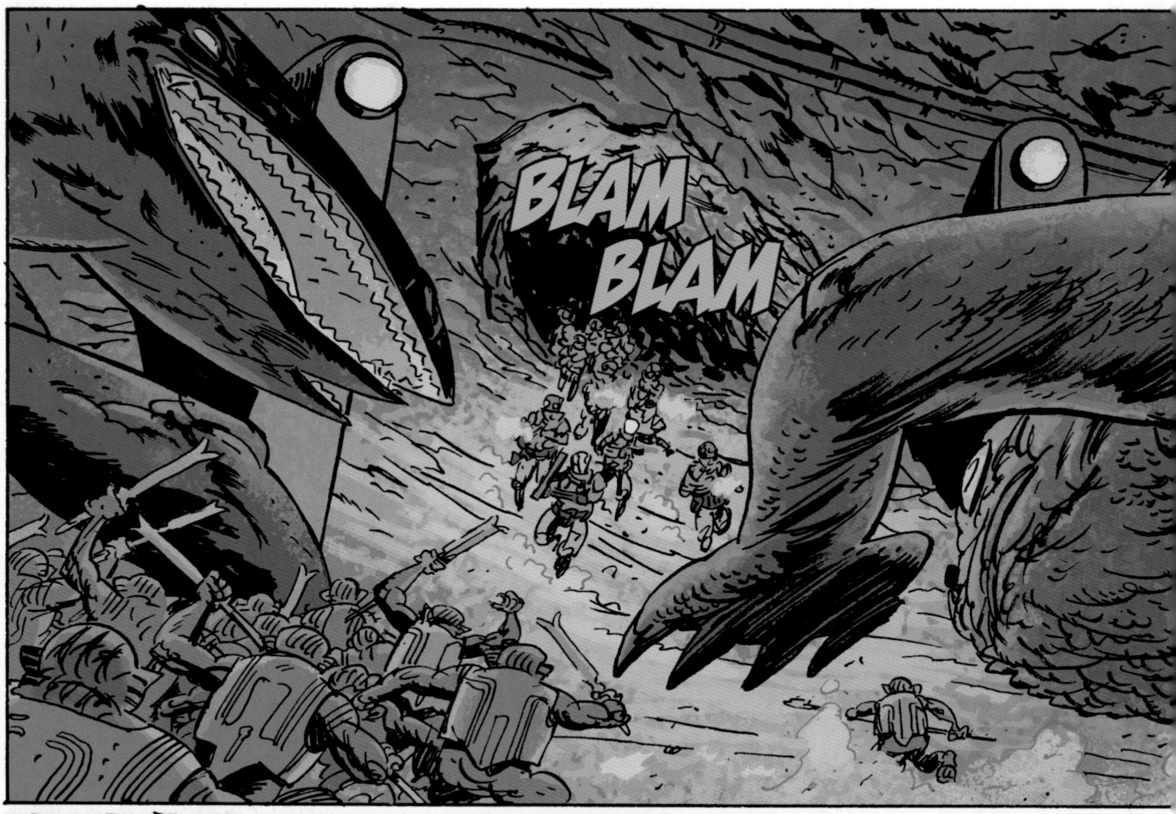
BLAM
BLAM
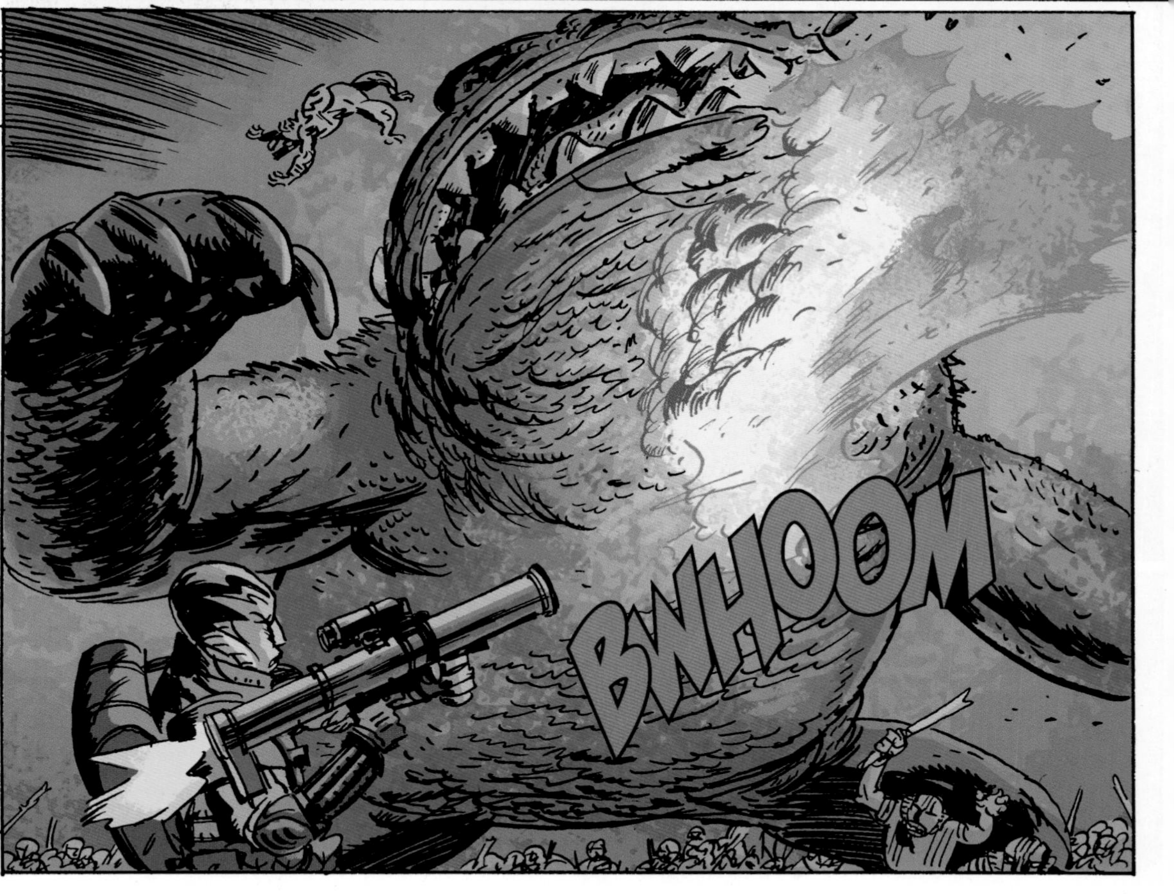
BWHOOM

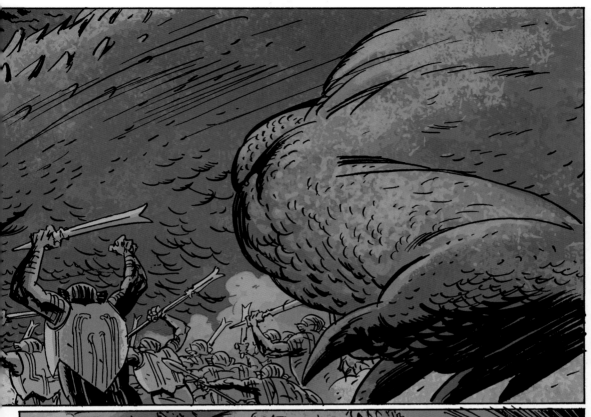

JOHANN!

YES. OF COURSE. I SHOULD HAVE THOUGHT OF IT MYSELF.

BLAM BLAM

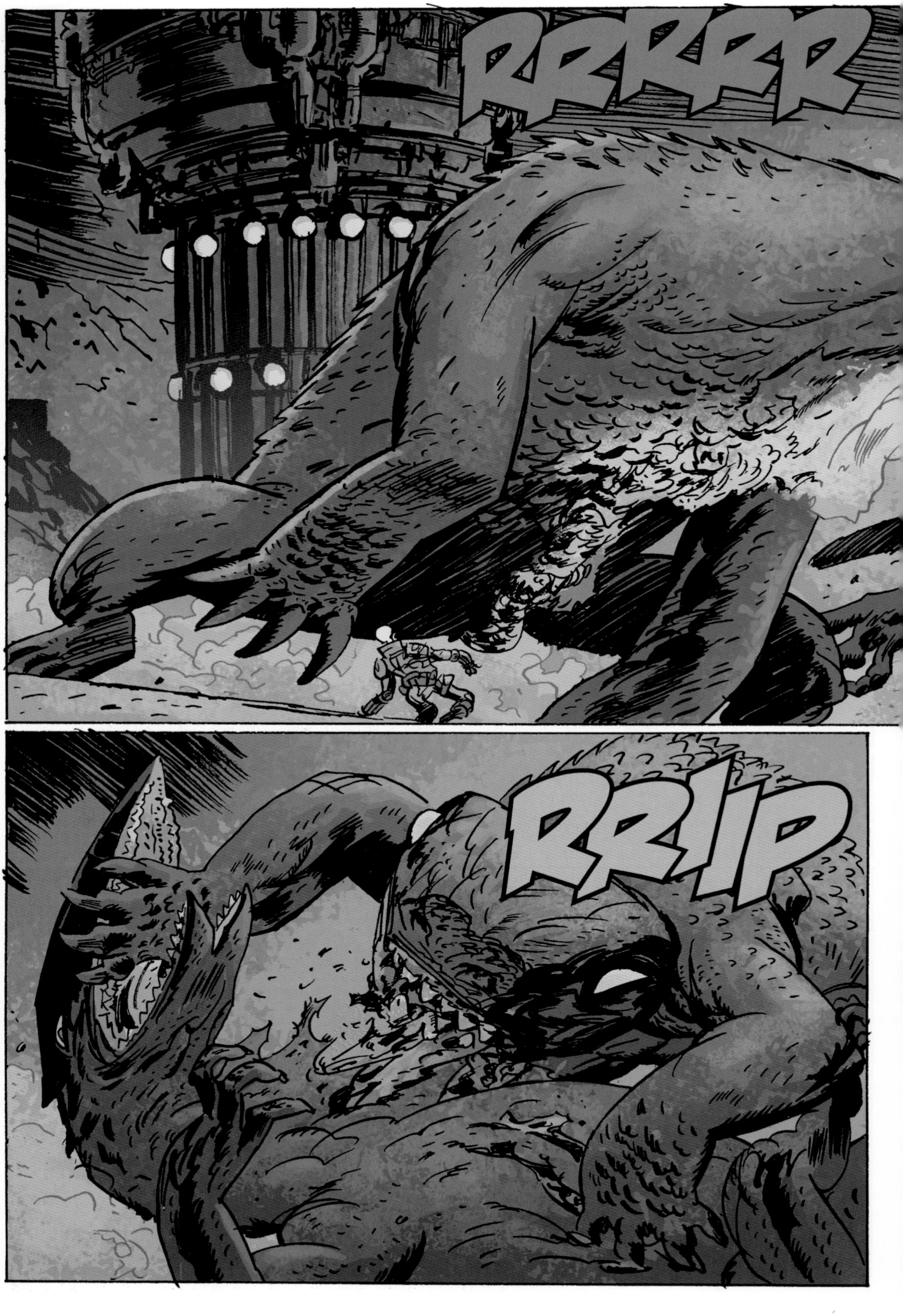
RRRRR
RRIP

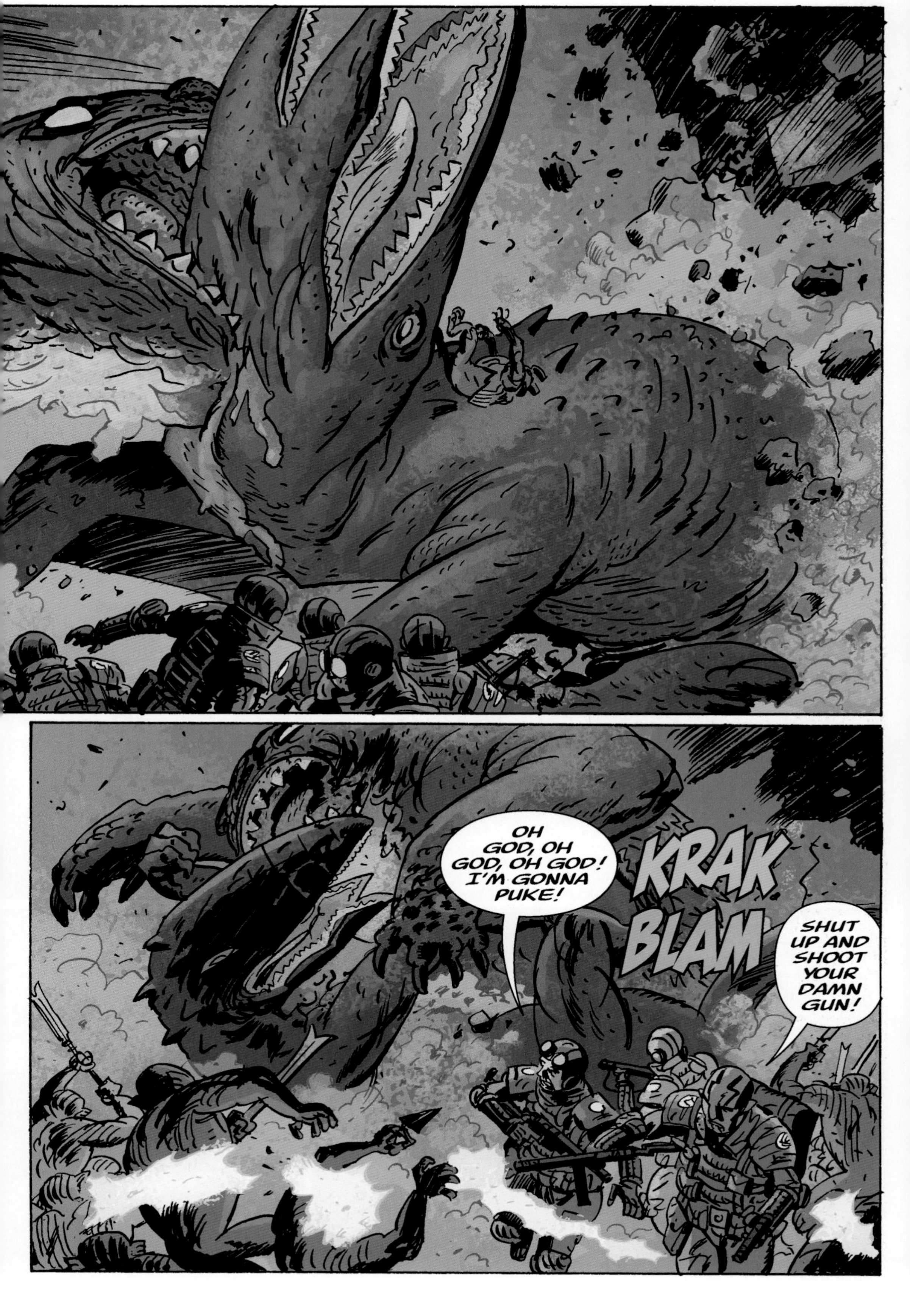
OH GOD, OH GOD, OH GOD! I'M GONNA PUKE!
KRAK
BLAM
SHUT UP AND SHOOT YOUR DAMN GUN!

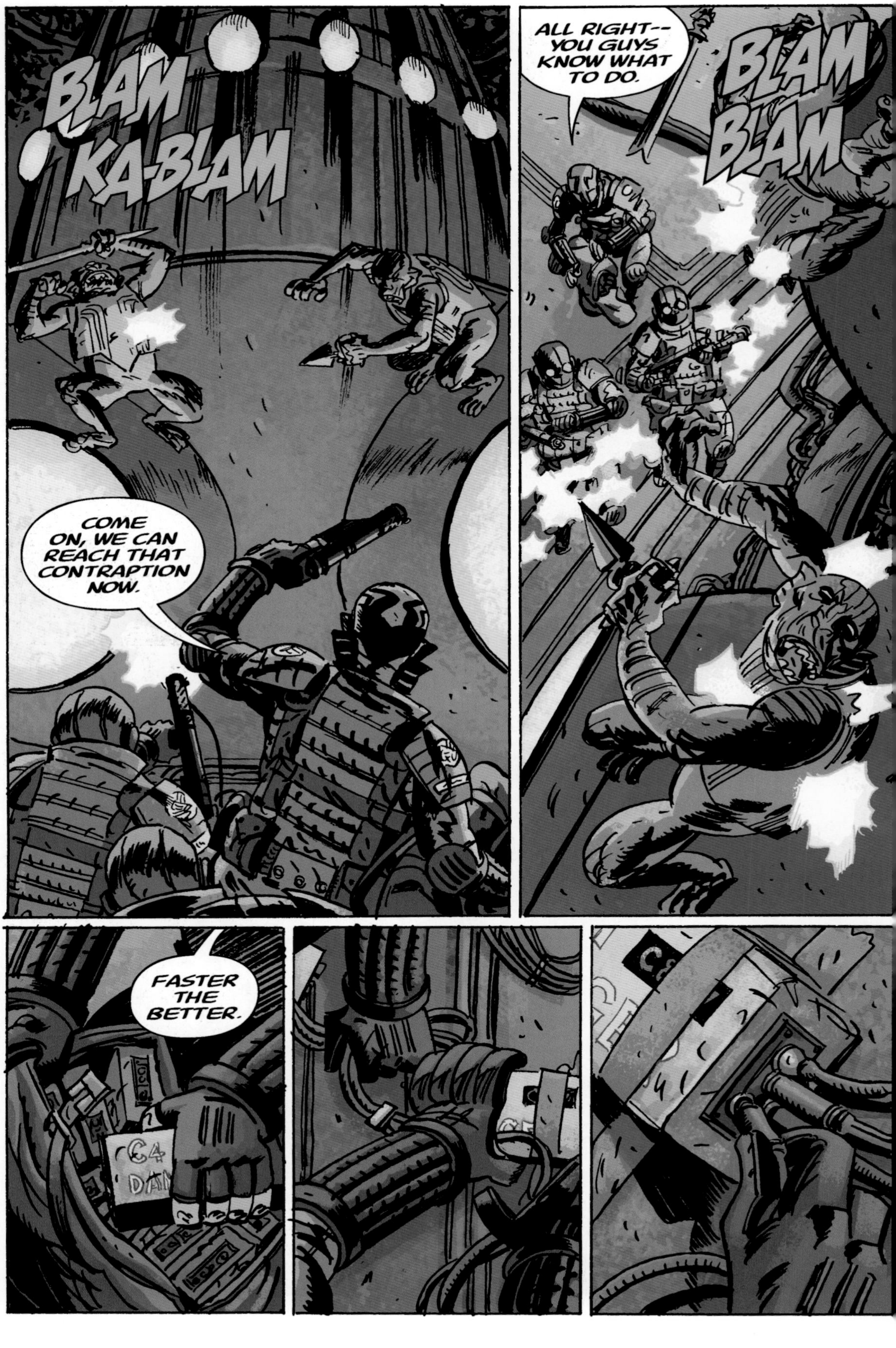
BLAM
KA-BLAM
COME ON, WE CAN REACH THAT CONTRAPTION NOW.
ALL RIGHT-- YOU GUYS KNOW WHAT TO DO.
BLAM BLAM
FASTER THE BETTER.
C4

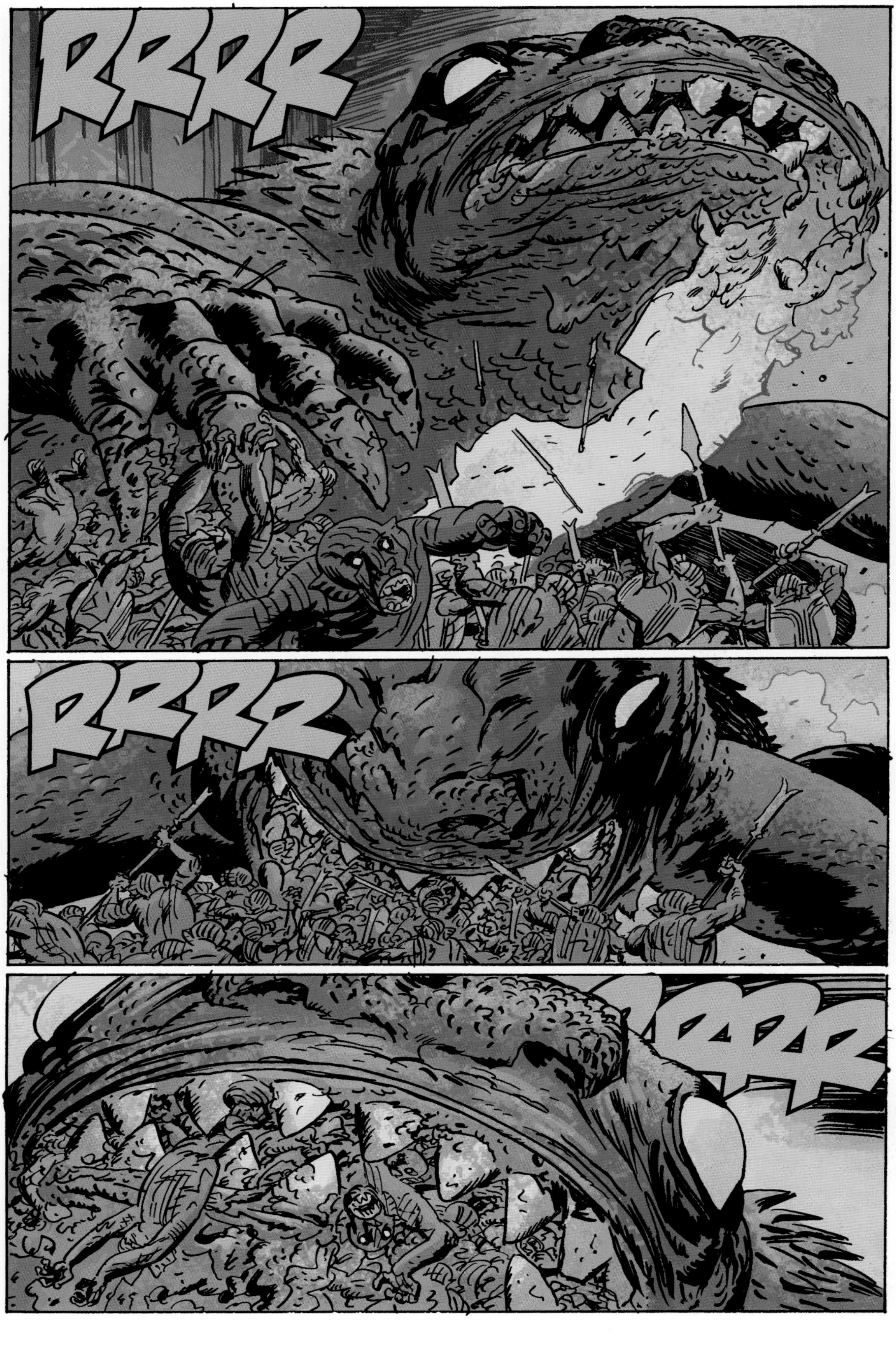
RRRR
RRRR
RRR

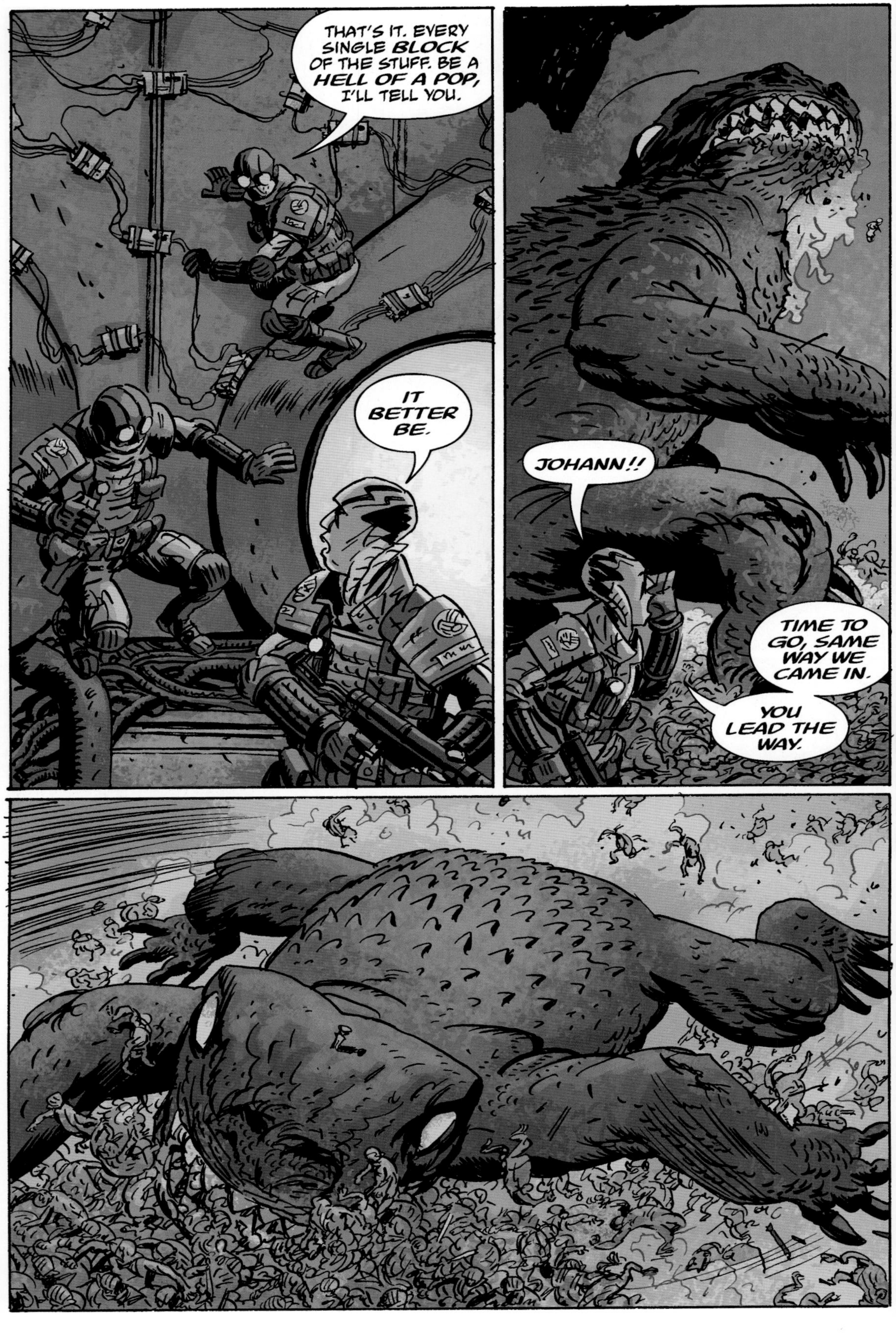
THAT'S IT. EVERY SINGLE BLOCK OF THE STUFF. BE A HELL OF A POP, I'LL TELL YOU.
IT BETTER BE.
JOHANN!!
TIME TO GO, SAME WAY WE CAME IN.
YOU LEAD THE WAY.

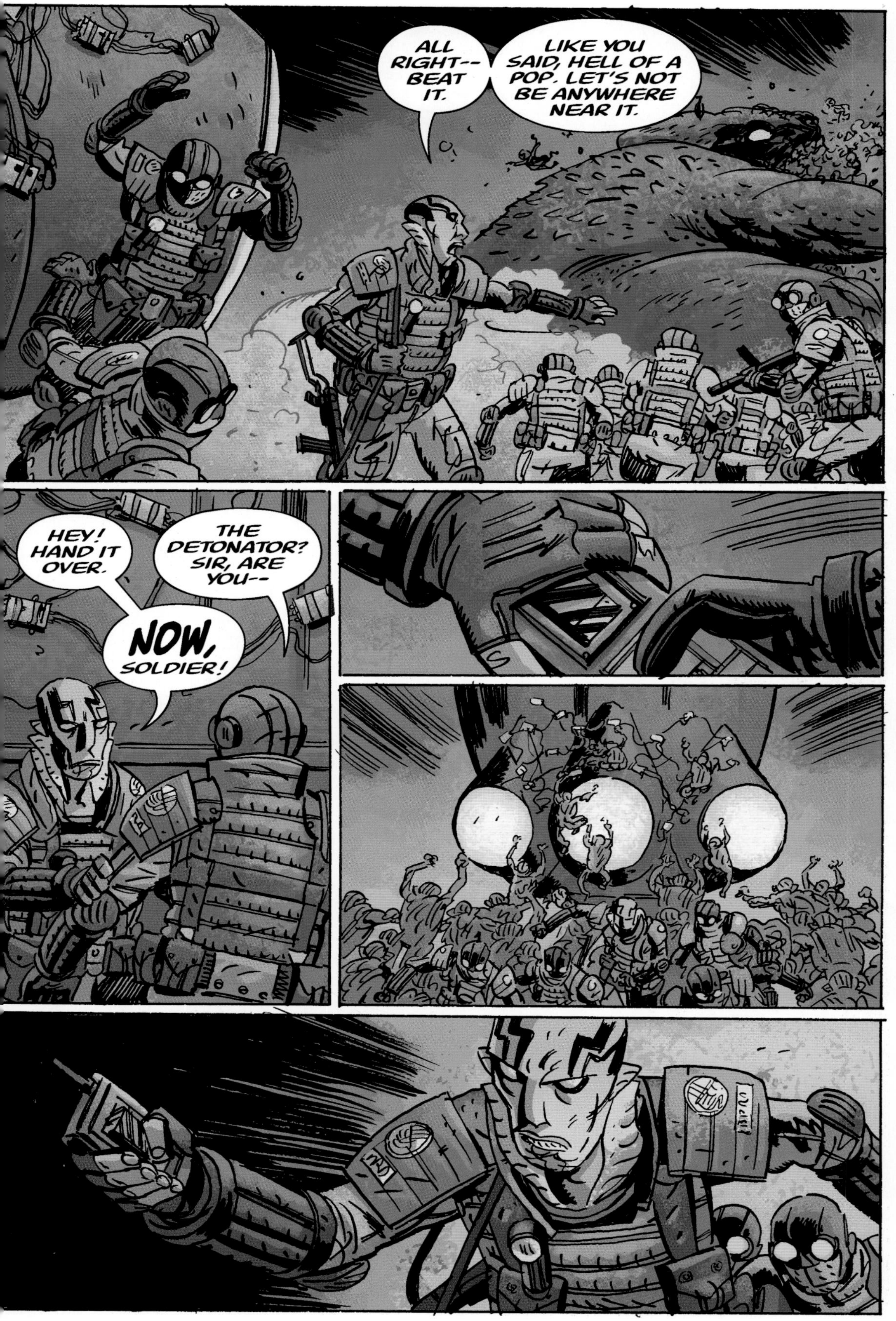
ALL RIGHT--BEAT IT.
LIKE YOU SAID, HELL OF A POP. LET'S NOT BE ANYWHERE NEAR IT.
HEY! HAND IT OVER.
THE DETONATOR? SIR, ARE YOU--
NOW, SOLDIER!

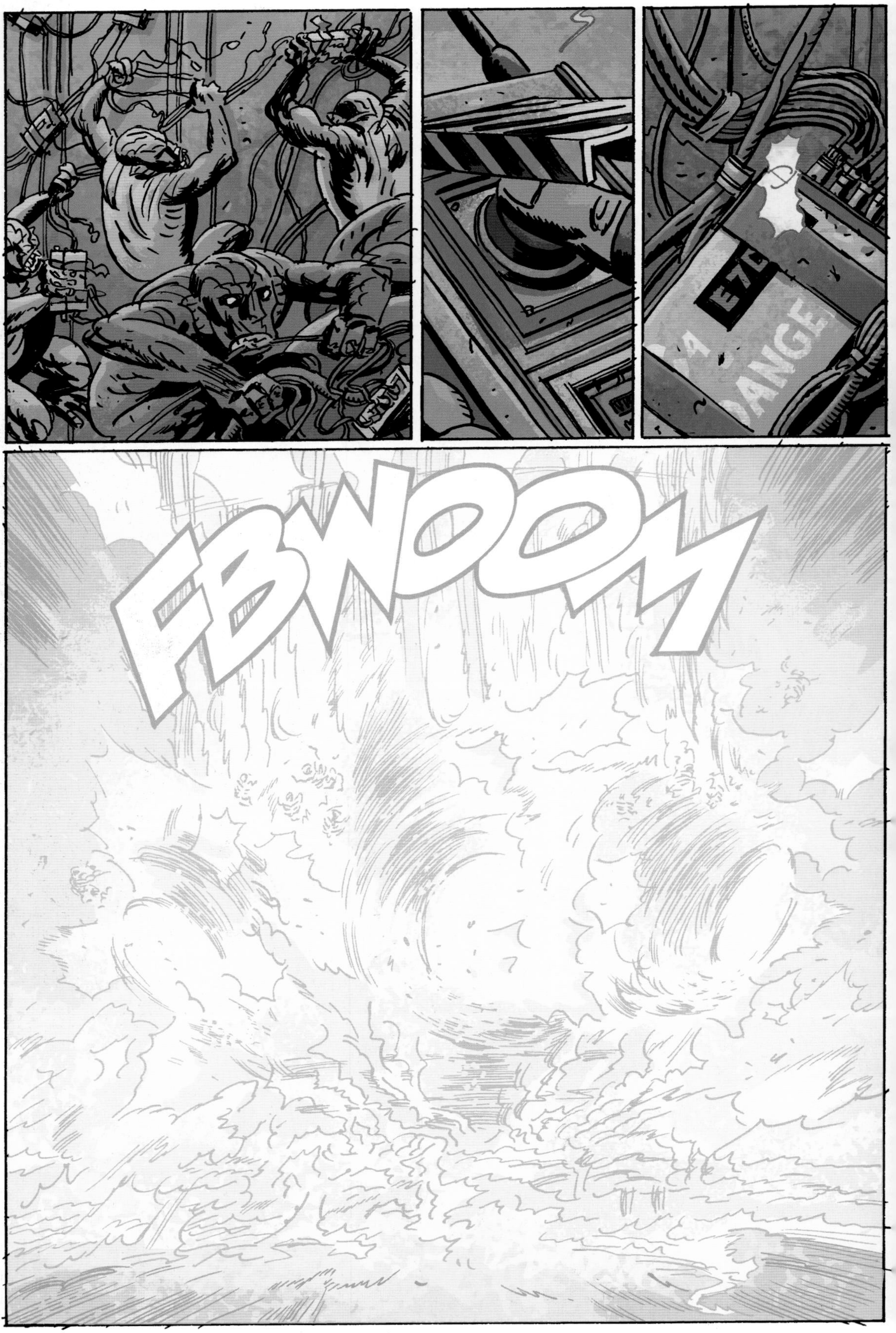
DANGE
FBWOOM

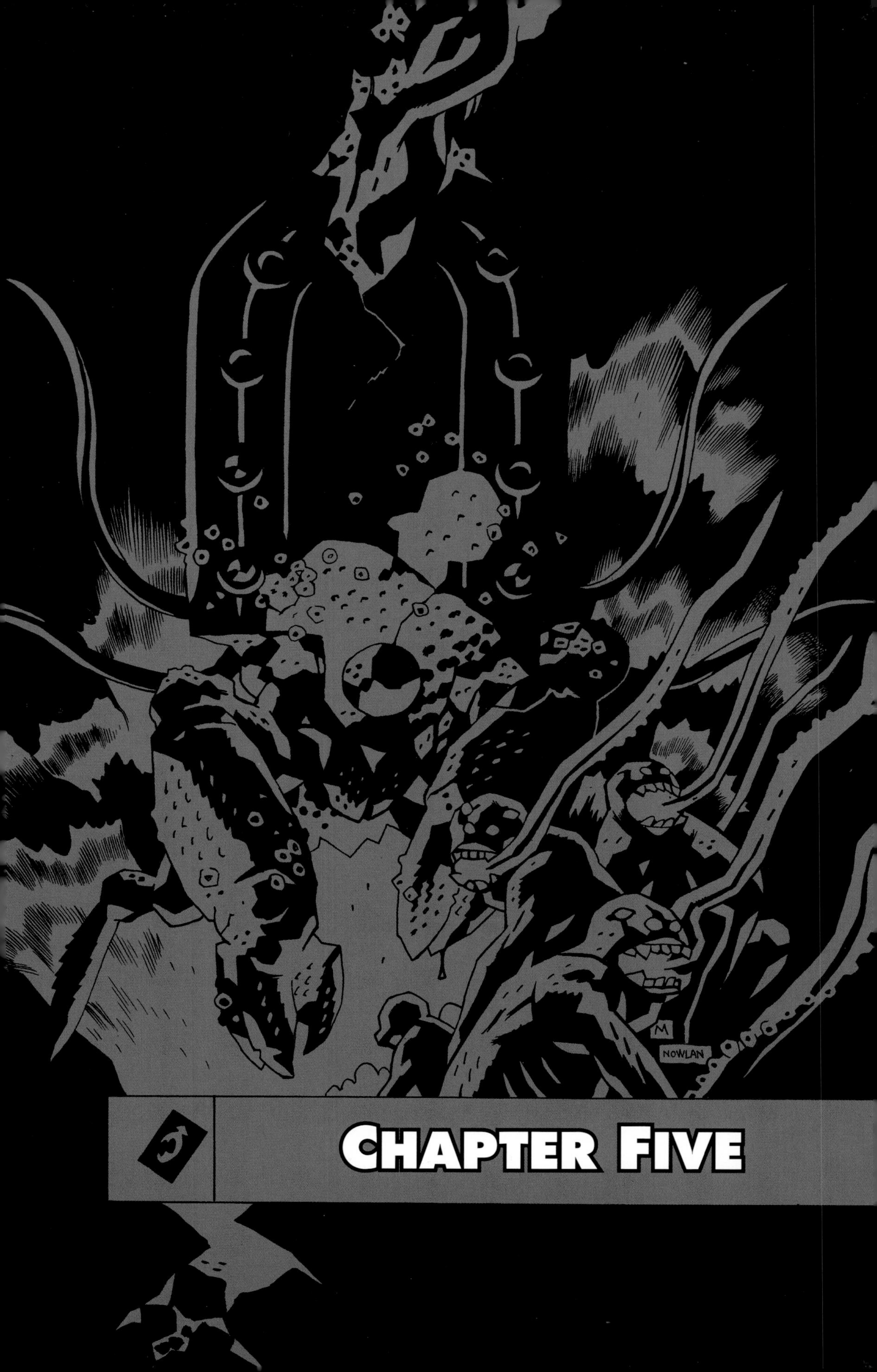
M
NOWLAN

CHAPTER FIVE

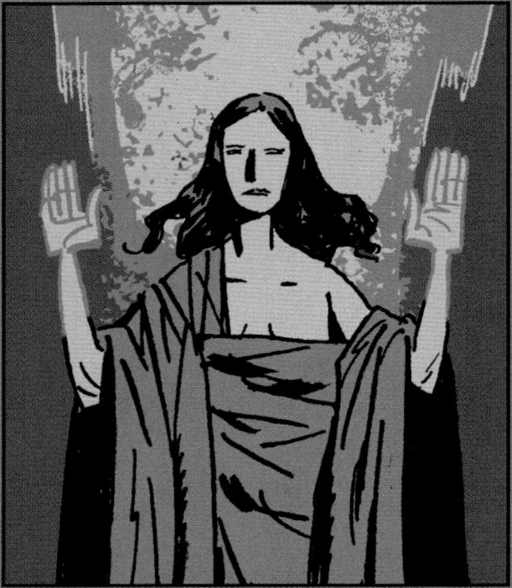

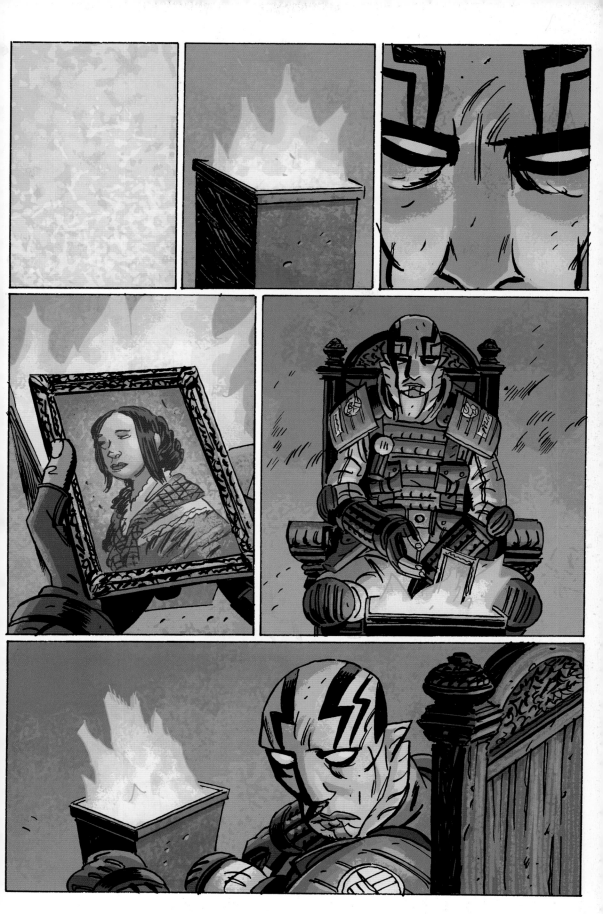

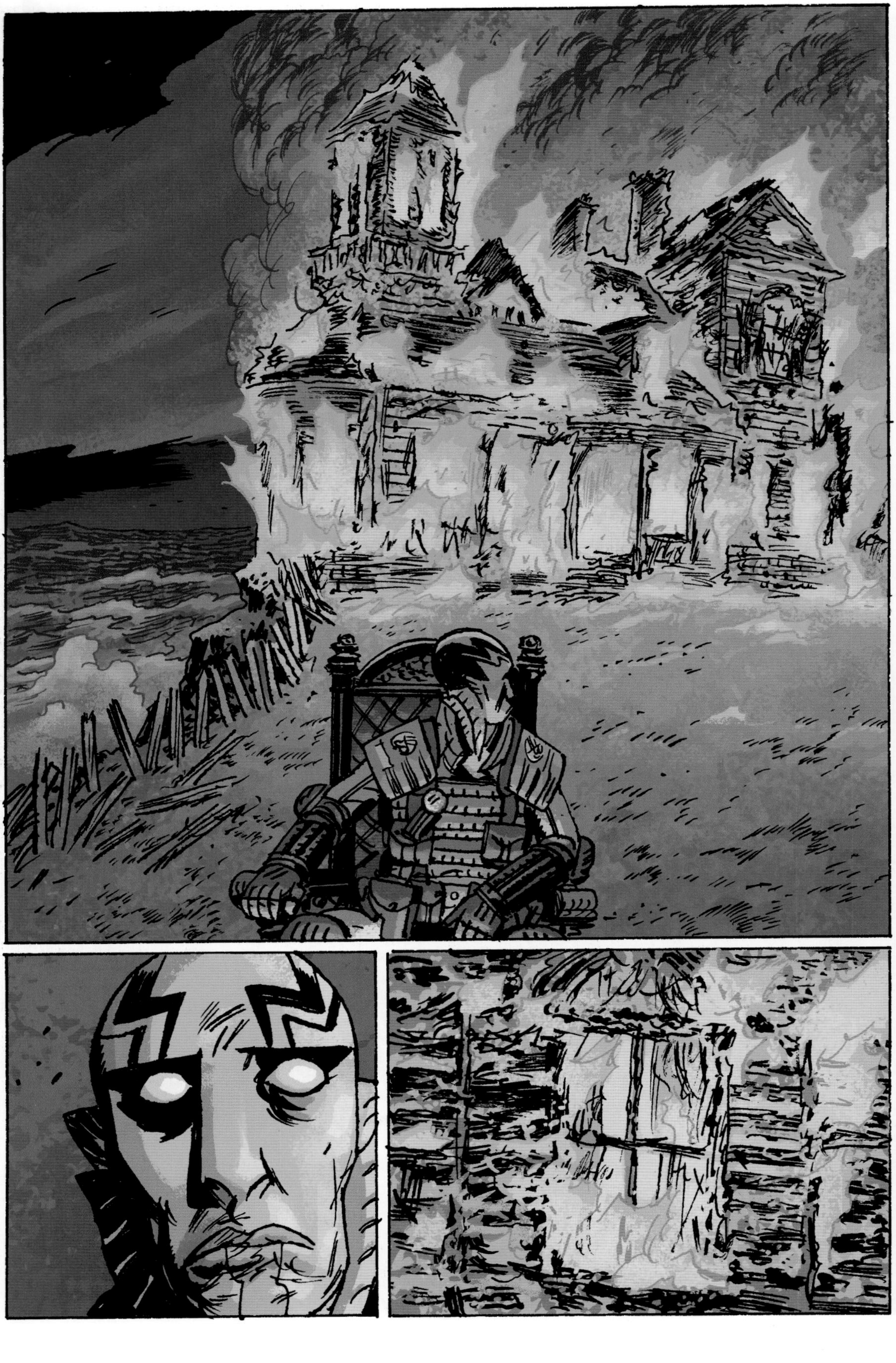

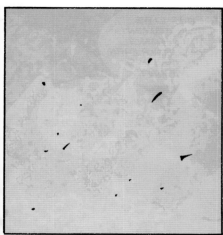
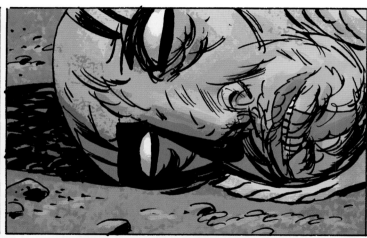

YOUR WORLD IS *SAFE* NOW? YOU END MY *MACHINE* AND *WHAT IS TO BE*--YOU TURN ASIDE?

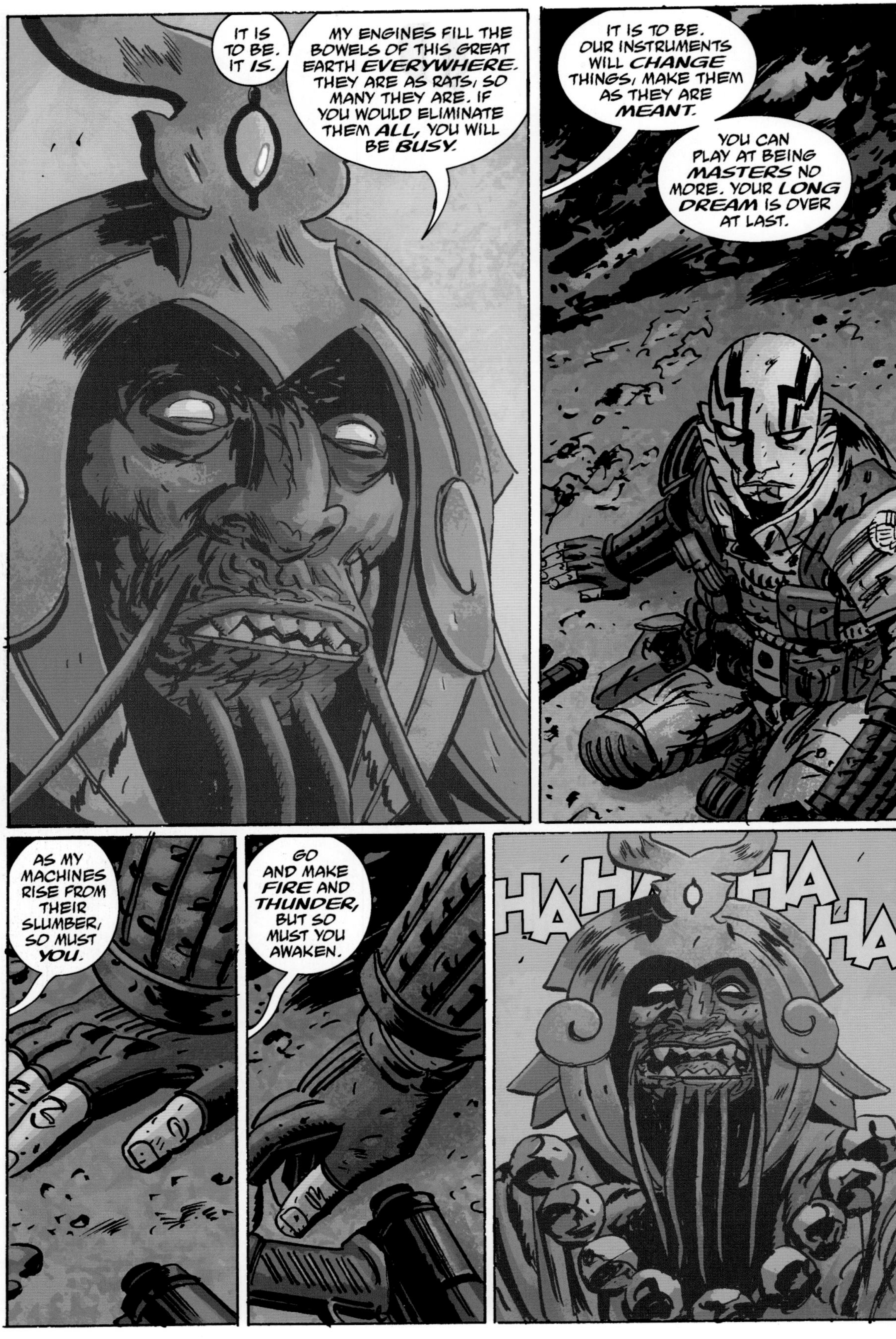
IT IS TO BE. IT *IS*.
MY ENGINES FILL THE BOWELS OF THIS GREAT EARTH *EVERYWHERE*. THEY ARE AS RATS, SO MANY THEY ARE. IF YOU WOULD ELIMINATE THEM *ALL*, YOU WILL BE *BUSY*.
IT IS TO BE. OUR INSTRUMENTS WILL *CHANGE* THINGS, MAKE THEM AS THEY ARE *MEANT*.
YOU CAN PLAY AT BEING *MASTERS* NO MORE. YOUR *LONG DREAM* IS OVER AT LAST.
AS MY MACHINES RISE FROM THEIR SLUMBER, SO MUST *YOU*.
GO AND MAKE *FIRE* AND *THUNDER*, BUT SO MUST YOU AWAKEN.
HA HA HA HA HA HA

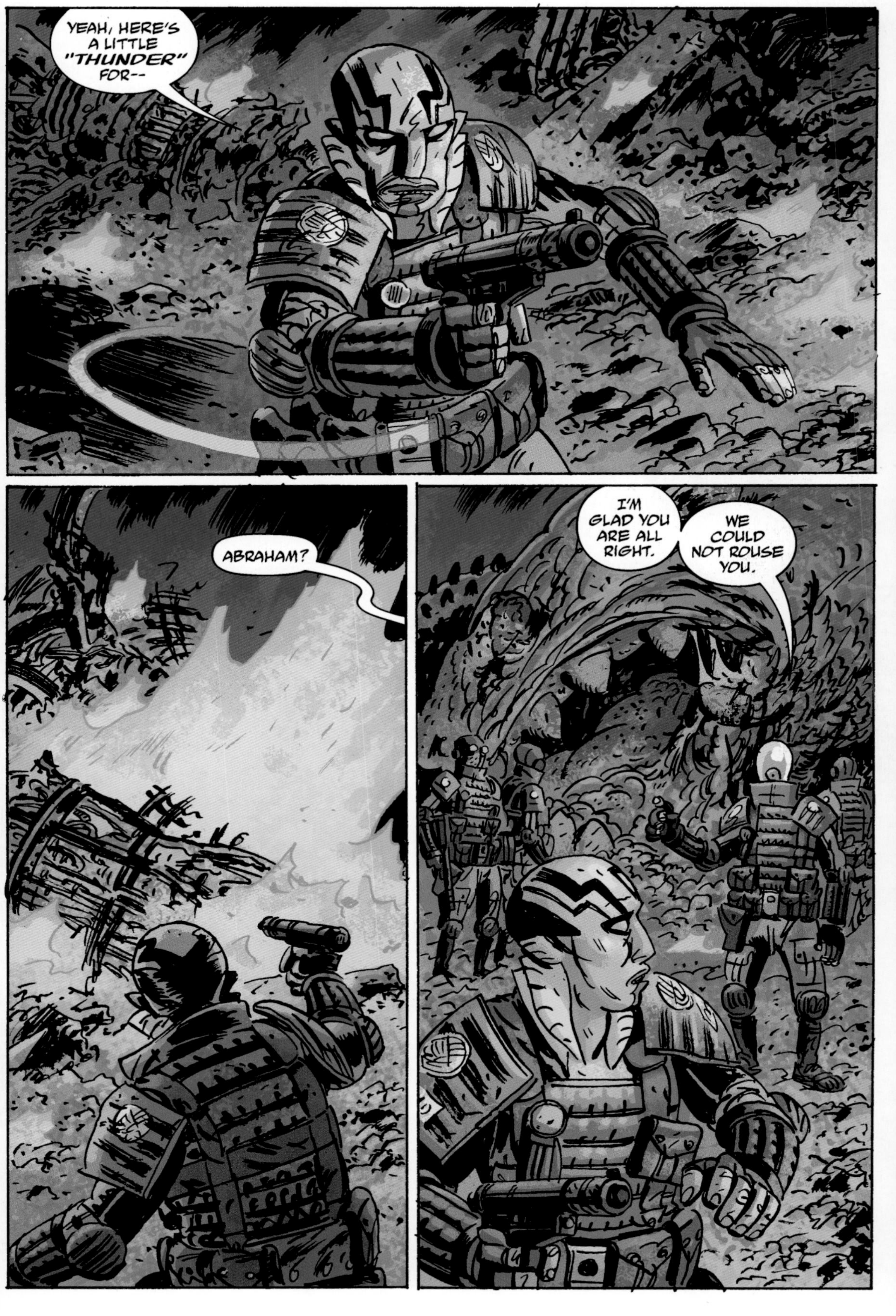
YEAH, HERE'S A LITTLE "THUNDER" FOR--
ABRAHAM?
I'M GLAD YOU ARE ALL RIGHT.
WE COULD NOT ROUSE YOU.

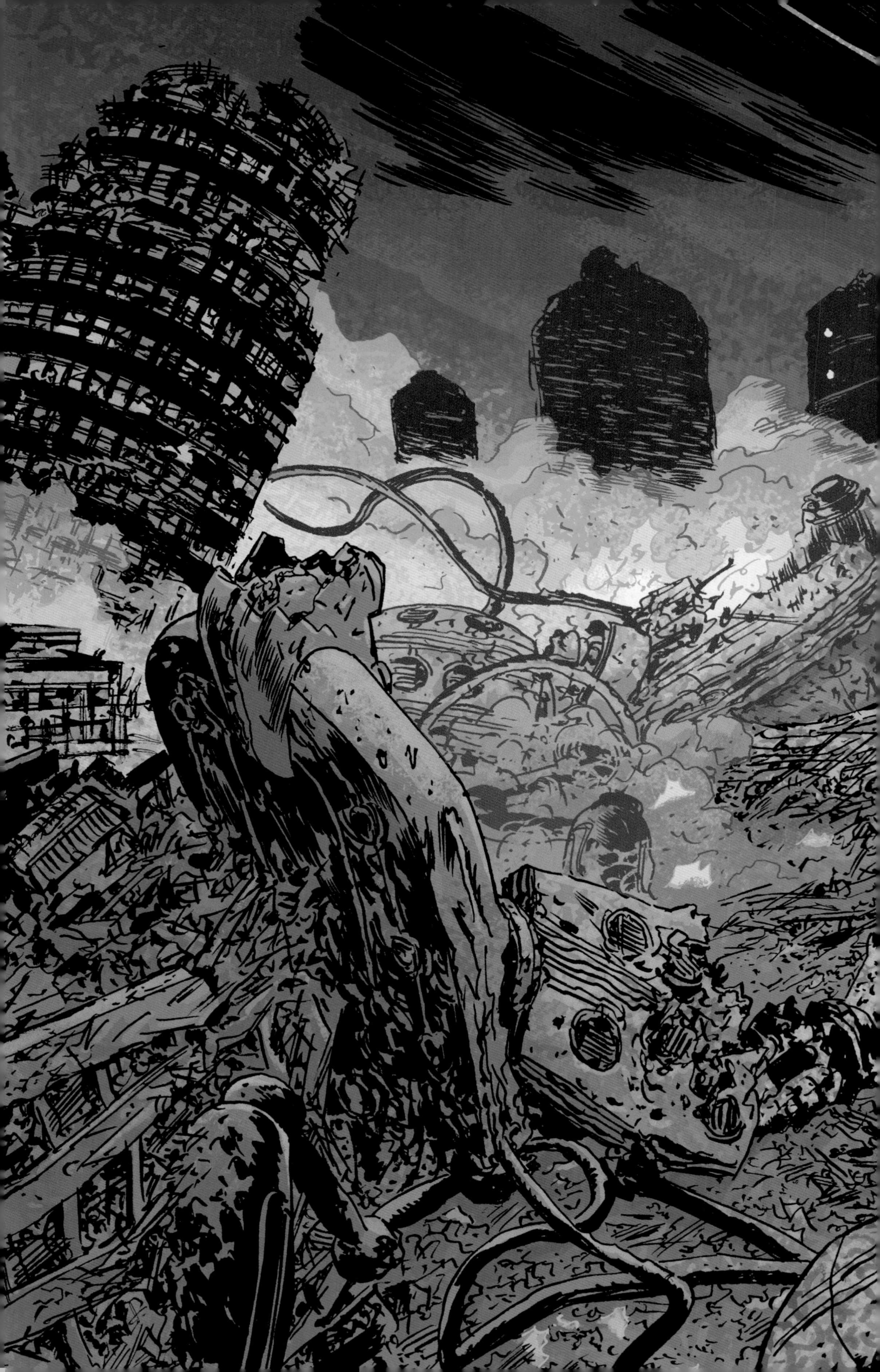

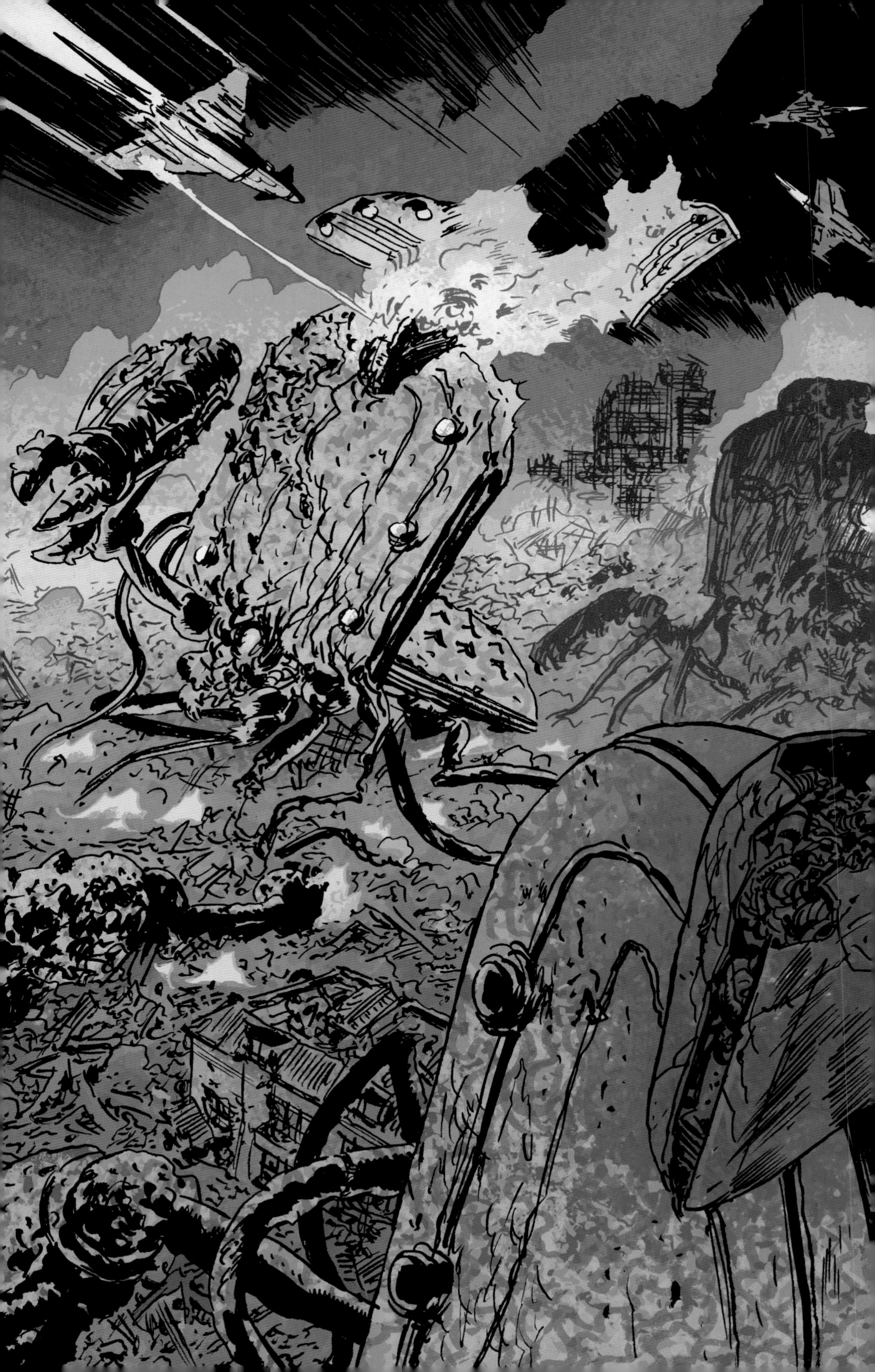

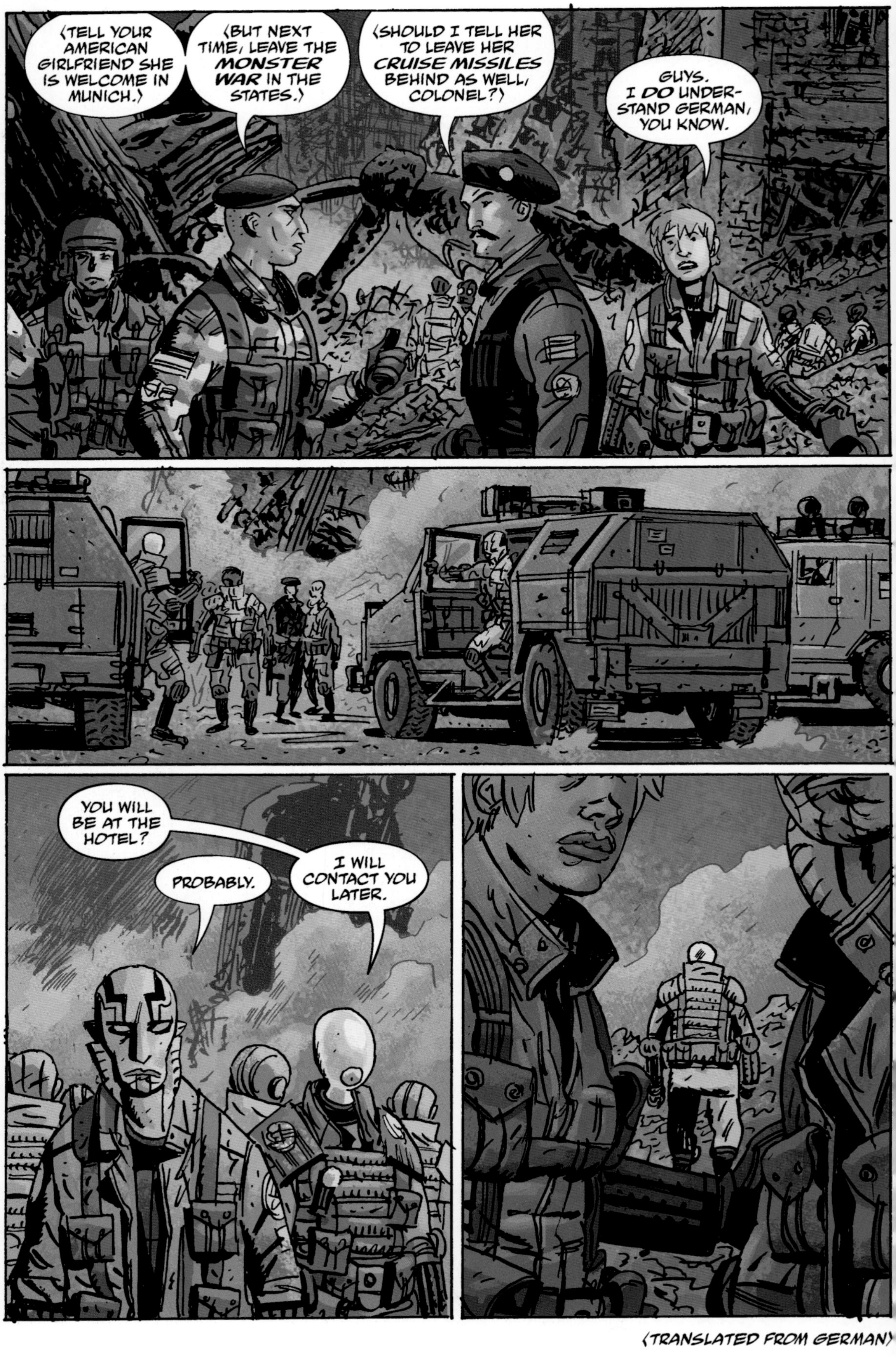
⟨TELL YOUR AMERICAN GIRLFRIEND SHE IS WELCOME IN MUNICH.⟩
⟨BUT NEXT TIME, LEAVE THE MONSTER WAR IN THE STATES.⟩
⟨SHOULD I TELL HER TO LEAVE HER CRUISE MISSILES BEHIND AS WELL, COLONEL?⟩
GUYS. I DO UNDERSTAND GERMAN, YOU KNOW.
YOU WILL BE AT THE HOTEL?
PROBABLY.
I WILL CONTACT YOU LATER.

⟨TRANSLATED FROM GERMAN⟩

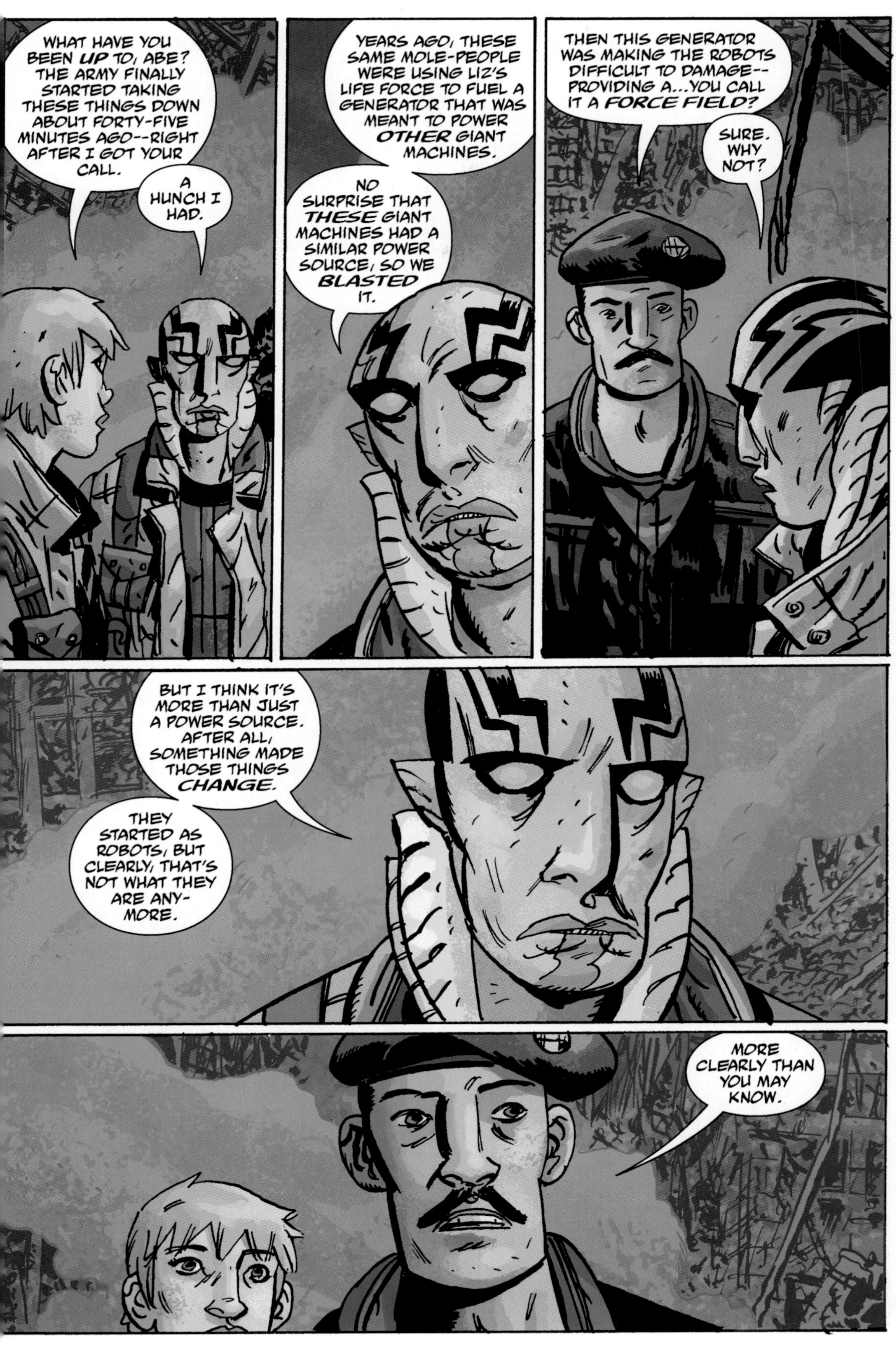
WHAT HAVE YOU BEEN UP TO, ABE? THE ARMY FINALLY STARTED TAKING THESE THINGS DOWN ABOUT FORTY-FIVE MINUTES AGO--RIGHT AFTER I GOT YOUR CALL.
A HUNCH I HAD.
YEARS AGO, THESE SAME MOLE-PEOPLE WERE USING LIZ'S LIFE FORCE TO FUEL A GENERATOR THAT WAS MEANT TO POWER OTHER GIANT MACHINES.
NO SURPRISE THAT THESE GIANT MACHINES HAD A SIMILAR POWER SOURCE, SO WE BLASTED IT.
THEN THIS GENERATOR WAS MAKING THE ROBOTS DIFFICULT TO DAMAGE--PROVIDING A...YOU CALL IT A FORCE FIELD?
SURE. WHY NOT?
BUT I THINK IT'S MORE THAN JUST A POWER SOURCE. AFTER ALL, SOMETHING MADE THOSE THINGS CHANGE.
THEY STARTED AS ROBOTS, BUT CLEARLY, THAT'S NOT WHAT THEY ARE ANYMORE.
MORE CLEARLY THAN YOU MAY KNOW.

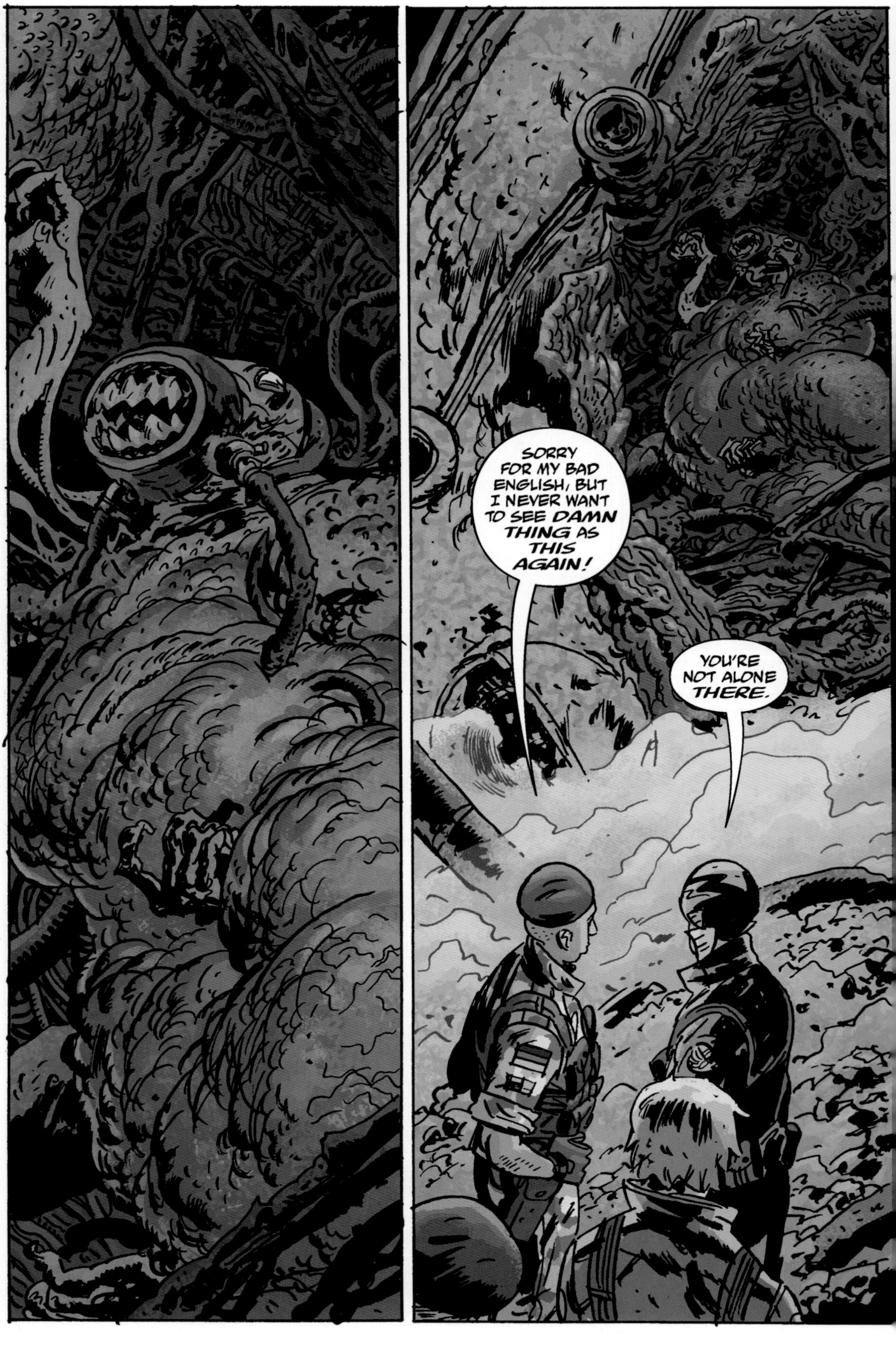

SORRY FOR MY BAD ENGLISH, BUT I NEVER WANT TO SEE DAMN THING AS THIS AGAIN!
YOU'RE NOT ALONE THERE.

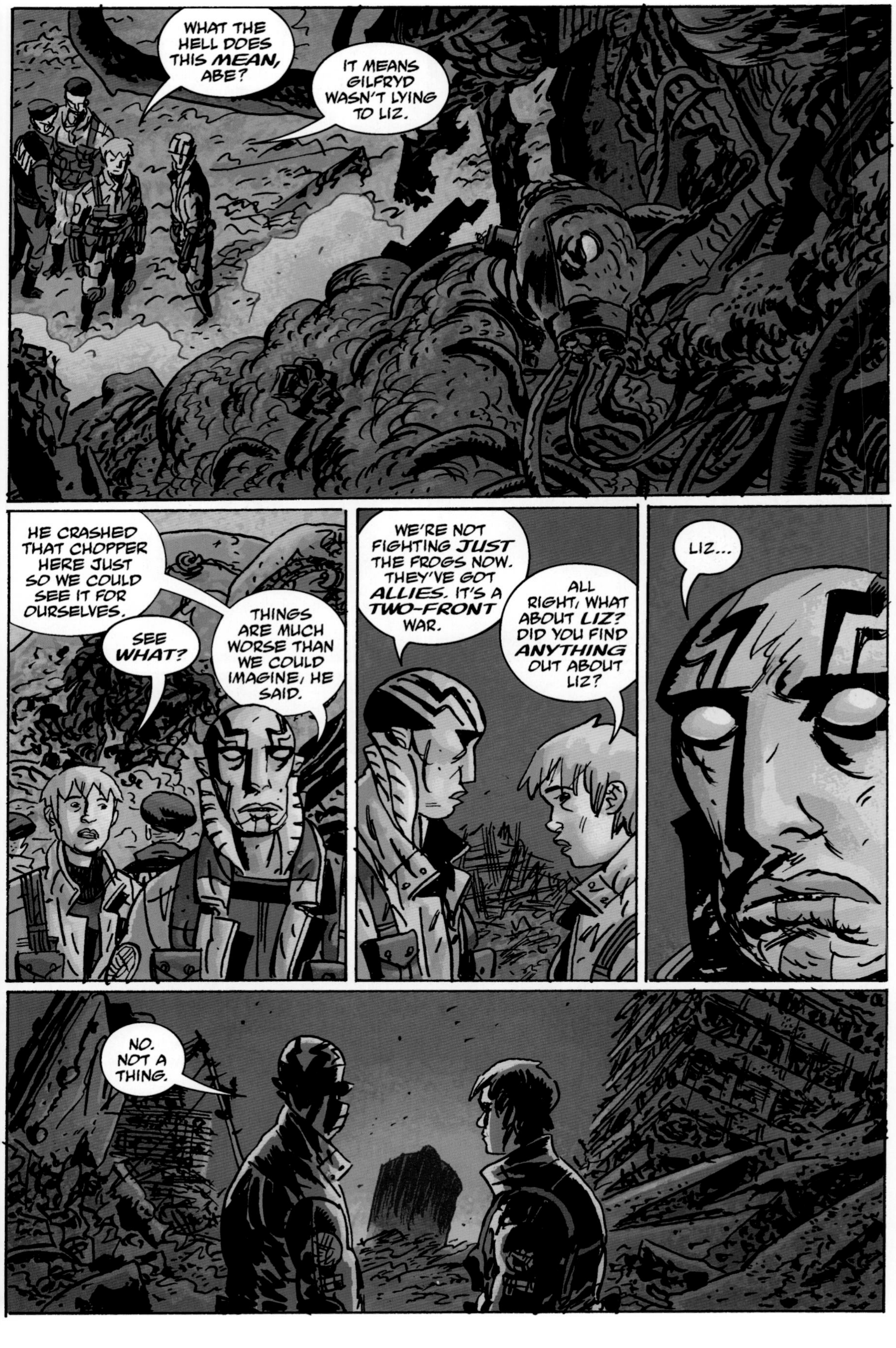

WHAT THE HELL DOES THIS MEAN, ABE?
IT MEANS GILFRYD WASN'T LYING TO LIZ.
HE CRASHED THAT CHOPPER HERE JUST SO WE COULD SEE IT FOR OURSELVES.
SEE WHAT?
THINGS ARE MUCH WORSE THAN WE COULD IMAGINE, HE SAID.
WE'RE NOT FIGHTING JUST THE FROGS NOW. THEY'VE GOT ALLIES. IT'S A TWO-FRONT WAR.
ALL RIGHT, WHAT ABOUT LIZ? DID YOU FIND ANYTHING OUT ABOUT LIZ?
LIZ...
NO. NOT A THING.

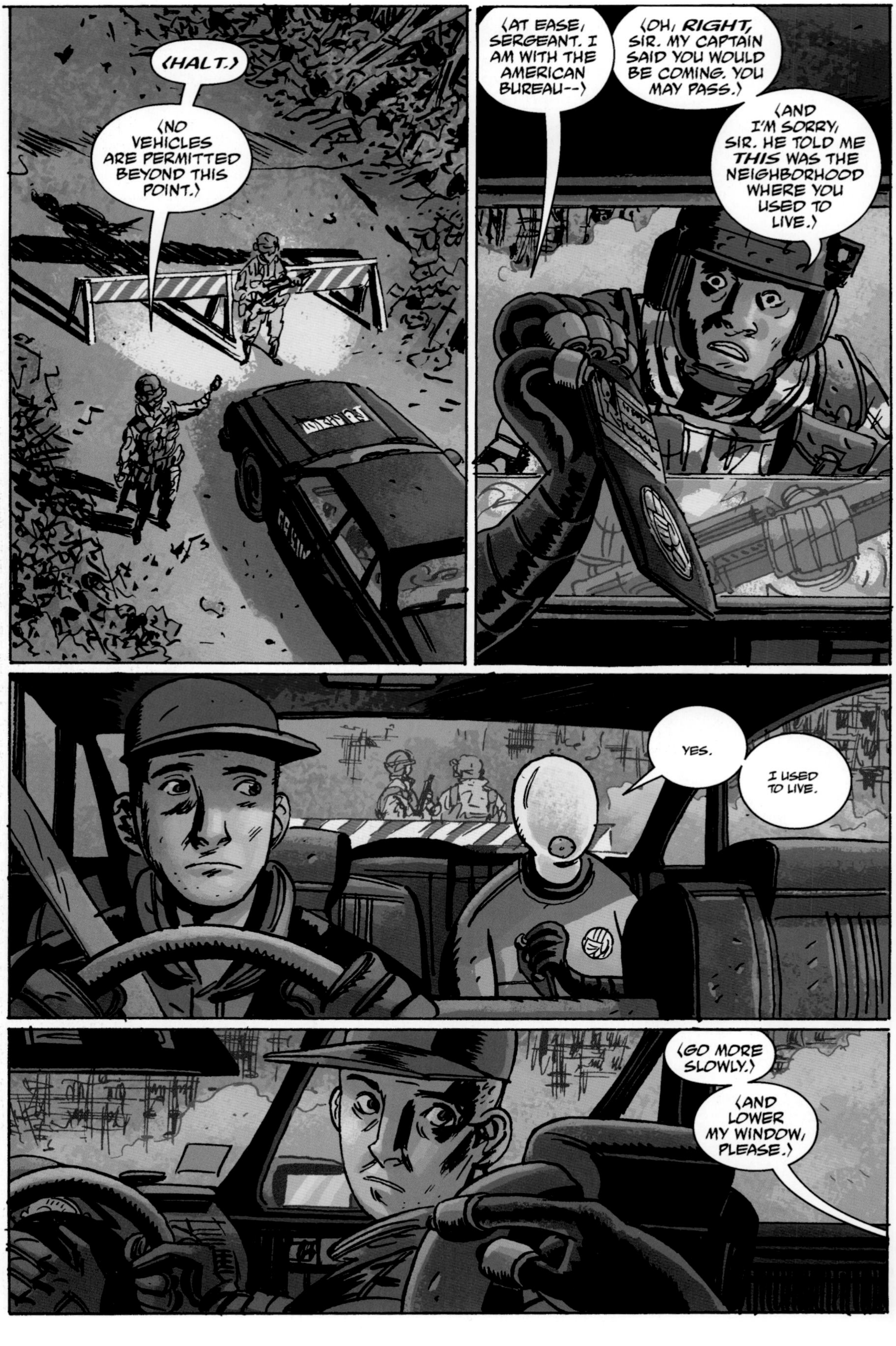

⟨HALT.⟩
⟨NO VEHICLES ARE PERMITTED BEYOND THIS POINT.⟩
⟨AT EASE, SERGEANT. I AM WITH THE AMERICAN BUREAU--⟩
⟨OH, RIGHT, SIR. MY CAPTAIN SAID YOU WOULD BE COMING. YOU MAY PASS.⟩
⟨AND I'M SORRY, SIR. HE TOLD ME THIS WAS THE NEIGHBORHOOD WHERE YOU USED TO LIVE.⟩
YES.
I USED TO LIVE.
⟨GO MORE SLOWLY.⟩
⟨AND LOWER MY WINDOW, PLEASE.⟩

⟨THERE! THERE IT IS.⟩

⟨MY HOME. GONE.⟩

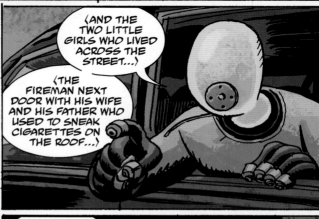

⟨AND THE TWO LITTLE GIRLS WHO LIVED ACROSS THE STREET...⟩

⟨THE FIREMAN NEXT DOOR WITH HIS WIFE AND HIS FATHER WHO USED TO SNEAK CIGARETTES ON THE ROOF...⟩

⟨SIR, THEY PROBABLY WERE WARNED. MAYBE THEY ALL ESCAPED.⟩

⟨NO. NO, THEY DIDN'T.⟩

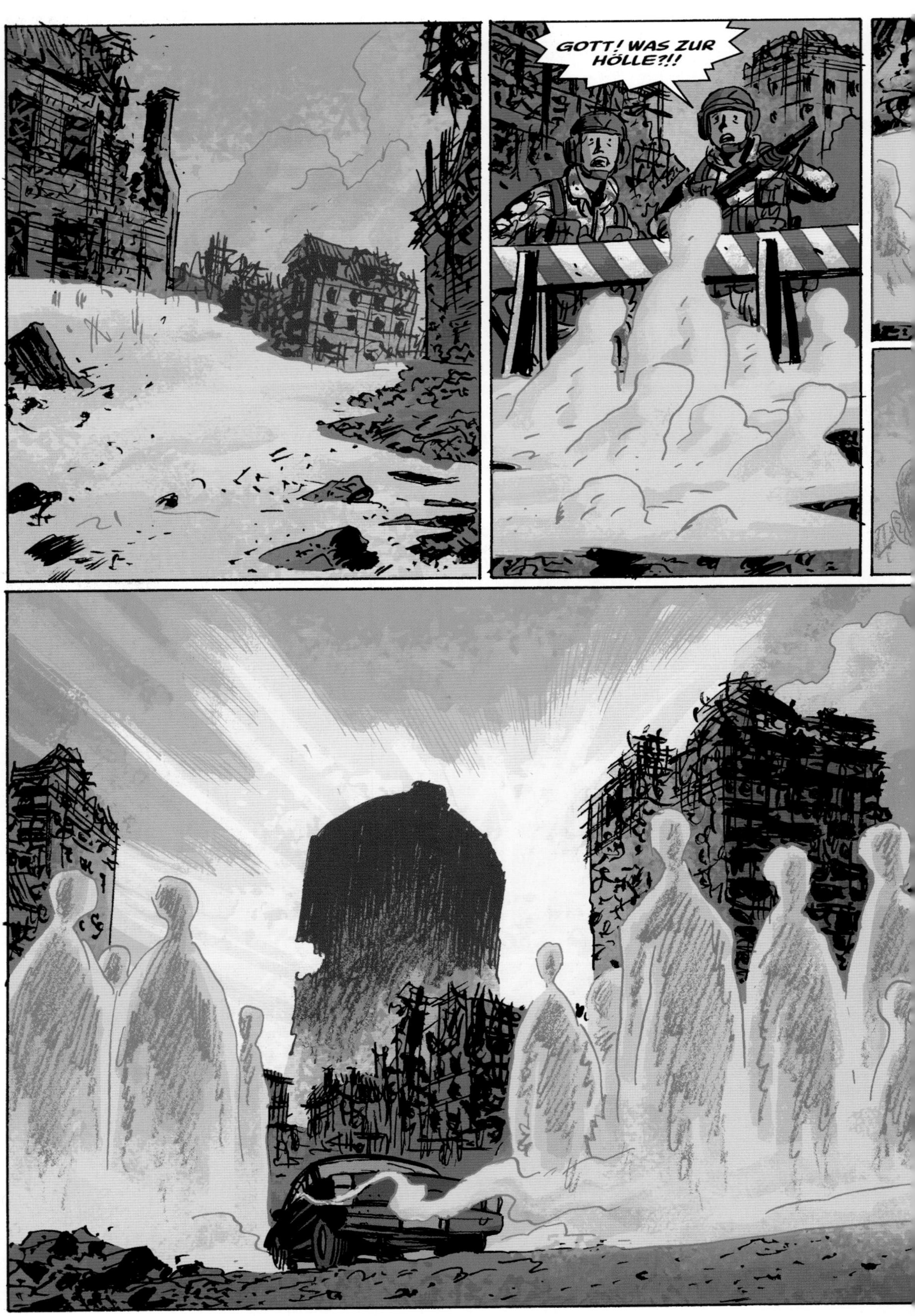
GOTT! WAS ZUR HÖLLE?!!

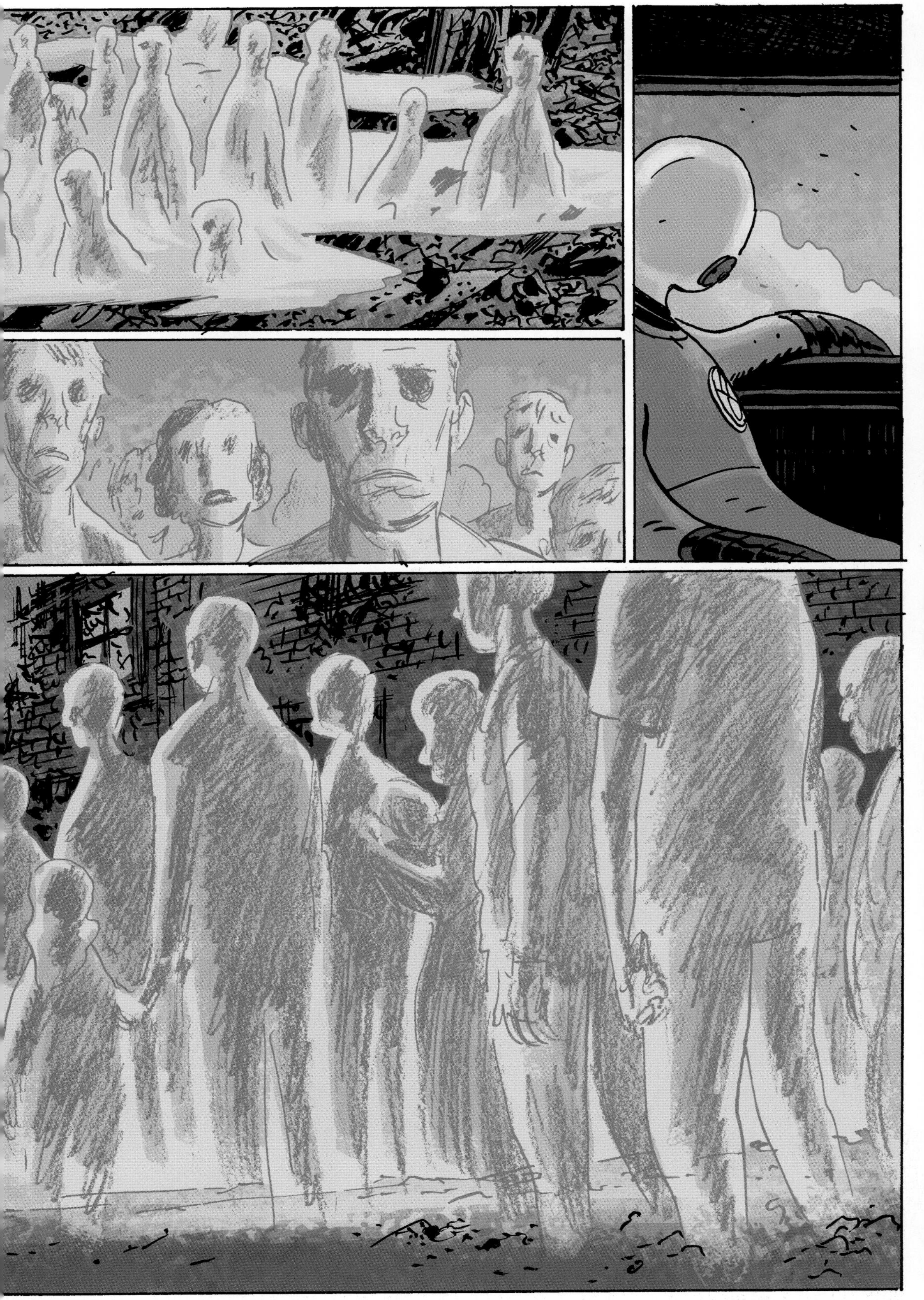

I'M SORRY ABOUT WHAT THE COLONEL SAID, KATE, BUT HE HAS MADE ME THINK.

WHY ALL OF A SUDDEN HAS THIS STARTED? WHY ARE THESE CREATURES HERE NOW?

THEY'VE ALWAYS BEEN AROUND-- LONGER THAN WE HAVE, ACTUALLY.

BUT FOR A LONG TIME THEY WERE OPERATING... WELL, UNDER OUR RADAR, YOU COULD SAY.

UNDERGROUND?

PARTLY THAT, YES, BUT THERE IS A BIGGER WORLD OUT THERE THAT ONLY SORT OF... BRUSHES UP AGAINST OURS.

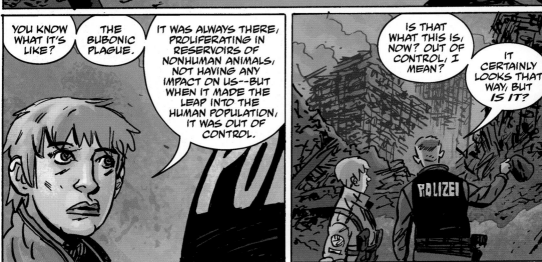

YOU KNOW WHAT IT'S LIKE?

THE BUBONIC PLAGUE.

IT WAS ALWAYS THERE, PROLIFERATING IN RESERVOIRS OF NONHUMAN ANIMALS, NOT HAVING ANY IMPACT ON US--BUT WHEN IT MADE THE LEAP INTO THE HUMAN POPULATION, IT WAS OUT OF CONTROL.

IS THAT WHAT THIS IS, NOW? OUT OF CONTROL, I MEAN?

IT CERTAINLY LOOKS THAT WAY, BUT IS IT?

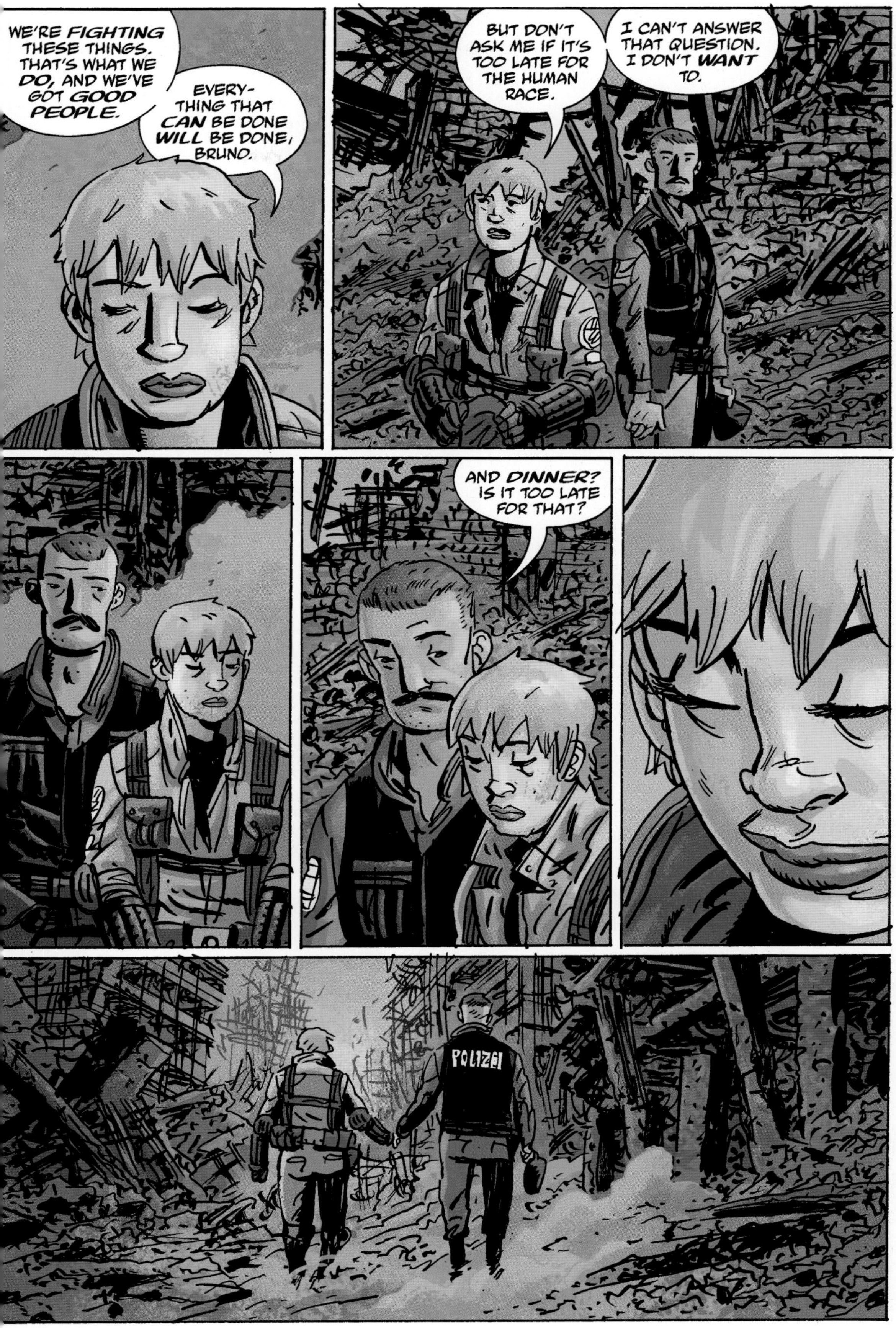
WE'RE FIGHTING THESE THINGS. THAT'S WHAT WE DO, AND WE'VE GOT GOOD PEOPLE.
EVERY-THING THAT CAN BE DONE WILL BE DONE, BRUNO.
BUT DON'T ASK ME IF IT'S TOO LATE FOR THE HUMAN RACE.
I CAN'T ANSWER THAT QUESTION. I DON'T WANT TO.
AND DINNER? IS IT TOO LATE FOR THAT?
POLIZEI

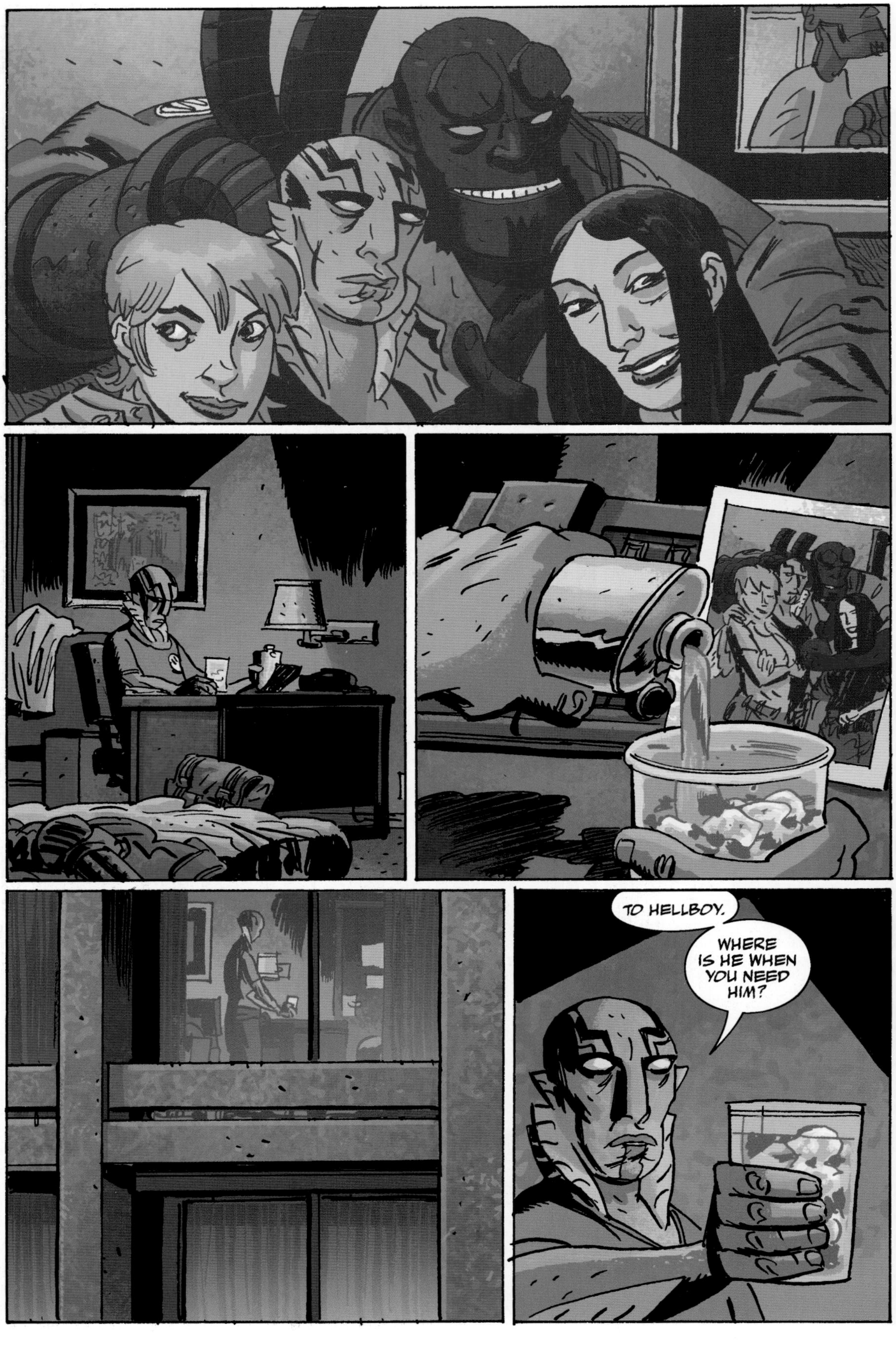
TO HELLBOY.
WHERE IS HE WHEN YOU NEED HIM?

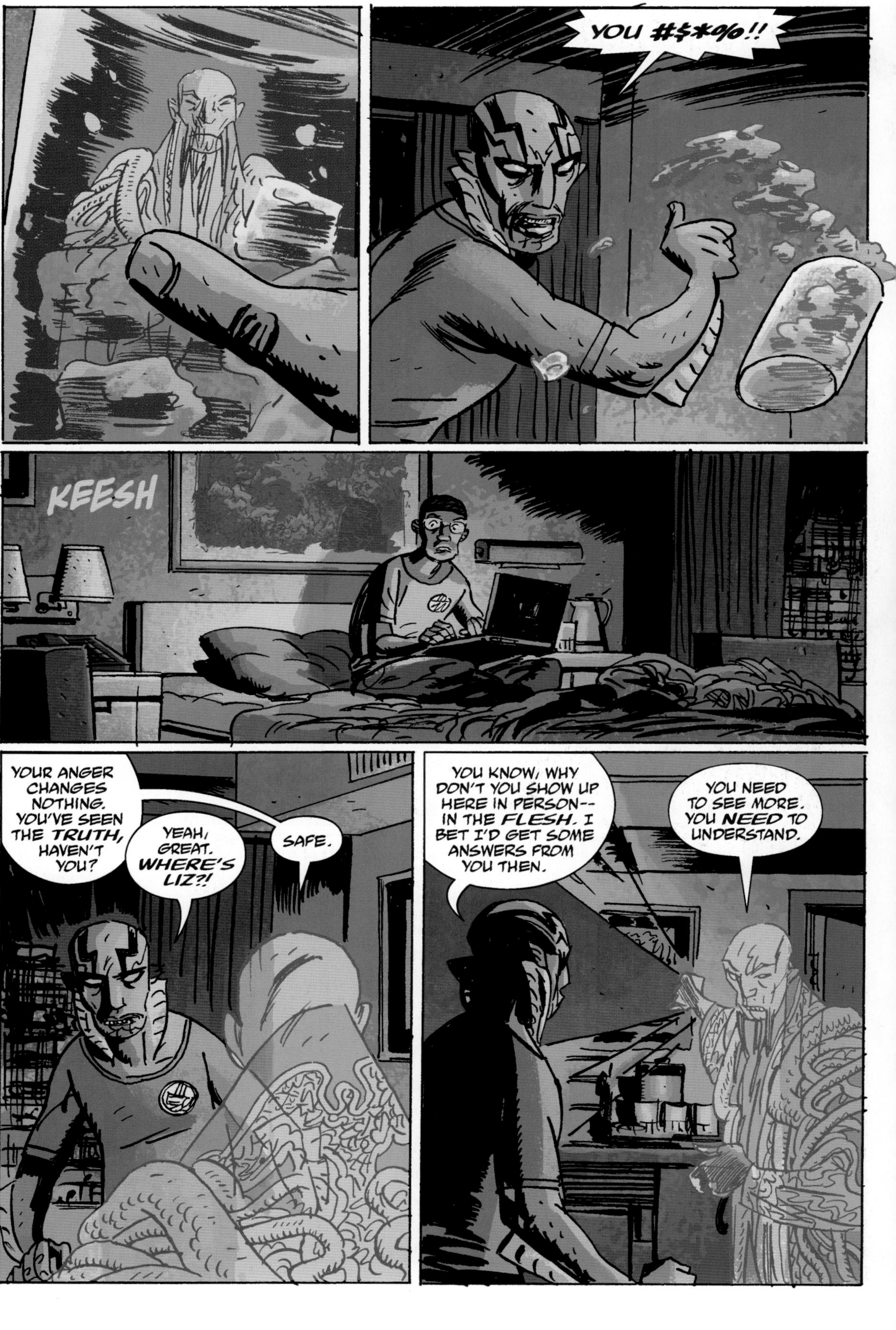
YOU #$*%!!
KEESH
YOUR ANGER CHANGES NOTHING. YOU'VE SEEN THE *TRUTH*, HAVEN'T YOU?
YEAH, GREAT. ***WHERE'S LIZ?!***
SAFE.
YOU KNOW, WHY DON'T YOU SHOW UP HERE IN PERSON-- IN THE *FLESH*. I BET I'D GET SOME ANSWERS FROM YOU THEN.
YOU NEED TO SEE MORE. YOU ***NEED*** TO UNDERSTAND.

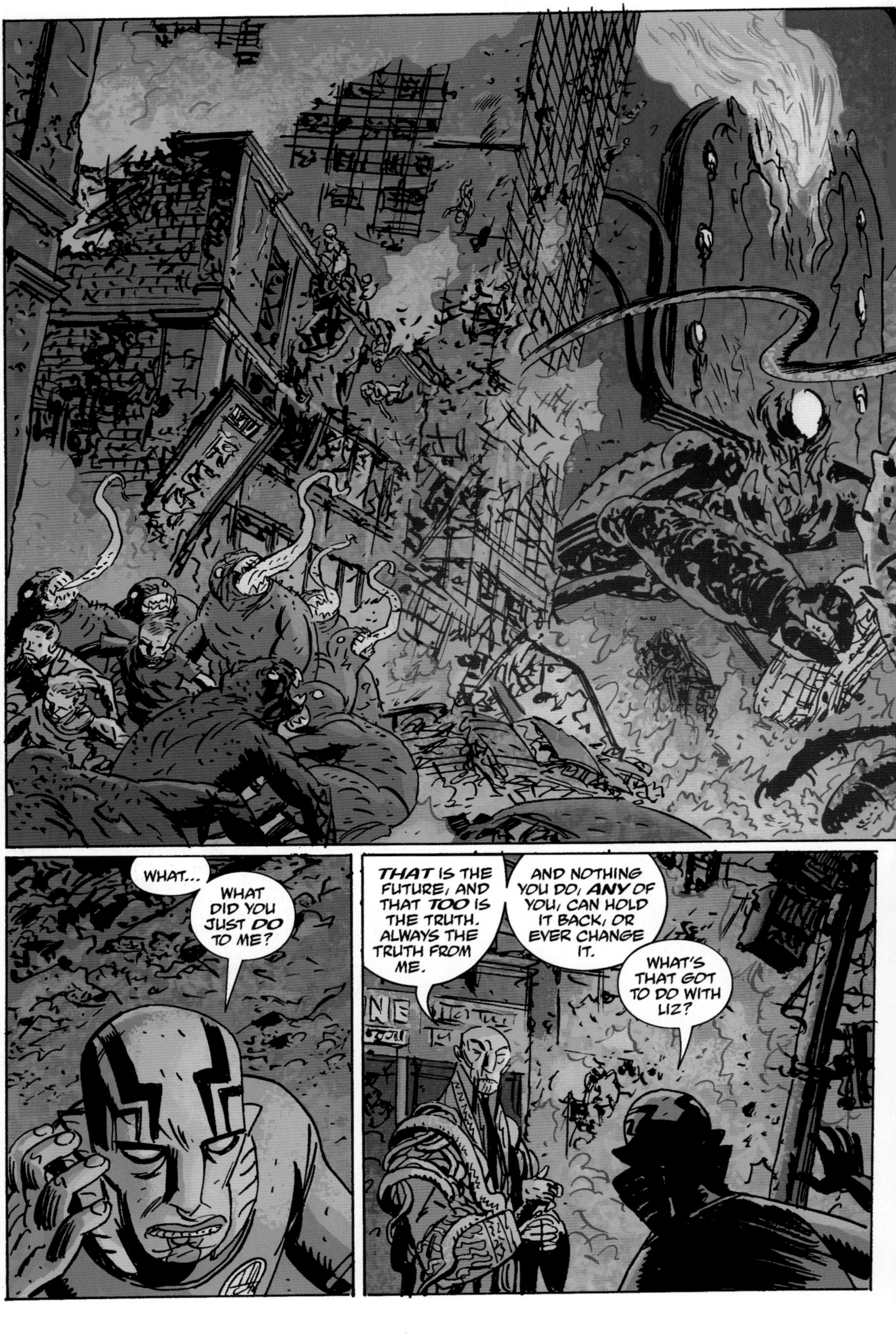
WHAT...
WHAT DID YOU JUST DO TO ME?
THAT IS THE FUTURE, AND THAT TOO IS THE TRUTH. ALWAYS THE TRUTH FROM ME.
AND NOTHING YOU DO, ANY OF YOU, CAN HOLD IT BACK, OR EVER CHANGE IT.
WHAT'S THAT GOT TO DO WITH LIZ?

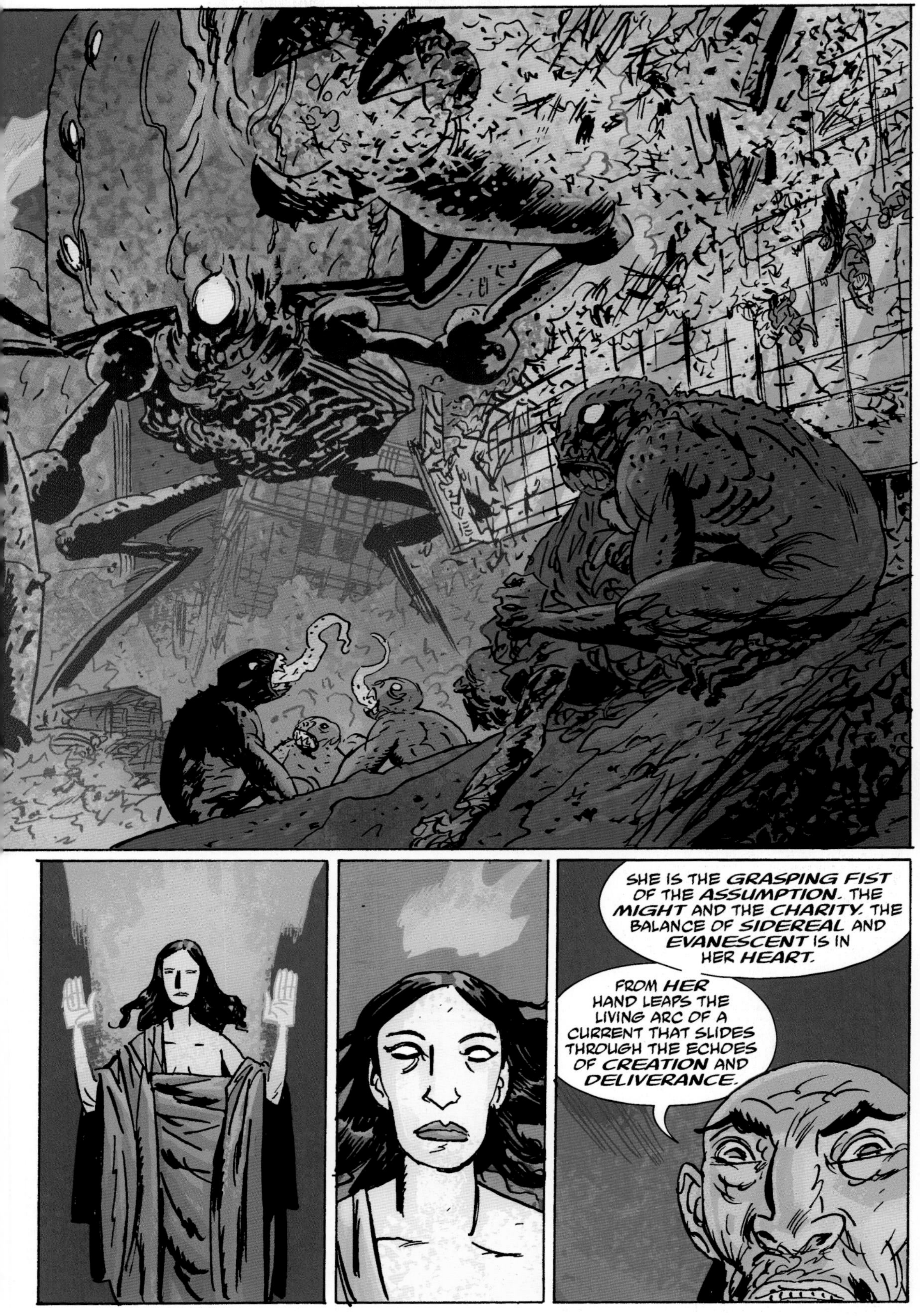
SHE IS THE GRASPING FIST OF THE ASSUMPTION. THE MIGHT AND THE CHARITY. THE BALANCE OF SIDEREAL AND EVANESCENT IS IN HER HEART.
FROM HER HAND LEAPS THE LIVING ARC OF A CURRENT THAT SLIDES THROUGH THE ECHOES OF CREATION AND DELIVERANCE.

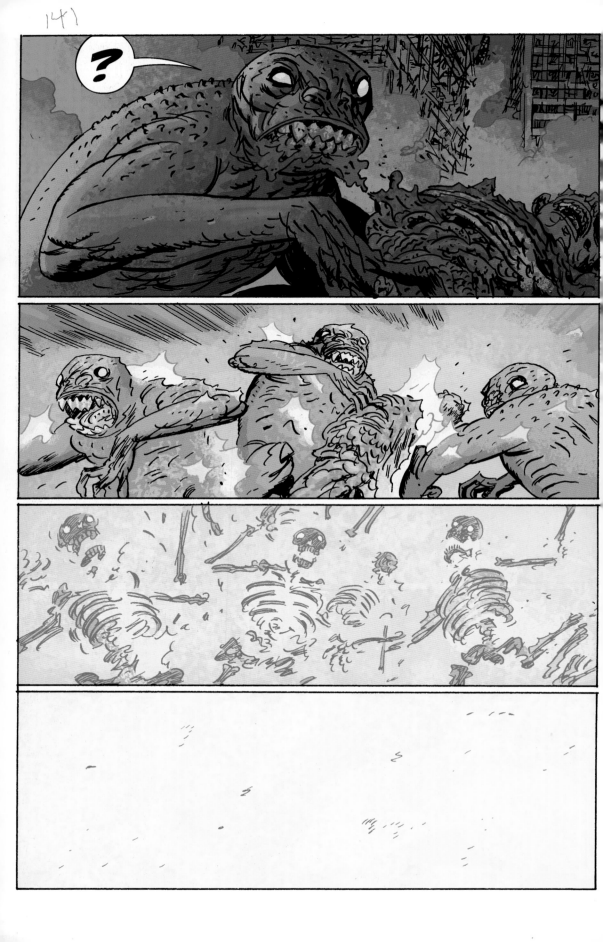

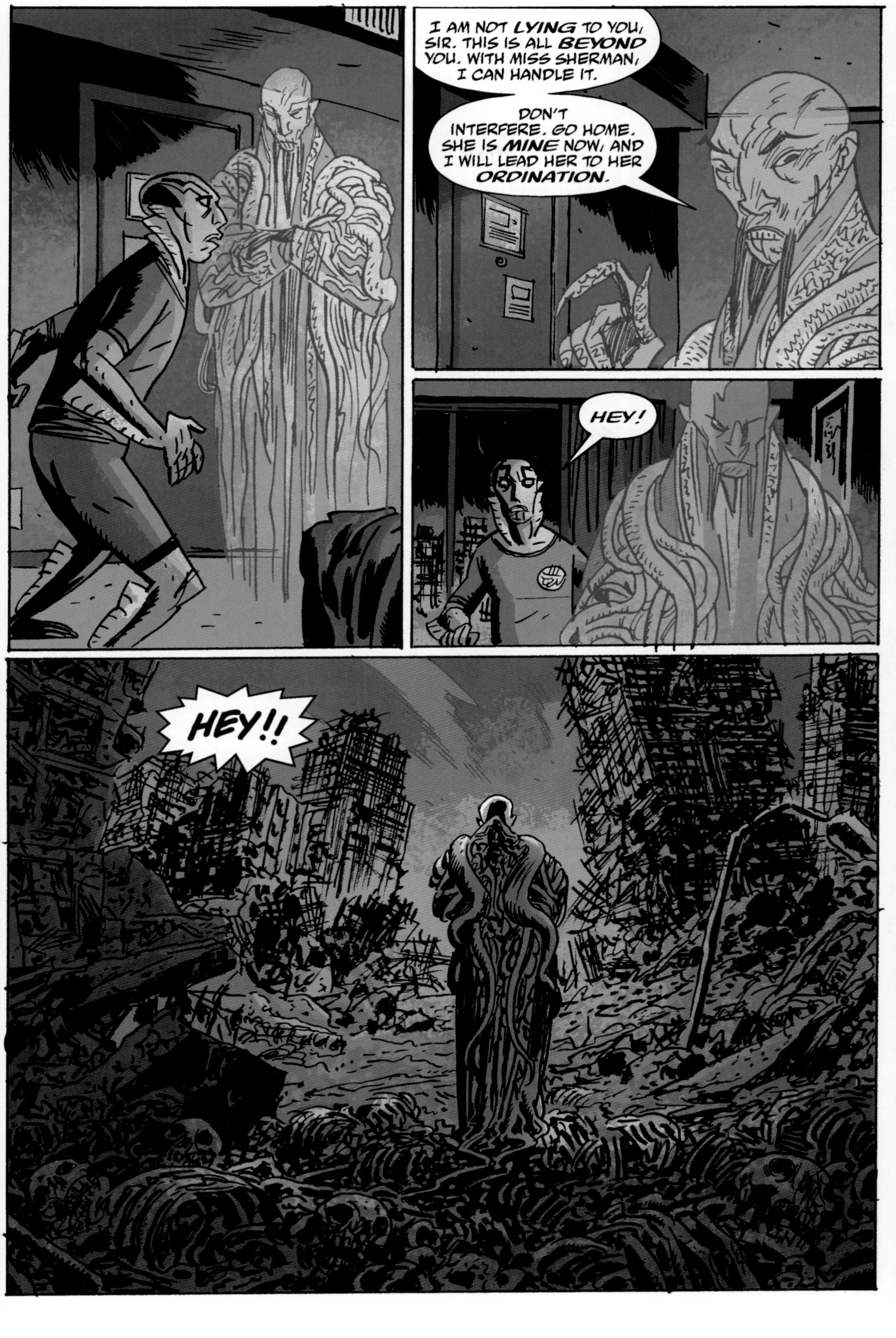
I AM NOT LYING TO YOU, SIR. THIS IS ALL BEYOND YOU. WITH MISS SHERMAN, I CAN HANDLE IT.
DON'T INTERFERE. GO HOME. SHE IS MINE NOW, AND I WILL LEAD HER TO HER ORDINATION.
HEY!
HEY!!

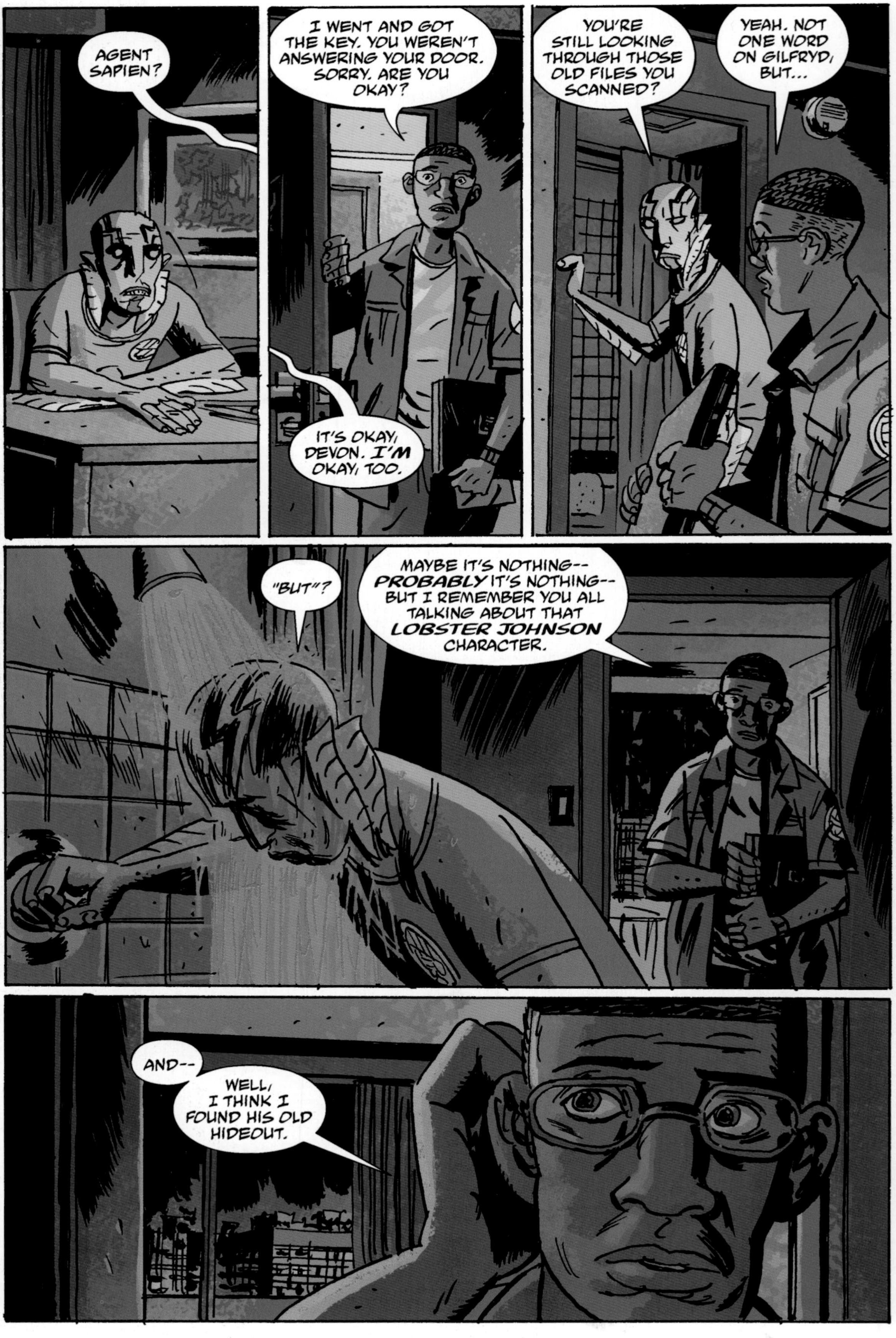
AGENT SAPIEN?
I WENT AND GOT THE KEY. YOU WEREN'T ANSWERING YOUR DOOR. SORRY. ARE YOU OKAY?
IT'S OKAY, DEVON. I'M OKAY, TOO.
YOU'RE STILL LOOKING THROUGH THOSE OLD FILES YOU SCANNED?
YEAH. NOT ONE WORD ON GILFRYD, BUT...
"BUT"?
MAYBE IT'S NOTHING-- PROBABLY IT'S NOTHING-- BUT I REMEMBER YOU ALL TALKING ABOUT THAT LOBSTER JOHNSON CHARACTER.
AND--
WELL, I THINK I FOUND HIS OLD HIDEOUT.

THE END

AFTERWORD

The Warning. That's right: Liz Sherman gets kidnapped, the B.P.R.D.'s entire fleet of helicopters gets wiped out, and gigantic robots trample Munich into rubble, but this is only a "warning."

Nobody ever accused Mike Mignola of thinking small, and that's where *The Warning* was born: one of triplets, from the incredibly fertile mind of Hellboy's very own daddy. As the title vaguely hints, this loud story of massive destruction is just the first chapter in a trilogy of much more massive destruction and far-reaching consequences. Mike and I really wanted to move forward with this Memnan Saa/Liz Sherman storyline, but Mike wanted to do it big. Really big. Bigger than anything I think I've ever seen in a continuing comic series. No kidding. You'll see.

Now, one could argue that this storyline had its origins in the *Plague of Frogs* series, where Mike reintroduced the frog monsters into the B.P.R.D. universe as a world-eating legion that spread faster than it could be killed off. Once he set that into motion, a massive conflict was bound to come about eventually, but that's not news to you. You, the faithful readers, have watched this story develop for a long time, and what you want to know is the background stuff. The story behind the story. Boy, I wish I could tell it to you. See, as Mike and I were brainstorming on our first collaboration (*B.P.R.D.: The Dead*) we came up with a gag in issue #3. Not to get too deeply into it, but you'll find in that issue that Johann discovered an old scrapbook deep in the subbase-

ment of the Colorado B.P.R.D. headquarters. We decided to do a full double-page splash of the open scrapbook, depicting World War II characters. This was just a little playful foreshadowing for future series wherein we planned to use the characters and props shown (most notably, the Black Flame and a certain suit of armor). At the last minute, Mike said, "Throw a Fu Manchu–looking guy in there." And there he was. Right there on the page (once Guy drew it, that is). Just so you know, Mike and I honestly do split the plotting chores on this book pretty evenly. Sometimes I do a lot more work on a plot than he, and sometimes he does a lot more than I, but we're both into it up to our elbows all the time. That said, if you want me to be honest, I'd have to tell you that I had no idea who that "Fu Manchu–looking guy" was, or who he would turn out to be. Clearly, however, the inscrutable Mike Mignola did. He just wasn't telling. Maybe he thought I'd be scared off by the magnitude of what he was planning (which is to say, five years of escalating nightmarish tales paying off in what appears to be a sort of prelude to Armageddon) or maybe he thought I'd think he was nuts for planning that far into the future. Hard to say, but anyway, I do know all about Memnan Saa now (hey, we couldn't just keep calling him "that Fu Manchu–looking guy") and very soon, so will you.

—John Arcudi
Philadelphia

B.P.R.D.™

SKETCHBOOK

Guy Davis: With more and more dangers lurking ahead for the B.P.R.D., I wanted to start modifying their combat dress with *The Warning*. Mostly it was just cluttering it up with belts and pouches to give them more of a foot-soldier feel.

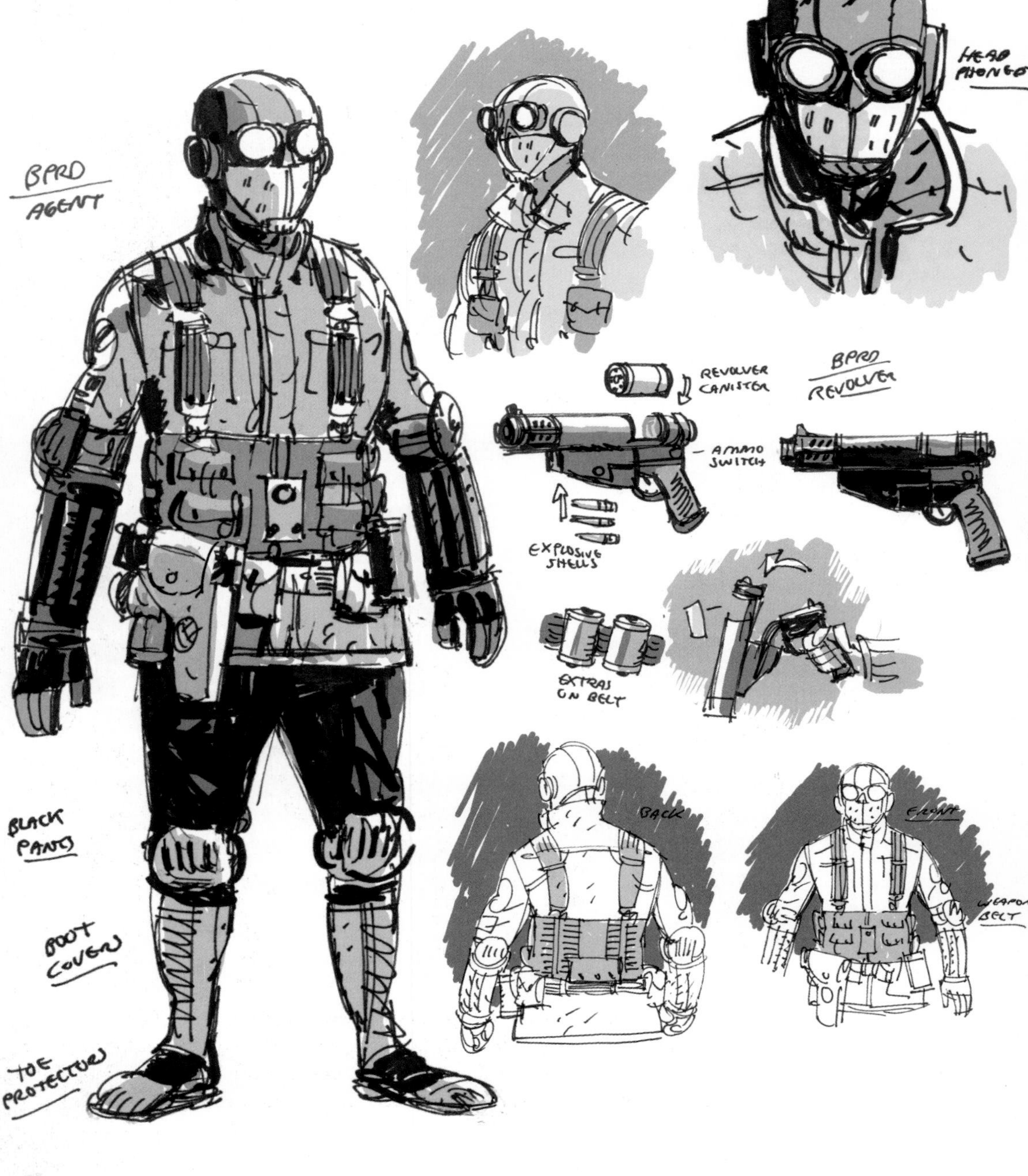
BPRD AGENT
HEAD PHONES
REVOLVER CANISTER
BPRD REVOLVER
AMMO SWITCH
EXPLOSIVE SHELLS
EXTRAS ON BELT
BLACK PANTS
BACK
FRONT
WEAPON BELT
BOOT COVERS
TOE PROTECTORS

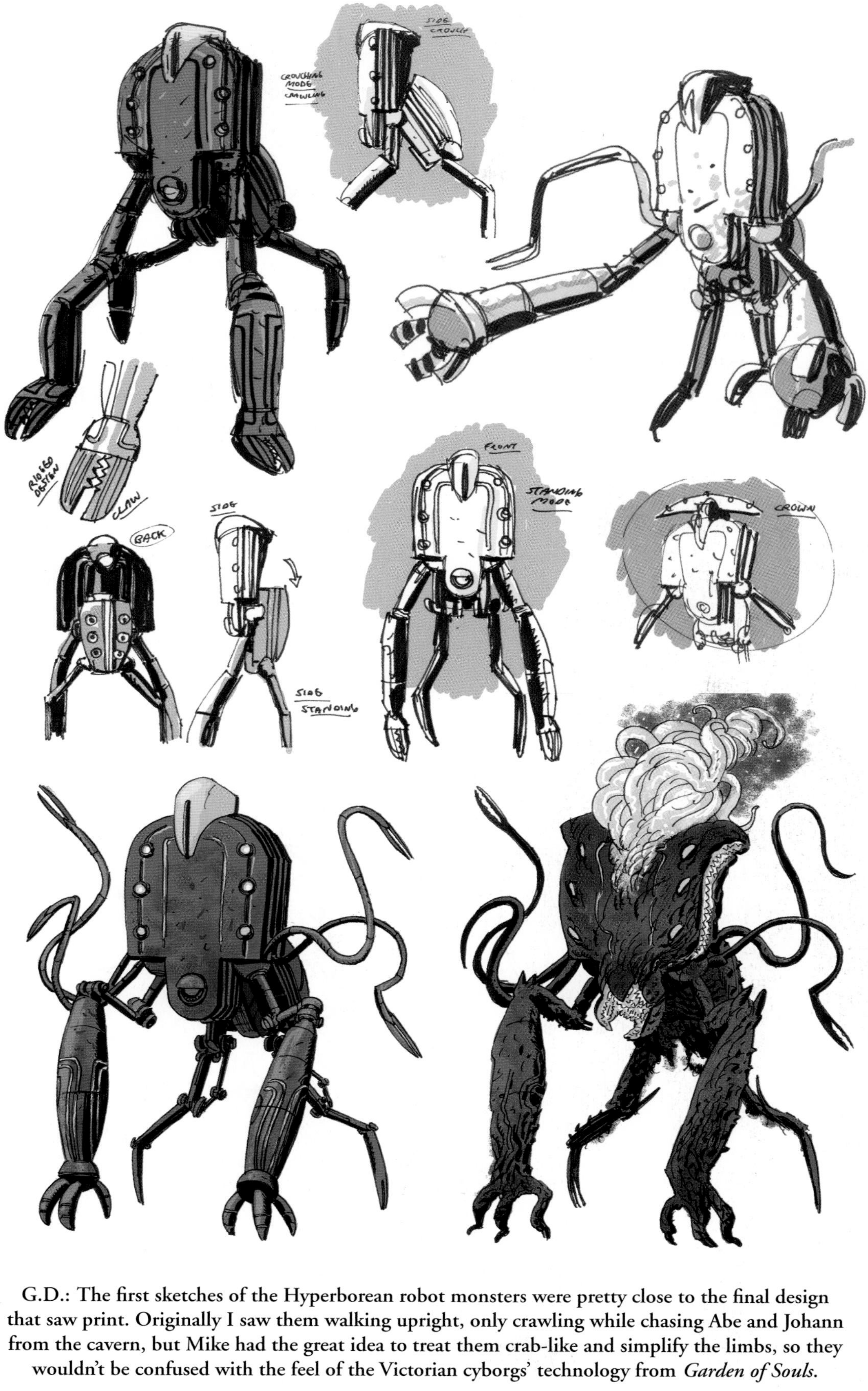
SIDE
CROUCH
CROUCHING
MODE
CRAWLING
RIDGED
DESIGN
CLAW
BACK
SIDE
SIDE
STANDING
FRONT
STANDING
MODE
CROWN

G.D.: The first sketches of the Hyperborean robot monsters were pretty close to the final design that saw print. Originally I saw them walking upright, only crawling while chasing Abe and Johann from the cavern, but Mike had the great idea to treat them crab-like and simplify the limbs, so they wouldn't be confused with the feel of the Victorian cyborgs' technology from *Garden of Souls*.

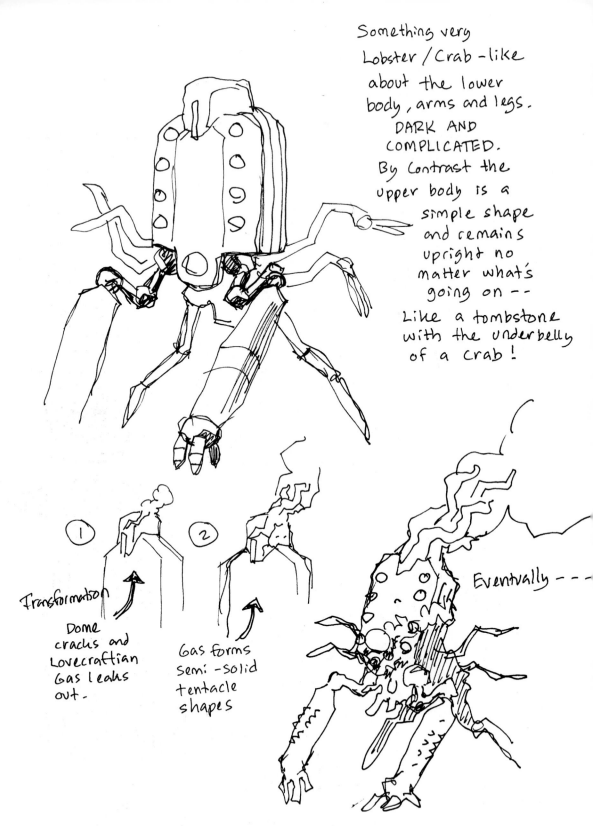

Something very Lobster / Crab-like about the lower body, arms and legs. DARK AND COMPLICATED. By Contrast the upper body is a simple shape and remains upright no matter what's going on --

Like a tombstone with the underbelly of a crab!

① Transformation
Dome cracks and Lovecraftian Gas leaks out.

② Gas forms semi-solid tentacle shapes

Eventually ---

Mike Mignola: In this book I didn't want to go *too* far with Hyperborean machines evolving into creatures. I stopped Guy from evolving their tombstone-like "heads." We don't yet know what's going on in there. Something bad, I suspect. The tentacle-like smoke coming out of the crack at the top of each machine hints at trouble yet to come.

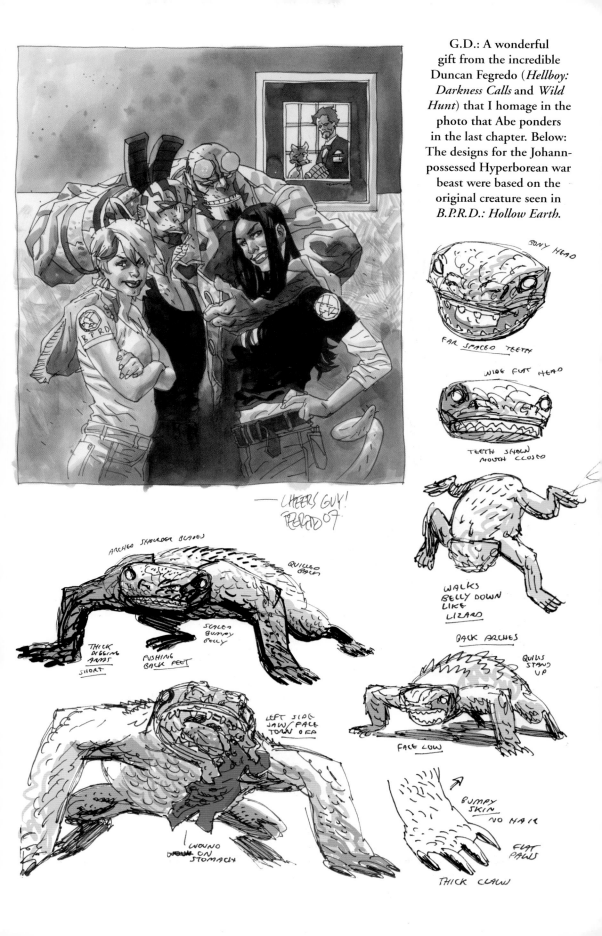

G.D.: A wonderful gift from the incredible Duncan Fegredo (*Hellboy: Darkness Calls* and *Wild Hunt*) that I homage in the photo that Abe ponders in the last chapter. Below: The designs for the Johann-possessed Hyperborean war beast were based on the original creature seen in *B.P.R.D.: Hollow Earth.*

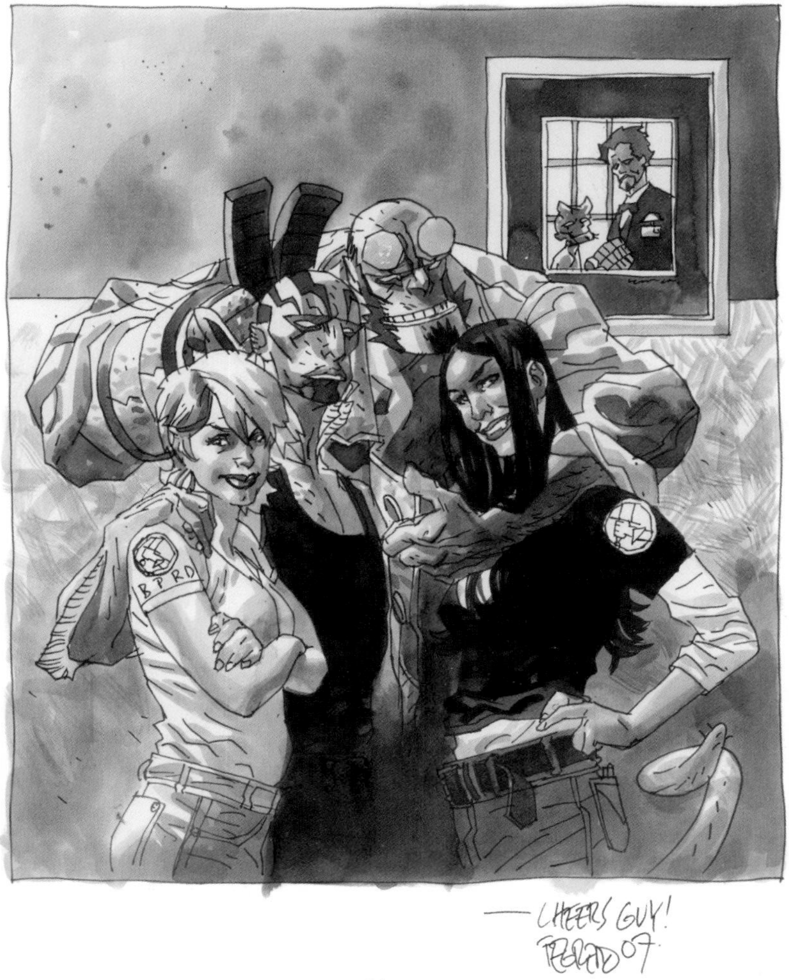
B P R D
—CHEERS GUY!
FEGREDO 07

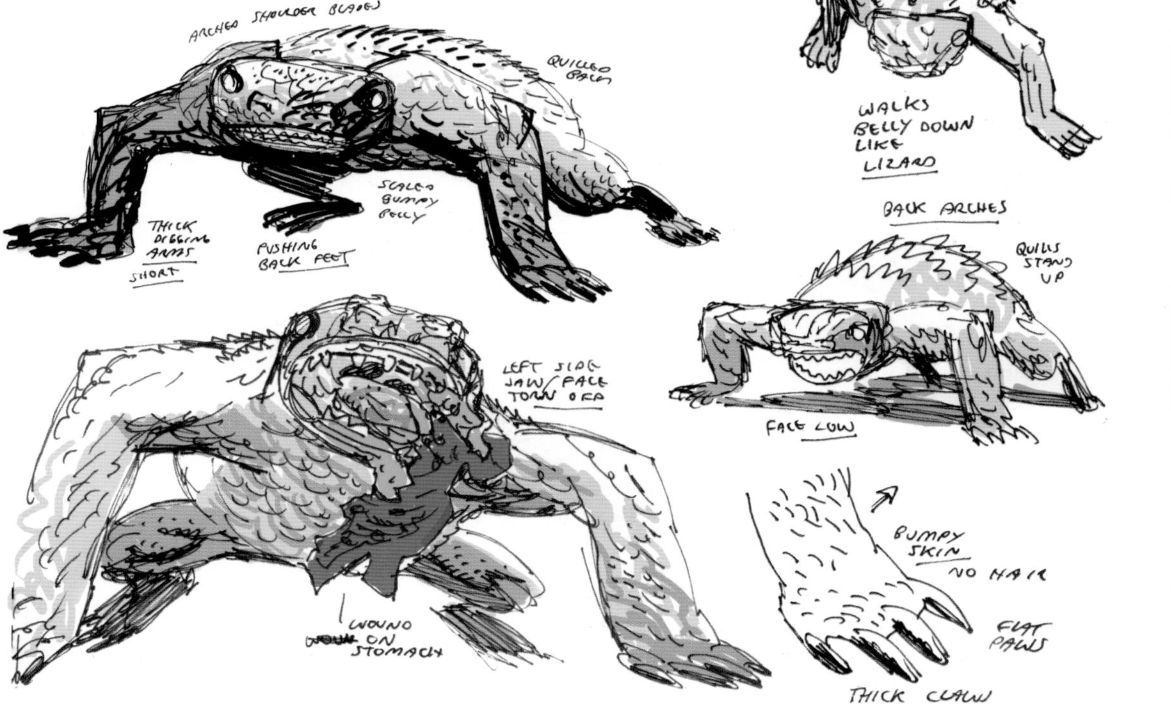
BONY HEAD
FAR SPACED TEETH
WIDE FLAT HEAD
TEETH SHOWN MOUTH CLOSED
WALKS BELLY DOWN LIKE LIZARD
ARCHED SHOULDER BLADES
QUILLED BACK
SCALED BUMPY BELLY
THICK DIGGING ARMS SHORT
PUSHING BACK FEET
BACK ARCHES
QUILLS STAND UP
FACE LOW
LEFT SIDE JAW/FACE TORN OFF
WOUND ON STOMACH
BUMPY SKIN NO HAIR
FLAT PAWS
THICK CLAW

G.D.: In the original script, John had the war beasts mounted with giant weapons that were a combination of Hyperborean and Black Flame mechanics.

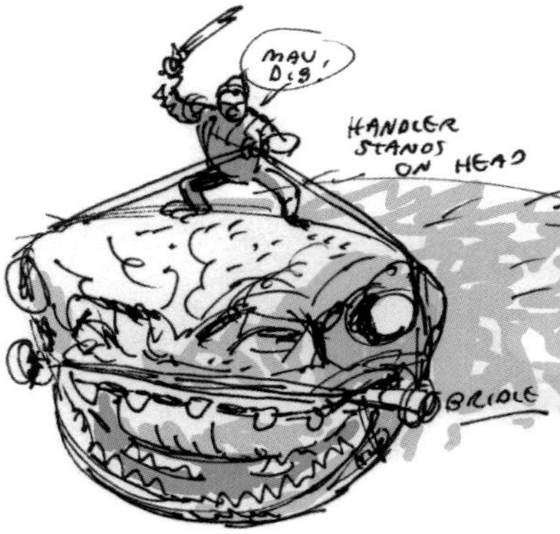
HANDLER STANDS ON HEAD
BRIDLE

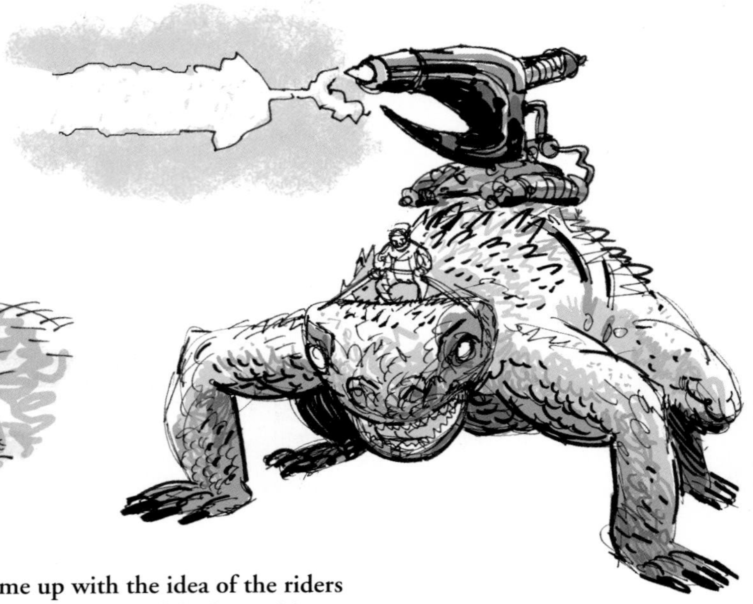

Instead of using reins, Mike came up with the idea of the riders holding onto a giant spike nailed into the skull of the beast, like some torturous steering column. A great detail that I wasn't able to show off due to limited space in the page layouts and scale of the creatures.

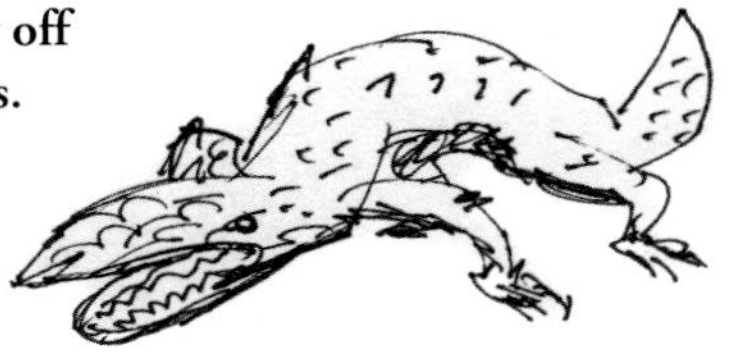

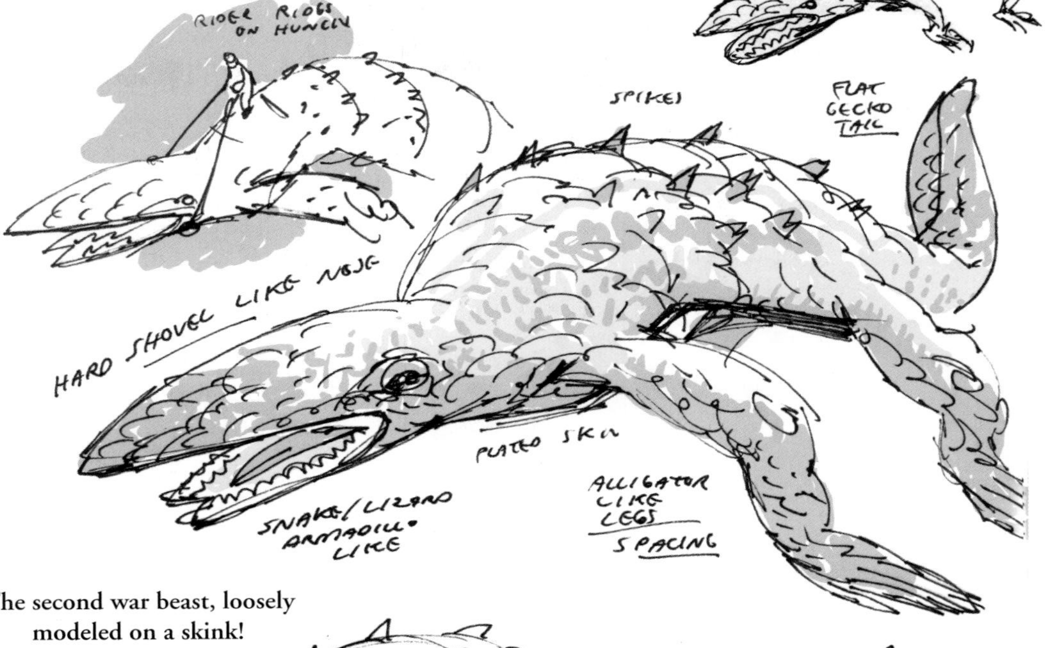
RIDER RIDES ON HUNCH
SPIKES
FLAT GECKO TAIL
HARD SHOVEL LIKE NOSE
PLATED SKIN
ALLIGATOR LIKE LEGS
SPACING
SNAKE/LIZARD ARMADILLO LIKE

The second war beast, loosely modeled on a skink!

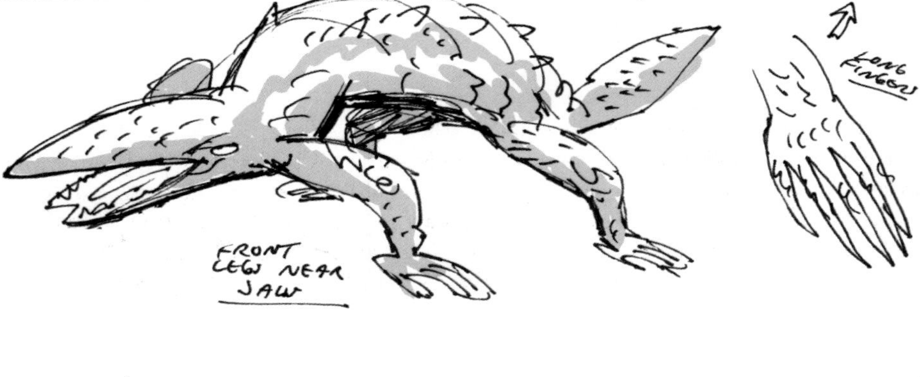
LONG FINGERS
FRONT LEGS NEAR JAW

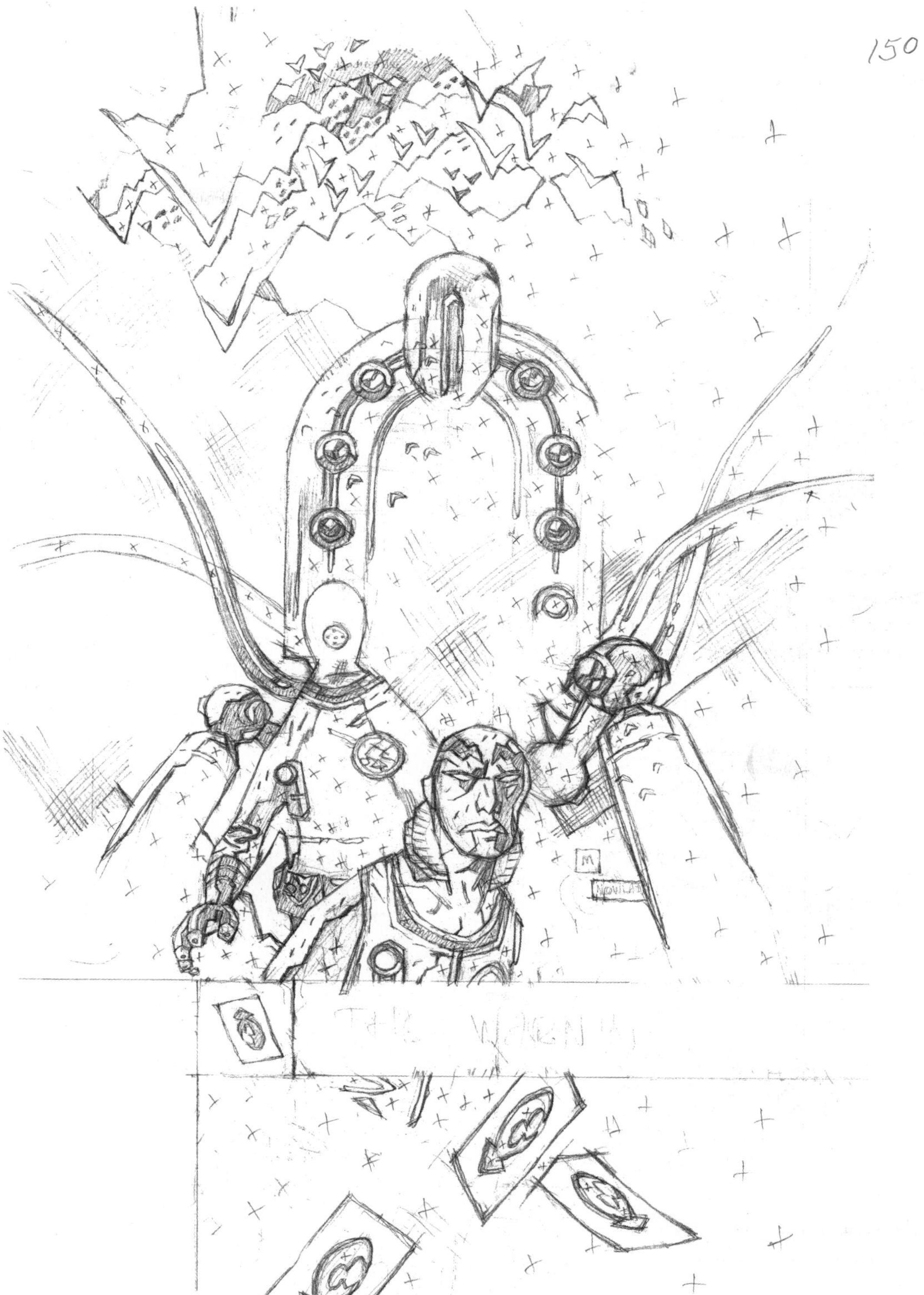

M.M.: My pencil art for the cover of issue #3. I threw a lot of crosshatching in there—something I almost never use these days—because no one is better at that super-fine crosshatching than Kevin Nowlan, who inked the covers of the series. I thought it would give these covers a misty atmosphere that would separate them from other *B.P.R.D.* covers. And I was right. And it was a thrill to work with Kevin again. He inked some of the first covers I did at Marvel—more years ago than either of us want to think about.

HELLBOY
by MIKE MIGNOLA

HELLBOY LIBRARY EDITION VOLUME 1:
SEED OF DESTRUCTION
AND WAKE THE DEVIL
ISBN 978-1-59307-910-9 | $49.99

HELLBOY LIBRARY EDITION VOLUME 2:
THE CHAINED COFFIN
AND THE RIGHT HAND OF DOOM
ISBN 978-1-59307-989-5 | $49.99

HELLBOY LIBRARY EDITION VOLUME 3:
CONQUEROR WORM AND STRANGE PLACES
ISBN 978-1-59582-352-6 | $49.99

SEED OF DESTRUCTION
With John Byrne
ISBN 978-1-59307-094-6 | $17.99

WAKE THE DEVIL
ISBN 978-1-59307-095-3 | $17.99

THE CHAINED COFFIN AND OTHERS
ISBN 978-1-59307-091-5 | $17.99

THE RIGHT HAND OF DOOM
ISBN 978-1-59307-093-9 | $17.99

CONQUEROR WORM
ISBN 978-1-59307-092-2 | $17.99

THE TROLL WITCH AND OTHERS
ISBN 978-1-59307-860-7 | $17.99

DARKNESS CALLS
With Duncan Fegredo
ISBN 978-1-59307-896-6 | $19.99

THE WILD HUNT
With Duncan Fegredo
ISBN 978-1-59582-352-6 | $19.99

THE CROOKED MAN AND OTHERS
With Richard Corben
ISBN 978-1-59582-477-6 | $17.99

THE ART OF HELLBOY
ISBN 978-1-59307-089-2 | $29.99

HELLBOY II: THE ART OF THE MOVIE
ISBN 978-1-59307-964-2 | $24.99

HELLBOY: THE COMPANION
ISBN 978-1-59307-655-9 | $14.99

To find a comics shop in your area,
call 1-888-266-4226
For more information or to order direct:
• On the web: darkhorse.com
• E-mail: mailorder@darkhorse.com
• Phone: 1-800-862-0052
Mon.–Fri. 9 AM to 5 PM Pacific Time

HELLBOY: WEIRD TALES
Volume 1
ISBN 978-1-56971-622-9 | $17.99
Volume 2
ISBN 978-1-56971-953-4 | $17.99

HELLBOY: MASKS AND MONSTERS
By Mignola, James Robinson, Scott
Benefiel, and Jasen Rodriguez
ISBN 978-1-59582-567-4 | $17.99

HELLBOY: EMERALD HELL
By Tom Piccirilli
ISBN 978-1-59582-141-6 | $12.99

HELLBOY: THE ALL-SEEING EYE
By Mark Morris
ISBN 978-1-59582-142-3 | $12.99

HELLBOY: THE FIRE WOLVES
By Tim Lebbon
ISBN 978-1-59582-204-8 | $12.99

HELLBOY: THE ICE WOLVES
By Mark Chadbourn
ISBN 978-1-59582-205-5 | $12.99

ODD JOBS
ISBN 978-1-56971-440-9 | $14.99

ODDER JOBS
With Frank Darabont, Charles de Lint,
Guillermo del Toro, and others
ISBN 978-1-59307-226-1 | $14.99

ODDEST JOBS
ISBN 978-1-59307-944-4 | $14.99

B.P.R.D.: HOLLOW EARTH
By Mignola, Chris Golden,
Ryan Sook, and others
ISBN 978-1-56971-862-9 | $17.99

B.P.R.D.: THE SOUL OF VENICE
By Mignola, Mike Oeming, Guy Davis,
Scott Kolins, Geoff Johns, and others
ISBN 978-1-59307-132-5 | $17.99

B.P.R.D.: PLAGUE OF FROGS
By Mignola and Guy Davis
ISBN 978-1-59307-288-9 | $17.99

B.P.R.D.: THE DEAD
By Mignola, John Arcudi, and Guy Davis
ISBN 978-1-59307-380-0 | $17.99

B.P.R.D: THE BLACK FLAME
By Mignola, Arcudi, and Davis
ISBN 978-1-59307-550-7 | $17.99

B.P.R.D: THE UNIVERSAL MACHINE
By Mignola, Arcudi, and Davis
ISBN 978-1-59307-710-5 | $17.99

B.P.R.D: THE GARDEN OF SOULS
By Mignola, Arcudi, and Davis
ISBN 978-1-59307-882-9 | $17.99

B.P.R.D.: KILLING GROUND
By Mignola, Arcudi, and Davis
ISBN 978-1-59307-956-7 | $17.99

B.P.R.D: 1946
By Mignola, Joshua Dysart, and Paul Azaceta
ISBN 978-1-59582-191-1 | $17.99

B.P.R.D.: THE WARNING
By Mignola, Arcudi, and Davis
ISBN 978-1-59582-304-5 | $17.99

B.P.R.D.: THE BLACK GODDESS
By Mignola, Arcudi, and Davis
ISBN 978-1-59582-411-0 | $17.99

B.P.R.D.: 1947
By Mignola, Dysart, Fábio Moon, and
Gabriel Bá
ISBN 978-1-59582-478-3 | $17.99

B.P.R.D.: WAR ON FROGS
By Mignola, Arcudi, Davis, and others
ISBN 978-1-59582-480-6 | $17.99

B.P.R.D.: KING OF FEAR
By Mignola, Arcudi, and Davis
ISBN 978-1-59582-564-3 | $17.99

ABE SAPIEN: THE DROWNING
By Mignola and Jason Shawn Alexander
ISBN 978-1-59582-185-0 | $17.99

LOBSTER JOHNSON:
THE IRON PROMETHEUS
By Mignola and Jason Armstrong
ISBN 978-1-59307-975-8 | $17.99

LOBSTER JOHNSON:
THE SATAN FACTORY
By Thomas E. Sniegoski
ISBN 978-1-59582-203-1 | $12.99

WITCHFINDER:
IN THE SERVICE OF ANGELS
By Mignola and Ben Stenbeck
ISBN 978-1-59582-483-7 | $17.99

THE AMAZING SCREW-ON HEAD
Hardcover
ISBN 978-1-59582-501-8 | $17.99

DARK HORSE COMICS *drawing on your nightmares*™
darkhorse.com